ELIZABETH CAIRNS was born in London in 1933. When she was four her parents moved to Oxford. She began her education at a boys' preparatory school where she learnt Latin and Greek but while the boys headed for Eton and Winchester she was deflected to the Oxford High School for Girls. After leaving school she spent a mind-stretching six months at the university of Aix-en-Provence before returning to Oxford to take a degree in History. On leaving university she taught in an East End secondary modern then worked as research assistant on a book about disarmament. In 1956 she won a scholarship to the Department of Education at the Hebrew University of Jerusalem and spent a year there during which she travelled extensively on both the Israeli and the Arab sides of the border and met her husband, an ex-Romanian Israeli. For many reasons, not least political, they decided to settle in Britain. She wrote a book, *Israel* (1967), and a number of articles and reviews. In the 1970s she became involved in the Women's Liberation Movement, a period she looks back on from today with nostalgia. In 1976 she trained as a teacher in Further Education and spent the next fourteen years teaching in Wandsworth – communications, study skills and women's courses. She now teaches on an Access course for adult returners to education in Tooting. She has three children and three grandchildren. She plans, as she is phased out of education, to phase herself into full time writing.

Singing in Tune with Time

STORIES AND POEMS ABOUT AGEING

Edited by Elizabeth Cairns

Published by VIRAGO PRESS Limited 1993
20—23 Mandela Street, Camden Town, London NW1 0HQ

Collection, Introduction and Notes Copyright
© Elizabeth Cairns 1993

The right of Elizabeth Cairns to be identified as the
editor of this work has been asserted by her in accordance
with the Copyright, Designs and Patents Act 1988

*A CIP catalogue record for this book
is available from the British Library*

Typeset By Florencetype Ltd, Kewstoke, Avon
Printed in Great Britain by
Cox & Wyman Ltd, Reading, Berkshire

CONTENTS

ACKNOWLEDGEMENTS

Permission to reproduce stories and poems by the following authors is gratefully acknowledged: Penelope Lively: to Murray Pollinger and Grove Press for 'The Party' from *Pack of Cards*, William Heinemann Ltd, 1986, published in the US by Grove Press, 1986, Copyright © Penelope Lively 1978; Elizabeth Smart: to Sebastian Barker and Flamingo, an imprint of HarperCollins Publishers Ltd for 'Old Woman, Flying' from *Collected Poems of Elizabeth Smart*, Paladin, 1992, Copyright © Sebastian Barker 1992; Daphne Glazer: to The Sumach Press for 'Out of the Dragon's Mouth' from *The Last Oasis*, The Sumach Press, 1992, Copyright © Daphne Glazer 1992; Grace Nichols: to Virago Press Ltd for 'Granny Granny Please Comb my Hair' from *Lazy Thoughts Of A Lazy Woman*, Virago Press, 1989, Copyright © Grace Nichols 1989; Nadine Gordimer: to Jonathan Cape Ltd and Russell and Volkening, as agents for the author, for 'Enemies' from *Six Feet of Country*, Jonathan Cape, 1975 Copyright © Nadine Gordimer 1975; Rosalind Brackenbury: to the author and to Taxus Press at Stride Publications for 'Odysseus and Penelope' from *Coming Home The Long Way Round The Mountain*, Taxus Press, 1993, Copyright © Rosalind Brackenbury 1933; Margaret Laurence: to McClelland and Stewart, A.P.Watt and Virago Press Ltd on behalf of New End Inc. for excerpts from *The Stone Angel*, McClelland and Stewart, Toronto, 1964, first published in Great Britain by Macmillan and Company Ltd 1964, Copyright © 1964 by Margaret Laurence; Susan Katz: to the author and Papier Mache Press for 'New Directions' from *When I Am An Old Woman I Shall Wear Purple*, Papier Mache Press, 1987, Copyright © 1987 by Susan Katz; Julia Birley: to the author for 'Rage', published for the first time in

Acknowledgements

this collection, Copyright © Julia Birley 1993; Kathleen Dayus: to
Virago Press Ltd for the excerpt from 'Granny Moves In' from *Her
People*, Virago Press, 1982, Copyright © Kathleen Dayus 1982;
Colette: to Peter Owen Publishers, London, for 'In The Flower of
Age', translated by Matthew Ward, from *The Collected Stories Of
Colette*, Secker and Warburg 1984, first published by Farrar, Strauss
and Giroux in the USA, 1983, Copyright © 1949 by Flammarion;
Mari Beinset Waagaard: to the author for 'The Sweet Old Lady Who
Cried Wolf', published in A-Magasinet, Oslo, in 1991 and for the
first time in Great Britain in this collection, translated by the author,
Copyright © Mari Beinset Waagaard 1991; Mary Cowan: to the
author for 'Sonnet, Consolation' published for the first time in this
collection, Copyright © Mary Cowan 1993; Elizabeth Taylor: to the
estate of the late Elizabeth Taylor and Virago Press for 'Mice and
Birds and Boy' from *A Dedicated Man And Other Stories*, Chatto and
Windus, 1965, Virago Press Ltd, 1993 Copyright © Elizabeth Taylor
1965; Pam Gidney: to the author for 'Time Travel' published for the
first time in this collection, Copyright © Pam Gidney 1993; Susan
Hill: to Richard Scott Simon Ltd for 'A Bit of Singing and Dancing'
from *A Bit of Singing and Dancing*, Hamish Hamilton, 1973,
Copyright © Susan Hill 1971, 1972, 1973; Ismat Chugtai: to Kali for
Women for 'Tiny's Granny', first published by the Sahitya Akademi,
Delhi, in the Literary Review, 1961, and in *Truth Tales: Contemporary
Writing by Indian Women* edited by Kali for Women, 1986, first pub-
lished in Great Britain by the Women's Press Ltd, 1987, translated
by Dr Ralph Russell, Copyright © Ismat Chugtai 1961; Muriel
Spark: to Macmillan Publishers Ltd and David Higham Associates
for Chapter Three of *Memento Mori*, Macmillan, 1959, Copyright ©
Copyright Administration Ltd 1959; Sarah Barnhill: to the author
and Papier Mache Press for 'Near Places, Far Places', first published
by *Appalachian Heritage* 1986, and in *When I Am An Old Woman I
Shall Wear Purple*, Papier Mache Press, 1987, Copyright © by Sarah
Barnhill 1986; Marion Molteno: to the author and The Women's
Press Ltd for 'The Uses of Literacy' from *A Language in Common*,
The Women's Press Ltd, 1987, Copyright © Marion Molteno 1987;
Stevie Smith: to the Executor James MacGibbon and the New
Directions Publishing Corporation, USA, for 'Autumn' from *The
Collected Poems of Stevie Smith*, first published as *Collected Poems*

of Stevie Smith, Penguin Allen Lane, 1975, Copyright © James MacGibbon 1975, 1978; Edna O'Brien: to George Weidenfeld and Nicolson Ltd for 'The Creature' from *A Scandalous Woman*, Weidenfeld and Nicolson, 1974, Copyright © Edna O' Brien 1974; Elizabeth Cairns: 'Echoes', published for the first time in this collection, Copyright © Elizabeth Cairns 1993; Paule Marshall: to the Feminist Press at the City University of New York and Virago Press Ltd for 'To Da-Duh, In Memoriam' from *Reena and Other Stories*, The Feminist Press, 1983, published in Great Britain as *Merle and Other Stories*, Virago Press, 1985, Copyright © 1967, 1983 by Paule Marshall; Adrienne Rich: to W.W. Norton & Company, Inc., for 'Aunt Jennifer's Tigers' reprinted from *The Fact Of A Doorframe, Poems Selected and New*, 1950–1984, by Adrienne Rich, Copyright © 1984 by Adrienne Rich, Copyright © 1975, 1978 by W.W. Norton & Company, Inc. Copyright © 1981 by Adrienne Rich; Penelope Gilliatt: to The New Yorker for 'Foreigners' from *Nobody's Business*, Viking Press, 1972, originally published in *The New Yorker*, Copyright © Penelope Gilliatt 1970.

Every effort has been made to trace copyright holders in all copyright material in this book. The editor regrets if there has been any oversight and suggests the publisher is contacted in any such event.

INTRODUCTION

It starts when we are born (before, even) but for the first quarter of our lives it is called growing up and earns us only approval. Not until its later stages does society's ambivalence towards the process show itself as we become increasingly visible symbols of the brevity of life.

I'm speaking of course, of ageing. And increasingly visible we oldies become because there are a lot of us, more every year. Average life expectancy has gone up from less than 50 years at the beginning of the century to well over 70 now (78.6 for women, 73.2 for men); and because of the fall in the birthrate this is creating what has been called a greying world. Is that why our currency has been devalued? Certainly, in societies where there are fewer old people they are treated as assets rather than liabilities, repositories of wisdom and worthy of particular respect. It has even been suggested that in prehistoric times the survival of the human race was only made possible because of the accumulated knowhow of the senior members of the group. Be that as it may, there is no doubt that today we have lost our rarity value; and we are on the increase. Statistics may seem dry but they are important, I believe, to enable us to get a sense of the scale of the demographic changes that have happened in this century; and these changes are affecting not only society's attitude to us but our attitudes to ourselves.

Since the census year of 1901 the number of over-60s in the

UK has risen four times, while the population as a whole has grown by about a half. That is to say, the oldest tranche in the population has increased eight times faster than any of the others. At the turn of the century the over-60s accounted for less than 8% of the population, now they account for over 20%. In another generation and a half it is estimated they will be well over a quarter of the whole population.

To talk about the 'over-60s', however, gives a picture of a compact, homogeneous age-group which we all know is not the case. The term may be useful to bureaucrats, but it means, in effect, lumping 20–30 years of life into one phrase, much as if one were to talk about the 'over-ones' and include in that people in their twenties. These last twenty or thirty years of life have their phases, just as much as the first: their growth and physical change, their 'adolescence', their maturity.

These labels are not just fanciful. Growth, transition, change, crisis, adjustment – these are some of the themes which can apply to both of these 30-year blocks of life. But because Nature gives us greying masks and we have learnt to conceal our feelings, the world is largely unaware of the stresses and dramas, the pains and joys in our older lives. 'Granny/you have all the time/in the world,' says the child in Nichol's beautiful poem. But what does Granny do with her time? When she brushes your hair what thoughts go fleeting through her mind?

Si la jeunesse savait, si la vieillesse pouvait, runs the French adage. If youth only *knew*, and if old age only *could* . . . Today, I feel, old age both knows and can. We are retired and still healthy (touch wood). While we brush our grandchildren's hair we can dream fantasies which can indeed be turned into reality. There are restrictions – like the carer's ties which Hill's Esme has just been released from at the beginning of her story, or the shock of compulsory retirement for Glazer's Ivy. But Ivy swims ('part of the frilling and the rippling') away from hers, while Esme finds opportunity knocking at her door; and she is able to open her mind to it feeling that the future is in her power; 'now I am answerable only to myself'. As Smart's flying woman exhorts us, 'Nothing is, aft/er all, too late.' The later years can, if we are lucky, give us the space we need to catch up on those unlived experiences.

These stories and poems have been chosen for the themes they illustrate: what I think of as the themes of ageing. Some are joyful, some are dark. The shadow side inevitably creeps in; it would be distorting the truth – like a mirror which showed only half a reflection – to keep it out. In the excerpt from Laurence's 'Stone Angel' we see the poignancy of old age from both sides, that of the battling eighty-year old mother and the trapped son and daughter-in-law. Love, compassion, loyalty – these are the qualities we'll look for at the end but may not always recognise, as Hagar Shipley can't, even as she mouths words which echo a dream of them.

The battling granny is the theme both of the extract from Dayus' 'Her People', the only piece of straight autobiography in the collection, and of Chugtai's story 'Tiny's Granny'. While the Birmingham granny of the 1900s is not so near the bread-line that she cannot weigh 16 stone, Tiny's Granny is the archetype of impoverished old age, sans teeth, sans hope, with nothing but a burning rage to survive. In Birley's story, 'Rage', the psychological battle seems to be a losing one in the after-math of late retirement, that dread moment which can take such toll. But here, as in Chugtai, the end offers hope. The maple tree in its autumn glory glows like a vast ruby, as red as the poppies which spring up on Tiny's Granny's grave. All these stories, I feel, can be read at the straight story ('yarn') level, but at the same time their symbolism makes subtle points which hold many messages for us.

Like the bags and baggage of Mrs Hansen's travelling companion on the Durban train, in Gordimer's 'Enemies'. Mrs Hansen ('her face withdrawn as a castle') has pared her life down till it is totally under her control. Aloneness shields her like a carapace. Her 'strong sense of survival' instantly makes her wary of the other woman passenger and smugly observant of her physical deterioration. Are we led to wonder if this woman is in fact Mrs Hansen's shadow self, the enemy she has so adroitly fought to distance herself from all her life? Her ultimate act of distancing, the telegram, expresses the *schaden-freude* and shameful relief we must all have experienced at one time or another when disaster struck elsewhere.

Survival is the name of the game too in the excerpt from Spark's 'Memento Mori', that great novel about ageing. Here old age seems to come full circle with youth as octogenarian Godfrey takes piquant delight in his peers' disabilities and pinches the iced cakes at the funeral tea. In the Colette story the same message comes in a succinct and charming variation: the old can be young and the young old. The cobwebs that cover young Paul Vasco's hair as he comes up from the wine cellar tell it all.

The corollary of this is the theme of discovery and growth which runs through many of these stories. This can involve a making sense of the past and building on it, or being released from it. In Barnhill's 'Near Places, Far Places' Momma announces that she's waited till she got old before she's begun to do her thinking; but it is her daughter's rethinking of priorities, sparked by her children's creativity, which transforms their lives like alchemy. A sense of gentle magic runs through Molteno's story too ('The Uses of Literacy'), with its image of a man waiting till the leisure of old age to achieve his life's ambition. Mrs Werle in Waagaard's story acts out her fantasies in a more macabre manner, but her motto – '*carpe diem*' – stands for all those who feel, near the end of their lives, they have nothing to lose, everything to gain.

Another word for this perhaps could be reconciliation: a refinding of self and the re-establishment of a relationship with sides of yourself or others which the intervening years have obscured. Brackenbury's poem takes the return of Odysseus to Penelope as the metaphor for this, perhaps one of the most important themes of ageing, that sense of fulfilment through the return to the roots of yourself ('all his journeying become simply/this return.'). In Katz' poem the roots are literally in the soil as she feels her 'flesh molding/itself to gravity'. At mid-life, she says, 'I am more comfortable/with the truth.' There is a sense in many of these stories and poems of a truth – about self, about life, about the world – being searched for and attained.

Sometimes at a price. In O'Brien's story, her 'Creature' is left bereft ('for twenty years she had lived on that last high tightrope of hope, it had been taken away from her'). As you read this it makes you remember again how fragile that hold on serenity can be. Like Aunt Jennifer's fingers tugging at the ivory needle in Rich's poem (or Hagar Shipley's, nervously pleating her skirt), our grip is not always as strong as we would like it to be, our hands can take on an uncontrolled life of their own. We will be lucky if they leave sleek and prancing tigers for us to be remembered by.

Children figure in several of the stories. There seems to be a natural kinship between the ageing and the very young – answering the question asked in Cowan's sonnet: 'Do you think . . . that it is time/to watch things grow?' Yes, the answer has to be, and not just because we have the time, like Nichol's Granny, but because at some deep level we share a vision with the young. This is beautifully expressed in Lively's story, 'Party'. Between the two chaotic gatherings going on in the house Ellen, the grandmother, and Paul, the eleven-year-old grandson, are 'alone in a state of unsullied consciousness'. Across the surrounding confusion they recognise and respond to the need for calm in each other as, perfectly in tune, they tinker the night away building his model planes.

But when children grow up they 'begin to lose their simple vision,' as the father in Taylor's story, 'Mice and Birds and Boy,' observes; and William, who has befriended lonely aged

Mrs May and suffered with her from the knowing looks and gravely-kept straight faces she is greeted with in the shops ('he felt, uncomfortably, that this behaviour was something children came to expect, but that an older person should neither expect nor tolerate'), loses his innocence and is irresistibly drawn to join the snide grown-ups. Solitude is a theme of this story, too, the loneliness which Gordimer's iron Mrs Hansen takes such care to distinguish from the 'aloneness' that she relishes. This also is one of the key themes of ageing; all the characters in these stories are dealing or have dealt with it in one way or another. In Marshall's 'To Da-Duh, in Memoriam', the grandmother, Da-Duh, though surrounded by family is isolated in her strong competitive certainties from the realities of her granddaughter's world until they finally break in, and break her too. The granddaughter has seen her grandmother as 'both child and woman, darkness and light, past and present, life and death,' a figure in which all of life is contained; to be obeyed and feared but, as the young perhaps ultimately have no choice but to do, also challenged.

The challenge of change and loss of certainty and the crisis this brings is the theme of Gilliatt's 'Foreigners'. Thomas Flitch, foreigner in the sense of being half-Indian, finds himself a foreigner in his own life. Again a child plays a key role, this time as the unwitting instrument of Thomas's retrieval of himself. The last words of the story – 'I'll leap into my life' – are a clarion call to all of us who have ever been brushed by the kind of uncertainties that have afflicted him, in an image which Glazer's Ivy (perhaps having a go at diving now?) would surely appreciate.

It is a clarion call too to everyone who feels that the older age is a time to celebrate. 'Good teeth,' Mrs Hansen admonishes herself and us, '. . . must be kept to oneself.' But whether we have good teeth or not, we are alive. We have like a gift from Time a span of life our forebears didn't dream of. It brings its problems and its pains, but we're learning to work things out, we're discovering strengths in ourselves with every extra day we live and we're learning to learn from each other.

Because I have learnt a lot from these stories in the course of collecting them and their characters have over the months become my companions, even my friends, I have a fantasy: of inviting them to my sixtieth birthday party. The absentees would include Mrs Hansen who, much as I respect her, I know would refuse outright, as would Madame Vasco (she would never trust my choice of champagne and the idea of a tea party would surely revolt her), and Da-Duh would not run the risk of catching sight of the Empire State building on her way; while Mrs Merle, I'm afraid, I would feel safer without . . .

The rest, I hope, would come, and it might be fun. Esme's Mr Curry could provide a bit of entertainment, though that would send Godfrey, cakes notwithstanding, to a hasty exit; but we would all enjoy a smidgin of the Creature's rhubarb wine (and she would surely help with the washing up, while Tiny's Granny would be lurking to clear up any remains . . .). Dayus' Gran I would sit in a corner and ply with tea to shut her up; and who would serve it, need I ask? Mr Ramgarhia would be standing like a sentinel watching for empty cups while his smiling wife would put everyone at their ease. Birley's couple would make a brief appearance – she in her cinnamon-coloured trouser suit – but her embarrassment if her husband had failed to change out of his old cardigan might make them early leavers. If I was lucky I might get a very special present from Barnhill's Momma, now that Mr Van Fleet no longer visits them . . . but that is wishful thinking. I just know that, across the heads crowded around the table, I would be happy to catch Ellen Greaves' amused and tolerant smile. And I would like Mr Flitch to stay on afterwards for a (soft) drink. There is a quotation I want to show him which sprang into my mind as I read of his 'wish to touch with his fingers a future which he knew was that of many others . . .

He had his hand on a way to proceed, and one that might be of some consequence, with luck.'

The quotation is from Shakespeare and I feel with a slight twist of context it could apply to us all, at this point in our lives:

'So thou through windows of thine age shalt see,
Despite of wrinkles, this thy golden time.'

PENELOPE LIVELY

Party

She gets out of the taxi, Ellen Greaves, the grandmother, and pays with the change that she has assembled, carefully, on the way from Paddington. Then she picks up her suitcase once more and climbs the short flight of steps to the front door of the house, her daughter's house. It is a tall, thin terrace house, nineteenth century, in the middle of a street of similar houses. Aircraft lumber overhead. She rings the bell.

The door is opened, by an adolescent she does not recognise, who explains that they are all in the kitchen. From down below, in the basement, her daughter's voice calls up, 'Hallooo . . . Mum? Down here . . . It's a shambles – be warned.' And Ellen dumps her case in the hall and goes with caution down the steep stairs to the basement kitchen which is full of people and certainly most untidy. There are bottles everywhere, and food, both cooked and uncooked, and many loaves of bread. She kisses, and is kissed. Her grandchildren are there: Toby who is seventeen and Sophie who is eighteen and Paul, the little one, who is only eleven. And there are others, a dark girl and two boys and yet another she does not at first see, who is apparently mending the back of the fridge. They smile and greet; they have nice manners. Ellen smiles and greets too, and notes their appearance: all are shabbily, not to say scruffily, dressed, but their voices suggest a reasonable prosperity. Ellen finds this interesting.

Her daughter, Louise (who has got very thin again – indeed

1

everyone is thin, they all have a lean and hungry look, despite the plenitude of things to eat) is furiously applied to something at the stove. She chops and stirs and flies to cupboards and despatches someone to the freezer and explains that *she* is doing the food for *their* party, for the grown-up dinner, and *they* are coping absolutely on their own with *their* stuff (and indeed, as Ellen now sees, Sophie is also chopping and stirring, though with what seems to be a less refined approach). The two parties, Louise explains, will coexist but there will be no mixing, in all probability – we shall be upstairs and they will do their own thing down here, and nobody will get in anyone else's hair that way. But, she adds, doing it like this means that we are here to keep an eye, Michael and I, there will be no hanky-panky, no nonsense. And she casts a look at the young, who grin.

Ellen sits down at the kitchen table and wonders if, amid all this, there will be a cup of tea going. She decides (rightly, as it turns out) that there probably will not. Someone goes out and comes back in with a crate of bottles which is put on the dresser; Louise shrieks no, no! not there, for heaven's sake! The crate is removed to the floor beside the fridge. There is a brief, whispered consultation among the young, two of whom leave; they move with slouching purposefulness. Louise, on the other hand, darts from point to point. Her mother observes her thoughtfully.

We, Louise explains, are having a salmon trout and a rather lavish pud that I haven't tried before. They – and there are to be absolutely no more than thirty, do you hear, as agreed, no last-minute additions (Sophie and Toby nod emphatically) – are having plonk and some goo that Sophie is fixing.

Chilli con carne, murmurs Sophie, stirring. She peers through her hair into the saucepan; the kitchen is very hot and close. Ellen looks at the window and at the same moment Louise dashes to it, throws up the sash, and returns to her chopping-board.

Ellen, who is really here for her annual visit to the dentist, says that she hopes she won't be in the way. If she had known, she says, she could quite easily have made it another day . . . But before she can finish Louise is saying that there is absolutely no question of her being in the way, her usual room is empty because no one is staying the night, that's for sure (another sharp look at the young), and this is an absolutely intergenerational night so in fact it is very appropriate that she should be here. Louise, in mid-chop and mid-stir, pauses to smile fondly at her mother. Not everyone's mum, she says, would fit in, as it happens, but you will be all right, I can count on you, I know, and actually you may rather like some of the people who are coming. There is Tony Hatch who . . . But Tony Hatch remains undeveloped, because at this moment the two departed young return bearing cardboard boxes full of glasses and there is an altercation over the disposal of these, which must not be put there, nor there, nor above all on the dresser . . . Indeed, the kitchen is silting up rapidly, there is not an uncluttered surface nor much uncluttered floor. Louise and the rest dart and shuffle amid the confusion with remark-able adroitness; Ellen decides that she is safest where she is. She sits there at the table, and looks at Paul, who is perched on a stool, intent on some map or plan he is studying; he seems quite impervious to what is going on around. Once, he says, 'Mum, have you got any glue, my tube's almost used up?' and Louise says, 'What?' and goes to the stairs to deal with Toby, who, with a friend, is trying to bring a table-tennis table down; there are accusations and denials concerning scraped paint. Louise comes back into the kitchen scowling (she is also sweating profusely, her mother observes, which is odd for someone so thin); Paul sighs, slithers from the stool, and goes out.

Ellen surreptitiously rewashes some crockery stacked on the draining-board, having noted its condition with disquiet.

Louise says, 'Oh, Christ, the man never came about the

stereo,' and rushes out. She can be heard upstairs, vehemently telephoning.

Ellen, who has been able to do some prospecting from her seat at the table, and has established the whereabouts of cups, tea, sugar etc., makes herself a cup of tea. She sits drinking it and listens to the conversation of two people at her feet. They are not so much exchanging observations or opinions as making statements, separate and unrelated. The girl says that she simply cannot stand anything fried nowadays, she doesn't know why, she thinks perhaps it is psychological, and the boy says there is this master at school, this bloke who has really got it in for him, it's a hassle. They are joined by another girl, who is concerned about the state of her fingernails. She sits peering at them and saying there are these little white spots, look, I'm worried, what should I do; then for a few moments these assorted themes come together in a united objection to honey (however did they get on to that?) before each is off again on a saga of personal revelation. Ellen, one of whose feet is being sat on, shifts, as unobtrusively as possible, and pours herself a cup of tea.

Louise returns, followed by Paul, who says again, 'Is there any glue anywhere, mum?' Louise says, 'Why?' and darts with exclamations of dismay to her saucepan. Paul begins, 'Because I haven't . . .', but now Louise remembers that no one has counted and allocated cutlery, so the group under the kitchen table are jolted into action, or rather into a state of gentle drift.

It is five o'clock.

At six o'clock Louise has the most ghastly headache. Further, she is seized with some compulsion that sends her on frequent brief and furtive excursions into the large room next to the kitchen, Toby's room, in which the youthful party is to take place. She seems to be hunting for something. During these hunts the young, in the kitchen, exchange glances and roll their eyes. Once or twice, Ellen cannot help hearing whispered snatches on the stairs, unspecified threats about what Louise will do if there is the slightest suspicion of, if anyone is so damn stupid as to bring, if anything other than absolutely straightforward . . . During one of these fraught exchanges, Paul reappears, sliding past his mother and siblings without paying them any attention. He delves in the breadbin, helps himself to bread, butter and jam, and sits once more upon the stool, lost in perusal of yet another printed sheet. Ellen says, 'What is that, dear?'

It is, Paul explains, the instructions for the assembly of the model aircraft on which he is currently working. He is stuck, he says, because he has run out of glue, almost, but also because there is a bit that he simply cannot get the hang of. It doesn't, he says, seem to make sense. The aeroplane is a De Havilland Mosquito, he explains, and the problem is that . . .

Ellen asks if she can have a look. She reads, frowns, puts her glasses on and reads again. After a few moments everything falls into place; the problem, as it turns out, is a semantic one. The model aircraft kit has been made in Japan, and the translation of the instructions, while for the most part admirable, has fallen down just at the end here, where in fact 'right' should read 'left', and 'front', 'back'. Paul is gravely grateful, and goes off again.

Michael arrives home. He kisses his mother-in-law, and immediately busies himself stowing bottles in the fridge, placing others by the stove; he says it is amazingly brave of Ellen to let herself in for all this, and Ellen, who is now repairing the zip on Toby's jeans (they have not been washed for some time, which makes the job a mite disagreeable), says not at all, a bit of gaiety will be a nice change, she leads a quiet enough life in the normal way of things. Louise, whose voice has become peculiarly shrill, interrupts to point out that the table needs laying; Sophie comes in and has an argument with Toby about some gramophone records; the telephone rings. Michael and Louise exchange clipped words about some gin, of which, it seems, there is not enough. Subdued accusations are made about responsibility.

Ellen goes up to her room, which is on the top floor. On the way, she passes the open door of Sophie's room. Sophie, within, can be seen seated at a dressing-table with tears pouring down her cheeks, a staggering sight, the incarnation of tragedy. Her grandmother, disturbed, ventures to ask if there is anything she can do, to be told, in tones of choked stoicism, that there is nothing, nothing, no one can help, it would be impossible to explain to anyone, it is to do with her friend, or rather ex-friend, Mike, and furthermore there is this dress she was to wear which is stained all down the front, ruined . . . Her grandmother nods understandingly and withdraws.

In her own room, Ellen unpacks her overnight case, hangs up a dress, and goes to the bathroom for a wash. She pats the hot-water tank in exploratory fashion; a hot-water bottle, she suspects, might be a comfort later on, but the water is not very hot. She will have to see about a kettle.

Downstairs, there are sudden bursts of loud music, as from a fairground. Louise is to be heard, also.

Ellen changes into her tidy dress and does her hair. Then she sits for a while on the edge of her bed, apparently looking out of the window over the ranges of grey London roof-tops. She was sixty-three last birthday, a small, neat person, a little fatter than in youth, her hands brown-mottled, her teeth not all her own. She sits so still, is so relaxed, that to an observer the room might appear to be empty. She watches the slow progress of an aeroplane along the line of a roof and thinks, in utter tranquillity, of her husband, ten years dead. She tells him, as is her habit, what has been happening to her today, and with the telling there is a faint, fragrant gust of sexual memory. Come now, she tells herself, this won't do, I am not here to be unsociable, and she gathers herself to go downstairs.

The house is strung up now, like a bow, any minute something might snap. As Ellen progresses downwards, people slip past her, dash from room to room, drop things. Louise comes from her bedroom, in a long dress, screwing on ear-rings, and says oh, there you are, mum, I say you do look smart, come down and Michael will find you a glass of sherry, would you believe it, the fridge has decided to play up again, now of all times. And she is gone down the stairs at a gallop, her skirt looped over her arm, her neat muscular calves visible beneath. Her mother remembers that at school she was good at games. It is not wise to mention this, though; for some reason that recollection is ill-received nowadays. Louise has a partnership in a small art gallery.

At eight, the guests begin to arrive. They arrive simultaneously on both floors – the young presenting themselves at the basement door, in twos and threes, furtive of manner, being admitted in silence, without greeting; Louise and Michael's friends climbing the steps to the front door, shedding coats in the hall, loud in greeting and comment. They are presented to Ellen: this tall thin man who is a psychiatrist, Tony Hatch, and his dark, shrieking wife; the small round unattached man who works at Sotheby's; two more couples whose allegiances she cannot for a while get straight, since they all arrive together and treat one another with indiscriminate familiarity. We are all such *old* friends tonight, declares Louise, flying from drinks cupboard to guests, it is lovely, everyone knows everyone else, I don't have to do any of that tiresome sorting people out. Except of course you, mum, she adds – and you are such a splendid adaptable lady, aren't you? She beams upon her mother and the other guests smile kindly. Ellen, who is not deaf, though it is apparently expected of her, has already heard Louise in the hall explaining that her mum is here for the night which actually is not the snag you'd think because she is really marvellous for that generation, nothing bothers her, she is amazingly well-adjusted, you'll love her.

Drinks are drunk. Ellen sits on the sofa beside the psychiatrist who tells her with boyish candour that he and Josie are recently married, just this year. He is in his early forties, and wears jeans and a jacket that reminds Ellen of her husband's old tropical bush-shirt. He is a little stout for the jeans and during the course of the evening the zip of the fly is to descend, which worries Ellen, not for herself but because embarrassment in others distresses her. As it turns out, though, there is no cause for distress; he is never aware of his plight. He talks to Ellen with nostalgia of his first wife, his divorced wife, who was the most super person; across the room, the new wife bites her fingernails and occasionally shouts out some personal comment; the niceties of social intercourse do not seem to interest her.

The volume of noise from the basement is increasing; several times Louise, or Michael, go to the stairs and remonstrate.

Dinner is had in the dining-room, which glows agreeably with candlelight and furniture polish and silver. Louise and Michael have some nice things. Ellen sits between the man from Sotheby's and one of the other husbands (she has sorted out now who is attached to whom, for what that is worth). The man from Sotheby's turns to her and says (in pursuit of the tail-end of a subject that had been bandied around earlier upstairs) what does she think about the Mentmore sale, and does she feel that the government should or shouldn't have stepped in earlier, but while she is giving proper consideration to what she thinks (and she does, in fact, have a number of thoughts on the matter) it turns out that what he really intended was to tell her what he thinks, which he proceeds to do. Ellen listens with attention; he is telling her, in fact, a great deal more than he realises. I . . . he says . . . my opinion is that . . . personally, I feel . . . consulted me earlier . . . Ellen nods thoughtfully. Down at the other end of the table, the second wife of the psychiatrist screams that Tony is getting a bald pate, just look at him, look at his pate! Everybody laughs; the psychiatrist blows his wife a kiss; the husband on Ellen's right says that Josie is a riot, she is such a direct person, she says just what comes into her head.

By now, everybody has had a good deal to drink, except Ellen, for whom a glass of sherry has always been quite enough.

There is a muffled crash, from below; Louise, who is listening to an anecdote told by the psychiatrist, leaves the room, sharply, a frozen smile on her lips. She returns and serves the salmon trout with what seems an unnecessary amount of clatter. Everybody says what a lovely treat.

Ellen, who has got up to help Louise pass the vegetables, asks if Paul has had something earlier, or what, and is told that he is absolutely fine, he is up in his room with a plate of bangers and beans, of course he is rather out on a limb tonight, poor love, neither one thing nor t'other. Michael, who is circulating more wine, says it is a tiresome time for him, poor chap, he longs to be out in the great wide world like the others.

The psychiatrist has finished his anecdote, and the man from Sotheby's is now having his turn; people are very given to interruption, Ellen notes, they do not so much listen as interject. She watches the young woman opposite her, who has been trying for the past hour to make various points about herself, without success, chiefly because she has to compete, at the end of the table, with Louise and the psychiatrist's wife, both of whom have louder voices. The psychiatrist's wife, at this moment, bawls to Michael that Tony gets awfully randy in hot weather, it's a real sweat. Ellen, interested, is trying to define her origins (Ellen likes to know where she is about people). She thinks she can detect, beneath that stridency, a residual hint of the west country, and would like to know if she is right – in a momentary lull she leans forward and asks the girl where her home is, but she is busy now picking her teeth with a fingernail and does not hear, or does not care to.

Downstairs, there is a steady thump of music, with intermittent louder bursts; Louise occasionally frowns, but her reactions are becoming slower. A sound of splintering glass escapes her altogether, engaged as she is in banter with the man from Sotheby's. She forgets to pass the biscuits with the pudding; Ellen rescues them from the sideboard and puts them on the table.

They move back to the sitting-room, for coffee. Ellen, following Louise down to the kitchen to give a hand, peeks through the half-open door of Toby's room at a scene of semi-darkness, peopled with murky, shifting presences like an aquarium. Louise, juggling a trifle unsteadily with hot water, coffee and a strainer, is muttering darkly about having a good mind to go in there and just have a thorough check . . . Sophie comes in, hand in hand with a boy, wreathed in smiles; she says 'Hello, gran' warmly, and her grandmother says, 'Good, so everything's all right now'; Sophie beams uncomprehendingly.

They take the coffee upstairs. In the sitting-room, there is an impression of dishevelment, as though everyone had slumped a notch or two, in every sense. Michael has been handing out brandy; the psychiatrist's wife has her shoes off and is sprawled over the arm of the sofa; the man from Sotheby's is reading a book; there is talk, a little incoherent, Ellen thinks. She picks up, without anyone noticing, a couple of glasses that are threatened by people's feet.

Coffee is dispensed. Ellen takes the opportunity to go upstairs to the bathroom for a minute; on the way, she looks in at Paul's room. He sits cross-legged on the floor, in a dressing-gown, the dismembered De Havilland Mosquito around him. He says, 'You were quite right, gran – I've got the tail on now, all but.' Together they examine his achievement; he points out a further technical hitch; Ellen, who is steady-fingered, is able to complete a tricky matter of inserting a door. Regretfully, she goes downstairs again.

The telephone rings. The neighbours, it appears, are less than happy about the noise emanating from the basement. Louise makes soothing remarks and assurances of action;

putting the receiver down she says that really it is a bit thick, I mean, it's only once in a blue moon. She goes to the stairs and bawls, 'Turn that thing *down*, do you hear, Toby . . .' The noise is reduced by a decibel or two.

Ellen goes down to see if there is any more coffee; she has been inspecting one of the male guests, unobtrusively, and thinks it would be a good idea if he had some, at least if he is intending to drive home. She glances again into Toby's room; there are many more than thirty people there, it seems to her. She makes coffee, humming to herself; she straightens a picture that has gone awry; she peeks into the freezer and is surprised by the orderly array of bags and parcels within, labelled and classified. 'For Xmas dinner,' she reads, '6 helps'. A boy, unfamiliar to her, slinks into the room, takes something from the fridge and slinks out again, with a deprecating smile.

Upstairs, there is further deterioration. The man from Sotheby's talks, but no one listens. Michael, on the sofa, has his arm round one of the girls. Louise, on the floor, talks intently to the psychiatrist. Someone else says something about Dorchester; the psychiatrist's wife looks up suddenly and shouts, 'Dorchester? I know Dorchester – Tony and I first copulated at Dorchester, in the back of a car.'

Ellen thinks, you poor dear, what a time you do have. She pours coffee for the man she feels could do with it; he is effusively grateful, but forgets to drink it.

The neighbours complain again.

At midnight, Ellen gets up and goes quietly from the room. To those who register her departure, she says a polite good-night.

The light is still on in Paul's room. She goes in. They get to work. The De Havilland Mosquito is almost finished. A quarter of an hour later, it is complete. They contemplate it with pleasure. Almost casually, Paul produces the box containing the Heinkel 447 which he has not yet opened. They look at it; it presents, they agree, an interesting challenge. After a minute or two they open the box. They spread the pieces out and study the instructions. They look at one another: it is half past twelve.

Conspiratorially, Ellen says that if they are going to do it a cup of cocoa might be nice; also, she would like to get into something comfortable.

She goes up to her room and puts on her housecoat and a pair of slippers. On her way down again she is joined by Paul and the two of them pad down the stairs. They pass the sitting-room, from which, now, there is the sound of music (quieter, though, and different in style from the music below). Ellen remembers her glasses, which are on the mantelpiece; she slips in to get them, with a murmur of apology, but in fact no one pays her any attention. The psychiatrist's wife would seem to be weeping; someone else is asleep; there is a kind of heaving on the sofa which Ellen does not stop to investigate.

In the hall, they are passed by Louise, who is saying something sourly about someone being stoned out of their mind. She must be talking to herself, though, for the sight of her mother and younger son does nothing for her, in any sense. She lurches back into the sitting-room.

It is a good deal quieter now, in Toby's room. The door is closed.

Ellen and Paul make a large jug of cocoa, which they load on to a tray, along with mugs, and a plate of cheese and biscuits. They open up the freezer, because Paul fancies there is probably an ice-cream; others appear to have been here first, though – there is a certain dishevelment and depletion of the bags and parcels. 'For Xmas dinner' has gone, Ellen notices, and so, to Paul's annoyance, has the ice-cream. He stands for a moment in the middle of the kitchen, hitching his dressing-gown (which has lost its cord) around him; he sighs; he says, with a toss of the head that includes both the room next door and the sitting-room above, 'They are all being a bit silly tonight, aren't they?' After a moment he adds, 'I suppose they can't help it.'

Ellen says she doesn't think they can, poor dears. She suggests a mousse that she has found in the fridge as an alternative to ice-cream.

They take the tray upstairs, comfortable with anticipation. There are fifty-three people in the house now. Ellen and Paul alone are in a state of unsullied consciousness.

At ten past two in the morning they are well into the Heinkel, but they have quite run out of glue, as feared. Separately, they scour the house. Paul goes through the drawers of his mother's desk (which involves shifting the man from Sotheby's, who is asleep in front of it, no mean feat for an eleven year old). Louise does not seem to be around, nor yet the psychiatrist; nor, indeed, Michael, or the psychiatrist's wife. Paul draws a blank, so far as the desk is concerned, and turns to the drawers of the sofa table; he ignores the goings-on on the sofa, which do not interest him.

Downstairs, Ellen is systematically searching the kitchen. She comes across a girl, deeply asleep (or something) between the dresser and the sink, and covers her with a rug that she fetches from the cloakroom; the child is inadequately clad as it is. She rummages in drawers, and on the shelves of the dresser, and at last, in triumph, turns up a nearly full tube of something that will certainly do. She sets off up the stairs, and then becomes aware that the gramophone in Toby's room is most irritatingly stuck; no one seems to be doing anything about it. She goes into the darkening room, and gropes her way across, to where in the muted light of a table-lamp, the record is hiccuping away; on the way she stumbles several times on recumbent forms. 'Sorry, dear,' she says. 'Excuse me just a minute . . .' She adjusts the instrument, and goes out again.

She meets Paul on the stairs and they go up together.

At three-thirty a policeman, who has been tipped off by a disgruntled would-be gatecrasher, knocks on the front door. He has reason to believe that there is consumption of . . . But when the door is opened to him by an elderly woman, wearing her dressing-gown and holding, for some reason, the super-structure of a model aeroplane, he loses his nerve, apologises, and says there has probably been a mistake.

As the dawn seeps upwards into the sky, extinguishing the street lights and redefining the London roof-tops, they finish the Heinkel. It has gone almost without a hitch; it is a triumph. They sit back, weary but aglow with satisfaction, and contemplate their craftsmanship. The house is quite quiet now; they must be the only ones still capable of celebration. Paul goes down to the kitchen and fetches a bottle of cider, the sole survivor of the night. He pours them a helping each, in tooth-mugs, and in silence and in mutual appreciation they drink to one another.

ELIZABETH SMART

Old Woman, Flying

Why shouldn't an old woman fly?
The Duchess of Bedford amazed in aeroplanes.
But it's flights of fancy I'm thinking of, I
Feel fancy still tickling beloved epitomes.

Old Mr Yeats
Reached new heights
Contained his rage
Against old age
And caused the best poems to be won
When he was a very old person.

So much the better if he couldn't get it up.
When energy's oozing you should cherish each drop in a cup
Until enough is gathered for a celebratory draught
To share with contrary Muse. Nothing is, aft

er all, too late
If you don't insult or hate her
(and he never did)
Why should she not recur?
He was her friend:
Was it likely she'd desert him towards the end?

So, pale and pendulous on my shaky bough
I get ready for take-off, jeered by hoi polloi.
But wait! watch! follow with eyes, mind,
(There are so many things far better left behind)
And then like a good bird-watcher you just might
See useful manoeuvring in this late flight,

    A hello, a hooray,
    A greeting along the way
    A well, well, then
    So it can be done:
    An instigatory vesper
    In a setting sun.

DAPHNE GLAZER

Out of the Dragon's Mouth

On this morning when Ivy had been cleaning the glass tooth for thirty years, that nasty little woman, Whitney, had called her in.

'Mrs Smedley, I don't like to have to say this . . . no, I really don't, but I have no option . . .' And she'd drawn herself up real tall. She was only the supervisor, after all, but you'd think she'd been born in her little suit and stilettos, toting her shiny executive case.

Anyway, she'd been speaking for about ten minutes before Ivy had understood what she was on about.

'. . . so you being the age you are . . . I'm having to suggest that you retire.'

Retire! She went boiling hot and her heart fluttered at the word. Why, she'd come there cleaning when the kiddies were little. Her mother-in-law had suggested it.

'Look there, Ivy, they've opened that big new college – go over and ask 'em if they'd take you on. It 'ud be a nice little job, like. You could fit it in dead easy while the kiddies are small. It wouldn't be for long like.'

And she had done – first thing in a morning at six o'clock she'd be fettling away; back again at four-thirty till six-thirty.

It had started off as her helping to supplement Ron's wage, and then Ron had run off with the receptionist at his garage. So, there she'd been, on her own with her three.

She'd seen cleaners come and cleaners go, but there'd always been Marge, her friend, who was on floor five when she was on four. They'd brewed up at eight in one of the classrooms on her floor, and Billy and George, the two caretakers, would drop in for a cuppa as well, bringing the tea-bags they'd dried out on the radiator. They'd have a good groan about council rents, and Billy would complain about his mother, and George about 'our lass', his wife. And it had seemed that they might carry on like this for ever: bairns got married and had bairns; principals came and went; nameplates changed on doors; walls were painted; it was always freezing at the front when the west wind blasted in from the estuary, and roasting when sun shone. But she had to say it, she had begun to notice how, like her, that eight-storey glass tooth had started to fall apart. First it had been the great black gobs of tar which had started raining down on the seventh floor; then the window-frames had gone rotten. The doors in the foyer had smashed when there was a gale. The doors in the girls' lavs wouldn't fasten. The drinking-fountain puddled all over the toilets. Somebody had been poisoned by drinking water from the taps. There had been all sorts of rumours about dead things in the water-tanks.

As she'd watched everything gradually growing more battered, she'd felt how her back gave her twinges and noticed how her face was suet-coloured and her hair turning grey. Mind you, nobody knew that, because she'd been putting lightener on it for years.

So when that nasty Whitney gave her her cards, it had seemed like the end.

Marge and George and Billy had gathered round her at tea-time.

'Oh, she's a rotten bit o' work!' Billy had rumbled through his flappy lips. He never bothered to wear his dentures, said he couldn't master 'em.

'Too bad, lass,' George said, 'bad luck, love . . .' He'd given her a little cuddle in the broom cupboard underneath his topless-lady picture.

They'd taken her out for a tipple at The Star in the evening . . . and then that had been that. She was finished. No more work. Thirty years over and done with in a blink.

From wherever she was in her house, she could see that square glass fang rising up. Whatever was she going to do with herself now?

Sue, her daughter, had tried to suggest things. Mam, why don't you go to afternoon bingo? Or you could go and help out at the hospital with the goodies trolley.

But she didn't want to be pushed around. She'd been responsible for her own life and theirs all these years. Her floors had shone; the desks had been lined up in neat rows; waste-bins emptied and shiny; lavs spotless . . .

What was she going to do? How she missed Marge and George and Billy! They belonged to a different world. She had to stop herself getting up at five-thirty to hurry off to college. At six she'd be looking at the wall-clock and imagining them all in their blue uniforms working the mops over the corridors. Billy and George would be slamming doors and seeing to waste-bins. Eight o'clock, snap-time. They were sitting round sipping milky tea and yawning.

Ivy felt deeply unhappy and unsettled. Was this the end?

And then she had the dream. Before her was a rippling expanse of blue water. Little eddies and frills twitched upon it. There she was, climbing down the steps into it; she, who had been terrified of water all her life, ever since a big kid had pushed her in when they'd gone to Madeley Street Baths from school. The best of it was, she didn't feel any fear. It seemed quite natural. Off she struck. She was gliding through the water. It made her feel so happy she wanted to sing, and it was warm, beautifully warm. She was soaring like some seagull, skimming weightlessly.

When she woke up, she was smiling. It was seven-thirty as well and not five o'clock. Around her clung the feeling of gladness. Nothing like that had ever happened to her before – not even with Ron.

Sue appeared with the push-chair and little Donna mid-morning.

'Listen, Sue, I've had this dream.' And she described it for her. 'I'm going to get down to the baths and learn to swim. I want to do like I did in the dream.'

'Don't you think you're knocking on a bit for that, our Mam?'

'Maybe, but I'm going to try.'

If she hadn't told Sue that she was going to learn, she would have abandoned the idea, but she kept looking out of the window at that big glass block and she knew she must do something. She was falling apart, like it was.

The next day she went into a sports shop in search of a bathing-costume. The last time she'd possessed one, it had had moulded bits like halved tennis-balls in the front. She'd bought it in the early days of her marriage to wear at Brid. on the sands, and every now and then she'd find her bust under her armpits or practically hitting her chin, and Ron had said, Eh up, our lass, what's up with yer knockers? Which had put her off even more.

Now she touched the swimsuits on the rails with nervous hands, looking for the infrastructure. There was none. They were just a smooth second skin with a few straps at the back. The assistant hovered nearby.

'Can I help?'

'Yes, love. I want one for me, you know.'

'I wouldn't have the legs too cut away, dear, if I were you. They're for the, you know, younger end.'

'Yes,' Ivy said, 'a thirty-six – that pink-and-white-stripe Speedo looks smart . . . Oh,' and then as an afterthought, 'do you sell them orange armbands?'

'For non-swimmers?'

'Yes, love.'

Me, she thought, me in a Speedo swimsuit . . . they didn't appear to be called 'bathing-costumes' any more!

She decided the great event would take place that after-noon. Alone in her bedroom she struggled into the striped Speedo number. Although gravity had conquered most of her, her stomach still bulged and that wasn't padding.

She was too excited to eat any dinner, and anyway she remembered dire warnings from childhood about not eating before going in the water or your heart would give out and you'd sink.

The swimming baths was a bus ride away. And then she saw it; one like she'd visited in childhood. Its green onion domes pierced the sky. She took a deep breath and went in. She had to keep reminding herself of the dream as she faltered in front of the glass doors.

Before her lay the pool, blue and twitching slightly, as in her dream, but it wasn't empty. Youths with navy-blue squiggles on their arms and chests were plunging in, and young women in goggles threshed up and down the length, avoiding little lads who nose-dived constantly. One or two small children wearing orange armbands huddled uncertainly at the shallow end.

In the cubicle she struggled out of her anorak, navy-blue Crimp. trousers and jumper. On no account would she be taking her glasses off.

What a fool she felt as she eased herself down the metal steps into the pool! Once there she thrust her arms into the orange bands. The warm water lapped about her waist. It seemed altogether unfamiliar, but she watched the bodies of young men and girls scything through the ripples and she remembered her dream. It looked so effortless, in the same way seagulls hang in air-currents; she used to see them from the college windows.

She waved her arms about a bit in the water and experi-mented, rowing them round as she had seen people doing when they were swimming. What would happen if she were to lie on the water? Would she sink?

Someone zoomed alongside her and came up for air, then set off again up the bath, rearing half out of the water, plunging back again like some weird bird or sea-monster. In seconds he was back.

'You learnin'?'

'Trying, love.'

'You should hold on to the side and I'll show you what to do with your legs.'

He took hold of her ankles and worked her legs so that she felt like a frog.

'Just lie on the water, kick out a bit! What you got your glasses on for?'

'I don't want to miss anything.'

She was all of a dither inside and thought maybe she should go home. All right, she couldn't do it; too old . . . just not right. She was coming to bits; past it.

Nevertheless, when the man galumphed off again up the pool Ivy tried one or two experimental lunges. As the water sprayed her face, she got a shock, but gradually the movement of the pool and the excitement of flapping forward a couple of inches became quite pleasurable.

That day, she stayed in the water about half an hour. I'll come again tomorrow, she told herself. I'll come every day. And she did.

'Mam, whatever's happened to you?' Sue asked. 'You're never in and you don't come round any more.'

'I'm too busy for now,' she said. 'Later on, love . . .'

One afternoon she forgot her armbands. I'll make do without, she thought, and she launched herself on the water. She hadn't sunk in the dream, had she? With frenzied kicking and dog-paddling she managed to stay afloat. It amazed and intrigued her.

In that way she covered a width. This is it, she registered, I've done it! But there was no gliding about it; it was painful, ungainly splashing.

The day she actually swam up to the deep end, she was convinced her heart would stop, it was pattering so fast, and she expected to sink glugging to the bottom like an empty bottle. She kept near the side and pulled horrible faces if any lad popped up near her.

'You're doing all right,' encouraged the man who'd first helped her.

'Yes,' she gulped, as she prepared for the vast distance back, wondering all the time whether she could ever make it.

Months went by as she battled on. Up and down, up and down. Ten, fifteen, twenty. Lads steered clear of her because she wasn't above kicking them if provoked. The water spumed and glittered. Her efforts were all geared to the strokes, and when she wasn't doing them she saw them in her head, and they were smooth and gliding and mesmerizing. She kept at it with the gritty determination that had got her out of bed at five-thirty all those years and made her floors gleam.

On the day that she'd been in the pool two hours and swum seventy lengths, she suddenly became aware that she wasn't forcing herself any more; she was part of the frilling and the rippling; she was going with it and not working against it, and it amazed her.

Arriving home for tea, she found Sue waiting for her.

'Mam, I was getting real worried.'

'Gerraway,' Ivy muttered absent-mindedly. She happened to glance out of the window and she saw there was scaffolding up the sides of the college.

'Mam, what are you grinning at?' Sue asked, astonished.

GRACE NICHOLS

Granny Granny Please Comb my Hair

Granny Granny please comb
my hair
you always take your time
you always take such care

You put me on a cushion
between your knees
you rub a little coconut oil
parting gentle as a breeze

Mummy Mummy
she's always in a hurry-hurry
rush
she pulls my hair
sometimes she tugs

But Granny
you have all the time
in the world
and when you're finished
you always turn my head and say
'Now who's a nice girl?'

NADINE GORDIMER

Enemies

When Mrs Clara Hansen travels, she keeps herself to herself. This is usually easy, for she has money, has been a baroness and a beauty and has survived dramatic suffering. The crushing presence of these states in her face and bearing is nearly always enough to stop the loose mouths of people who find themselves in her company. It is only the very stupid, the senile or the self-obsessed who blunder up to assail that face, withdrawn as a castle, across the common ground of a public dining room.

Last month, when Mrs Hansen left Cape Town for Johannesburg by train, an old lady occupying the adjoining compartment tried to make of her apologies, as she pressed past in the corridor loaded with string bags and paper parcels, an excuse to open one of those pointless conversations between strangers which arise in the nervous moments of departure. Mrs Hansen was giving last calm instructions to Alfred, her Malay chauffeur and manservant, whom she was leaving behind, and she did not look up. Alfred had stowed her old calf cases from Europe firmly and within reach in her compartment, which, of course, influence with the reservation office had ensured she would have to herself all the way. He had watched her put away in a special pocket in her handbag, her train ticket, a ticket for her de luxe bed, a book of tickets for her meals. He had made sure that she had her two yellow sleeping pills and the red pills for that feeling of pressure in her head, lying in cottonwool in her silver pillbox. He himself had seen that her two pairs of spectacles, one for distance, one for reading, were in her overnight bag, and had noted that her lorgnette hung below the diamond bow on the bosom of her dress. He had taken down the folding table from its niche above the wash-basin in the compartment, and placed on it the three magazines she had sent him to buy at the bookstall, along with the paper from Switzerland that, this week, had been kept aside, unread, for the journey.

For a full fifteen minutes before the train left, he and his employer were free to ignore the to-and-fro of voices and luggage, the heat and confusion. Mrs Hansen murmured down to him; Alfred, chauffeur's cap in hand, dusty sunlight the colour of beer dimming the oil shine of his black hair, looked up from the platform and made low assent. They used the half-sentences, the hesitations and the slight changes of tone or expression of people who speak the language of their association in the country of their own range of situation. It was hardly speech; now and then it sank away altogether into the minds of each, but the sounds of the station did not well up in its place. Alfred dangled the key of the car on his little finger. The old face beneath the toque noted it, and the lips, the infinitely weary corners of the eyes drooped in the indication of a smile. Would he really put the car away into the garage for six weeks after he'd seen that it was oiled and greased?

Unmindful of the finger, his face empty of the satisfaction of a month's wages in advance in his pocket, two friends waiting to be picked up in a house in the Malay quarter of the town, he said, 'I must make a note that I mustn't send Madam's letters on after the twenty-sixth.'

'No. Not later than the twenty-sixth.'

Did she know? With that face that looked as if it knew everything, could she know, too, about the two friends in the house in the Malay quarter?

She said – and neither of them listened – 'In case of need,

you've always got Mr Van Dam.' Van Dam was her lawyer. This remark, like a stone thrown idly into a pool to pass the time, had fallen time and again between them into the widening hiatus of parting. They had never questioned or troubled to define its meaning. In ten years, what need had there ever been that Alfred couldn't deal with himself, from a burst pipe in the flat to a jammed fastener on Mrs Hansen's dress?

Alfred backed away from the ice-cream carton a vender thrust under his nose; the last untidy lump of canvas luggage belonging to the woman next door thumped down like a dusty animal at Mrs Hansen's side; the final bell rang.

As the train ground past out of the station, Alfred stood quite still with his cap between his hands, watching Mrs Hansen. He always stood like that when he saw her off. And she remained at the window, as usual, smiling slightly, inclining her head slightly, as if in dismissal. Neither waved. Neither moved until the other was borne out of sight.

When the station was gone and Mrs Hansen turned slowly to enter her compartment to the quickening rhythm of the train, she met the gasping face of the old woman next door. Fat overflowed not only from her jowl to her neck, but from her ankles to her shoes. She looked like a pudding that had risen too high and run down the sides of the dish. She was sprinkling cologne onto a handkerchief and hitting with it at her face as if she were trying to kill something. 'Rush like that, it's no good for you,' she said. 'Something went wrong with my son-in-law's car, and what a job to get a taxi! *They* don't care – get you here today or tomorrow. I thought I'd never get up those steps.'

Mrs Hansen looked at her. 'When one is no longer young, one must always give oneself exactly twice as much time as one needs. I have learned that. I beg your pardon.' And she passed before the woman into her compartment.

The woman stopped her in the doorway. 'I wonder if they're serving tea yet? Shall we go along to the dining car?'

'I always have my tea brought to me in my compartment,' said Mrs Hansen, in the low, dead voice that had been considered a pity in her day but that now made young people who could have been her grandchildren ask if she had been an actress. And she slid the door shut.

Alone, she stood a moment in the secretive privacy, where everything swayed and veered in obedience to the gait of the train. She began to look anxiously over the stacked luggage, her lips moving, but she had grown too set to adjust her balance from moment to moment, and suddenly she found herself sitting down. The train had dumped her out of the way. Good thing, too, she thought, chastising herself impatiently – counting the luggage, fussing, when in ten years Alfred's never forgotten anything. Old fool, she told herself, old fool. Her ageing self often seemed to her an enemy of her real self, the self that had never changed. The enemy was a stupid one, fortunately; she merely had to keep an eye on it in order to keep it outwitted. Other selves that had arisen in her life had been much worse; how terrible had been the struggle with some of *them*!

She sat down with her back to the engine, beside the window, and put on her reading glasses and took up the newspaper from Switzerland. But for some minutes she did not read. She heard again inside herself the words *alone, alone*, just the way she had heard them fifty-nine years ago when she was twelve years old and crossing France by herself for the first time. As she had sat there, bolt upright in the corner of a carriage, her green velvet fur-trimmed cloak around her, her hamper beside her, and the locket with the picture of her grandfather hidden in her hand, she had felt a swelling terror of exhilaration, the dark, drowning swirl of cutting loose, had tasted the strength to be brewed out of self-pity and the calm to be lashed together out of panic that belonged to other times and other journeys approaching her from the distance of her future. *Alone, alone*. This that her real self had known years before it happened to her – before she had lived the journey that took her from a lover, or those others that took her from the alienated faces of madness and death – that same self remembered years after those journeys had dropped behind into the past. Now she was alone, lonely, lone – whatever you liked to call it – all the time. There is nothing of the drama of an occasion about it, for me, she reminded herself dryly. Still, there was no denying it, *alone* was not the same as *lonely*; even the Old Fool could not blur the distinction of that. The blue silk coat quivered where Alfred had hung it, the bundle of magazines edged along the table, and somewhere above her head a loose strap tapped. She felt again aloneness as the carapace that did not shut her off but shielded her strong sense of survival – against it, and all else.

She opened the paper from Switzerland, and, with her left foot (the heat had made it a little swollen) up on the seat opposite, she began to read. She felt lulled and comfortable and was not even irritated by the thuds and dragging noises coming from the partition behind her head; it was clear that that was the woman next door – *she* must be fussing with her luggage. Presently a steward brought a tea tray, which Alfred had ordered before the train left. Mrs Hansen drew in her mouth with pleasure at the taste of the strong tea, as connoisseurs do when they drink old brandy, and read the afternoon away.

She took her dinner in the dining car because she had established in a long experience that it was not a meal that could be expected to travel train corridors and remain hot, and also because there was something shabby, something *petit bourgeois*, about taking meals in the stuffy cubicle in which you were also to sleep. She tidied her hair around the sides of her toque – it was a beautiful hat, one of four, always the same shape, that she had made for herself every second year in Vienna – took off her rings and washed her hands, and powdered her nose, pulling a critical, amused face at herself in the compact mirror. Then she put on her silk coat, picked up her handbag and went with upright dignity, despite the twitchings and lurchings of the train, along the corridors to the dining car. She seated herself at an empty table for two beside a window, and, of course, although it was early and there were many other seats vacant, the old woman from the compartment next door, entering five minutes later, came straight over and sat down opposite her.

Now it was impossible not to speak to the woman and Mrs Hansen listened to her with the distant patience of an adult giving half an ear to a child, and answered her when necessary, with a dry simplicity calculated to be far above her head. Of course, Old Fool was tempted to unbend, to lapse into the small boastings and rivalries usual between two old ladies. But Mrs Hansen would not allow it and certainly not with this woman – this acquaintance thrust upon her in a train. It was bad enough that, only the week before, Old Fool had led her into one of these pathetic pieces of senile nonsense, cleverly disguised – Old Fool could be wily enough – but, just the same, unmistakably the kind of thing that people found boring. It was about her teeth. At seventy-one they were still her own, which was a self-evident miracle. Yet she had allowed herself, at a dinner party given by some young friends who were obviously impressed by her, to tell a funny story (not quite true, either) about how, when she was a week-end guest in a house with an over-solicitous hostess, the jovial host had hoaxed his wife by impressing upon her the importance of providing a suitable receptacle for their guest's teeth when she took them out overnight. There was a glass beside the jug of water on the bedside table; the hostess appeared, embarrassedly, with another. 'But, my dear, what is the other glass for?' The denouement, laughter, etc. Disgusting. Good teeth as well as bad aches and pains must be kept to oneself; when one is young, one takes the first for granted, and does not know the existence of the others.

So it was that when the menu was held before the two women Mrs Hansen ignored the consternation into which it seemed to plunge her companion, forestalled the temptation to enter, by contributing her doctor's views, into age's passionate preoccupation with diet, and ordered fish.

'D'you think the fish'll be all right? I always wonder on a train, you know . . .' said the woman from the next compartment.

Mrs Hansen merely confirmed her order to the waiter by lowering her eyes and settling her chin slightly. The woman decided to begin at the beginning, with soup. 'Can't go far wrong with soup, can you?'

'Don't wait, please,' said Mrs Hansen when the soup came.

The soup was watery, the woman said. Mrs Hansen smiled her tragic smile, indulgently. The woman decided that she'd keep Mrs Hansen company, and risk the fish, too. The fish lay beneath a pasty blanket of white sauce and while Mrs Hansen calmly pushed aside the sauce and ate, the woman said, 'There's nothing like the good, clean food cooked in your own kitchen.'

Mrs Hansen put a forkful of fish to her mouth and, when she had finished it, spoke at last. 'I'm afraid it's many years since I had my own kitchen for more than a month or two a year.'

'Well, of course, if you go about a lot, you get use to strange food, I suppose. I find I can't eat half the stuff they put in front of you in hotels. Last time I was away, there were some days I didn't know what to have at all for lunch. I was in one of the best hotels in Durban and all there was was this endless curry – curry this, curry that – and a lot of dried-up cold meats.'

Mrs Hansen shrugged. 'I always find enough for my needs. It does not matter much.'

'What can you do? I suppose this sauce is the wrong thing for me, but you've got to take what you can get when you're travelling,' said the woman. She broke off a piece of bread and passed it swiftly around her plate to scoop up what was left of the sauce. 'Starchy,' she added.

Mrs Hansen ordered a cutlet, and after a solemn study of the menu, the other woman asked for the item listed immediately below the fish – oxtail stew. While they were waiting she ate bread and butter and shifting her mouthful comfortably from one side of her mouth to the other, accomplished a shift of her attention, too, as if her jaw and her brain had some simple mechanical connection. 'You're not from here, I suppose?' she asked, looking at Mrs Hansen with the appraisal reserved for foreigners and the licence granted by the tacit acceptance of old age on both sides.

'I have lived in the Cape, on and off, for some years,' said Mrs Hansen. 'My second husband was Danish, but settled here.'

'I could have married again. I'm not boasting, I mean, but I did have the chance, if I'd wanted to,' said the woman. 'Somehow, I couldn't face it, after losing my first – fifty-two, thats all, and you'd have taken a lease on his life. Ah, those doctors. No wonder I feel I can't trust them a minute.'

Mrs Hansen parted the jaws of her large, elegant black bag to take out a handkerchief; the stack of letters that she always had with her – new ones arriving to take the place of the old with every airmail – lay exposed. Thin letters, fat letters, big envelopes, small ones; the torn edges of foreign stamps, the large, sloping, and small, crabbed hands of foreigners writing foreign tongues. The other woman looked down upon them like a tourist, curious, impersonally insolent, envious. 'Of course, if I'd been the sort to run about a lot, I suppose it might have been different. I might have met someone really *congenial*. But there's my daughters. A mother's responsibility is never over – that's what I say. When they're little, it's little troubles. When they're grown up it's big ones. They're all nicely married, thank God, but you know, it's always something – one of them sick, or one of the grandchildren, bless them . . . I don't suppose you've got any children. Not even from your first, I mean?'

'No,' said Mrs Hansen. 'No.' And the lie, as always, came to her as a triumph against that arrogant boy (Old Fool persisted in thinking of him as a gentle-browed youth bent over a dachshund puppy, though he was a man of forty-five by now) whom truly she had made, as she had warned she would, no son of hers. When the lie was said it had the effect of leaving her breathless, as if she had just crowned a steep rise. Firmly and calmly, she leaned forward and poured herself a glass of water, as one who has deserved it.

'My, it does look fatty,' the other woman was saying over the oxtail, which had just been placed before her, 'My doctor'd have a fit if he knew I was eating this.' But eat it she did, and cutlet and roast turkey to follow. Mrs Hansen never knew whether or not her companion rounded off the meal with rhubarb pie (the woman had remarked, as she saw it carried past, that it looked soggy), because she herself had gone straight from cutlet to coffee, and, her meal finished, excused herself before the other was through the turkey course. Back in her compartment, she took off her toque at last and tied a grey chiffon scarf around her head. Then she took her red-and-gold Florentine leather cigarette case from her bag and settled down to smoke her nightly cigarette while she waited for the man to come and convert her seat into the deluxe bed Alfred had paid for in advance.

It seemed to Mrs Hansen that she did not sleep very well during the early part of the night, though she did not quite know what it was that made her restless. She was awakened, time and again, apparently by some noise that had ceased by the time she was conscious enough to identify it. The third or fourth time this happened, she woke to silence and a sense of absolute cessation, as if the world had stopped turning. But it was only the train that had stopped. Mrs Hansen lay and listened. They must be at some deserted siding in the small hours; there were no lights shining in through the shuttered window, no footsteps, no talk. The voice of a cricket, like a fingernail screeching over glass, sounded, providing, beyond the old woman's closed eyes, beyond the dark compartment and the shutters, a landscape of grass, dark, and telephone poles.

Suddenly the train gave a terrific reverberating jerk, as if it had been given a violent push. All was still again. And in the stillness, Mrs Hansen became aware of groans coming from the other side of the partition against which she lay. The groans came, bumbling and nasal, through the wood and leather; they sounded like a dog with its head buried in a cushion, worrying at the feathers. Mrs Hansen breathed out once, hard, in annoyance, and turned over; the greedy old pig, now she was suffering agonies of indigestion from that oxtail, of course. The groans continued at intervals. Once there was a muffled tinkling sound, as if a spoon had been dropped. Mrs Hansen lay tense with irritation, waiting for the train to move on and drown the woman's noise. At last, with a shake that quickly settled into a fast clip, they were off again, lickety-lack, lickety-lack, past (Mrs Hansen could imagine) the endless telephone poles, the dark grass, the black-coated cricket. Under the dialogue of the train, she was an unwilling eavesdropper to the vulgar intimacies next door; then either the groans stopped or she fell asleep in spite of them, for she heard nothing till the steward woke her with the arrival of early-morning coffee.

Mrs Hansen sponged herself, dressed and had a quiet breakfast, undisturbed by anyone, in the dining car. The man sitting opposite her did not even ask her so much as to pass the salt. She was back in her compartment, reading, when the ticket examiner came in to take her ticket away (they would be in Johannesburg soon), and of course, she knew just where to lay her hand on it, in her bag. He leaned against the doorway while she got it out. 'Hear what happened?' he said.

'What happened?' she said uncertainly, screwing up her face because he spoke indistinctly, like most young South Africans.

'Next door,' he said. 'The lady next door, elderly lady. She died last night.'

'She died? That woman died?' She stood up and questioned him closely, as if he were irresponsible.

'Yes,' he said, checking the ticket on his list. 'The bed boy found her this morning, dead in her bed. She never answered when the steward came round with coffee, you see.'

'My God,' said Mrs Hansen. 'My God. So she died, eh?'

'Yes, lady.' He held out his hand for her ticket; he had the tale to tell all up and down the train.

With a gesture of futility, she gave it to him.

After he had gone, she sank down on the seat, beside the window, and watched the veld go by, the grasses streaming past in the sun like the long black tails of the widow birds blowing where they swung upon the fences. She had finished her paper and magazines. There was no sound but the sound of the hurrying train.

When they reached Johannesburg she had all her luggage trimly closed and ready for the porter from the hotel at which she was going to stay. She left the station with him within five minutes of the train's arrival, and was gone before the doctor, officials and, she supposed, newspaper reporters came to see the woman taken away from the compartment next door. What could I have said to them? she thought, pleased with her sensible escape. Could I tell them she died of greed? Better not to be mixed up in it.

And then she thought of something. Newspaper reporters. No doubt there would be a piece in the Cape papers tomorrow. ELDERLY WOMAN FOUND DEAD IN CAPE–JOHANNESBURG TRAIN.

As soon as she had signed the register at the hotel she asked for a telegram form. She paused a moment, leaning on the marble-topped reception desk, looking out over the heads of the clerks. Her eyes, which were still handsome, crinkled at the corners; her nostrils lifted; her mouth, which was still so shapely because of her teeth, turned its sad corners lower in her reluctant, calculating smile. She printed Alfred's name and the address of the flat in Cape Town, and then wrote quickly, in the fine hand she had mastered more than sixty years ago: 'It was not me. Clara Hansen.'

Odysseus and Penelope

The story is –
shipwreck. Ambition feeds
conquest and then loss, fatigue.

He's homeward and weary,
wiser, seamed by the ancient sea.
The journey's worn him

like an old coat. Threadbare,
serviceable at last, the hero
quests base.

And there's the white house
somewhere high above the sea
for waiting in.

Decades, she's sewn and torn,
discovered something
tougher than fidelity

or deeper than she'd known:
resistance, the power to make
and undo,

dissemble, keep counsel,
let nothing in,
her courtyards

but the daily work and wisdom
of discovering
what lasts.

A bent man aged with weather
mounts the steps
and the others

partying the hours
of their idleness away,
look up.

Who's this? Scarred
as a coastline, horizons
within his eyes

a homecoming sailor,
all his journeying become simply
this return.

What's made, she hides,
her solitary life knit
on the warp of absence.

The work's there,
solid to its edge and seam
and unrepeatable.

MARGARET LAURENCE

from *The Stone Angel*

'You all right, Mother?' Doris's voice. 'Dinner will be a few minutes yet. Marv's just got home.'

'Would Steven like the oak chair, do you think?' I ask, for it's in my mind to leave it to my grandson.

Doris looks doubtful. 'Well, I can't say. He's doing his apartment in Danish modern, and it mightn't fit in very well with what he's got.'

Danish modern? The world is full of mysteries, and I will not ask. Wouldn't she love to think me ignorant, wouldn't she just.

'It doesn't matter to me. I only thought he might like it. I want it clearly known, who's to have what. People should never leave these things to chance.'

'You always said the oak chair was to go to Marv and I,' she says, grieved.

I – me – she never gets it right. And isn't she the sly one?

'I never said any such thing.'

She shrugs. 'Have it your way. But you've said it a million times.'

'Tina's to have the brown jug, Doris.'

'I know. You've been telling her that for years.'

'Well? What if I have? I like things properly seen to. Anyway, none of you will get a thing yet. I'm only preparing against the day. But it won't be for a while yet, I can promise you that. You needn't think otherwise.'

'Nobody ever mentions it but you,' she says. 'I wish you wouldn't talk that way in front of Marv. It upsets him.'

'You needn't worry about Marvin.' I find myself snapping the words, like cards flung on a table. 'There is a boy who never gets upset, not even at what happened to his own brother.'

Her face becomes unknown before my eyes.

'Boy –' she shrills, like a tin whistle. 'He's sixty-four, and he has a stomach ulcer. Don't you know what causes ulcers?'

'Me,' I suppose. I suppose that's what you're saying. You must have some place to fix the blame, mustn't you? Well, go right ahead. See if I care.'

'Let's not discuss it. What's the sense? I'm sorry – there, will that do? I'm sorry. You just sit quiet now. We'll soon have dinner.'

Now I am exhausted and glad enough to change the subject. I will not give her the satisfaction of believing me cranky. I will make the effort, as much as she, to be agreeable.

'Will Tina be home for dinner?' A safe remark. We are both so fond of the girl, the only topic we can be certain of seeing eye to eye.

Doris's eyes stare widely for a revealing instant. Then she hoods them.

'Tina's hundreds of miles away. She left a month ago to take that job down east.'

Of course. Of course. Oh, I cannot look at her, for shame.

'Yes, yes. It slipped my mind, just for the moment.'

She goes back to the kitchen, and I hear her talking to Marvin. She makes no attempt to lower her voice.

'She thought Tina was still here –'

How is it that I have kept my hearing so acute? Sometimes I wish it would dim, and all voices be reduced to a wordless drone in my ears. Yet that would be worse, for I'd always be wondering what they were saying of me.

'We've got to have it out with her,' Marvin says. 'It's not a job I relish.'

Then, frighteningly, his voice, so low and solid, goes high and seeking.

'What will I say to her, Doris? How can I make her see?'

Doris does not reply. She only repeats over and over the mother-word. 'There, there. There, there.'

The ribs can scarcely contain the thudding of my heart. Yet I do not know what it is that frightens me so. Marvin comes into the living-room.

'How are you feeling tonight, Mother?'

'Fine. Just fine, thanks.'

One would make that polite rejoinder, presumably, even at the very moment of yielding up the ghost. But I want only to fend off his talk, whatever it may be.

'I left my cigarettes upstairs, Marvin. Would you kindly fetch them for me?'

'He's tired out,' Doris says, appearing in the doorway. 'I'll go.'

'It's okay,' Marvin says. 'I don't mind. I'll go.'

They shuffle in the doorway, elbowing over who is to go.

'I wouldn't have asked,' I say aloofly, 'if I'd thought it would be that much trouble.'

'Oh, for Pete's sake, do we have to start this?' Marvin says, and lumbers off.

'You've coughed worse in the nights lately,' Doris says accusingly. 'Those cigarettes aren't doing you any good.'

'At my age, I'll take my chances.'

She glares at me. Nothing is spoken at dinner. I eat well. My appetite is usually very good. I have always believed there could not be much wrong with a person if they ate well. Doris has done a roast of beef, and she gives me the inner slices, knowing I like it rare, the meat a faint brownish pink. She makes good gravy, to give her her due. It's never lumpy, always a silken brown. For dessert we have peach pie, and I have two helpings. Her crust's a little richer than I used to make, and not so flaky but quite tasty none the less.

'We thought we might go to a movie,' Doris says, over the coffee. 'I've asked the girl next door if she'll come in, case there's anything you want. Is that okay?'

I stiffen. 'You think I need a sitter, like a child?'

'It's not that at all,' Doris says quickly. 'But what would happen if you fell, Mother, or got a gall-bladder attack like last month? Jill's ever so nice, and won't bother you at all. She'll watch TV and just be here if you need –'

'No!' I am shouting, suddenly, and my eyes are like hot springs, welling up with scalding water. 'I won't have it! I won't.'

'Mother – wait, listen –' Marvin intervenes. 'It was fine while Tina was here, but now – we can't leave you alone.'

'Leave me alone, for all I care. A fat lot you'd mind.'

Oh, but that was not what I meant to say at all. How is it my mouth speaks by itself, the words flowing from somewhere, some half-hidden hurt?

'You left a cigarette burning last night,' Marvin says flatly, 'and it fell out of the ashtray. Lucky I found it.'

Now I can say nothing. I can see from his face that he's not making it up. We might all have been burned in our beds.

'We've not been out this entire month since Tina left,' Doris says. 'Maybe you hadn't noticed.'

As a matter of fact, I hadn't. Why didn't they say something before? Why let it go, and then blame me?

'I'm sorry if I tie you down,' I say, in fury and remorse. 'I'm sorry to be a –'

'Cut it out,' Marvin says. 'We won't go. Phone Jill, Doris, and tell her not to come.'

'Marvin – don't stay on my account. Please.' And in truth, I mean it now that it's too late.

'It doesn't matter,' he says. 'Let's forget it, for God's sake. It's all this talk of it I can't endure.'

I go to my room, not knowing whether I've won or lost.

* * *

I hear the footsteps on the carpeted stair. They sound muted and velvety, as though it were a smotherer. I do not like those footsteps. I don't trust them. *Who is it? Who is it?* I want to shout, but my voice emerges punily, a little squawk. A suspicion comes to mind. Have Doris and Marvin gone out after all, leaving me here? That is what they have done. I am certain of it. Oh, without even telling me, so I could bolt the doors. They have gone, flown like heedless children. I can just see the pair of them, giggling together as they sneak off, across the front porch, down the steps and away. And someone else is here, now. Doris read me from the papers not long ago, all about a molester who broke into women's apartments. The newspapers said he had small soft hands – how disgusting in a man. When the intruder opens the door, I won't be able to rise from my chair. How simple to strangle. A flick of a necktie and I'm done for. Well, he won't find me as helpless as he thinks, not by a long shot. Doris hasn't given me a manicure for a fortnight. I'll claw him.

A knock. 'Can I come in, Mother?'

Marvin. Why should I have thought otherwise? I must not let him see my agitation or he'll think me daft. Or if he doesn't, Doris will, trotting behind him.

'What's the matter, Marvin? What is it, for mercy's sake? What's the matter now?'

He stands there awkwardly, his hands held out. Doris sidles up to him, nudges his ribs with a brown rayon elbow.

'Go on now, Marv. You promised.'

Marvin clears his throat, swallows, but fails to speak.

'Stop fidgeting, Marvin, for heaven's sake. I can't bear people who fidget. What is it?'

'Doris and me, we've been thinking –' His voice peters out, goes thin as shadows, vanishes. Then, in a gunfire burst of words, 'She can't look after you any longer, Mother. She's not been well herself. The lifting – it's too much. She just can't do it –'

'Not to mention the disturbed nights –' Doris prompts.

'Yes, the nights. She's up and down a dozen times and never gets a decent sleep. You need professional care, Mother – a nurse who'll see to everything. You'd be much happier yourself, as well –'

'More comfortable,' Doris says. 'We've been to Silverthreads Home, Mother, and it's really cosy. You'd love it, once you got used to it.'

I can only gaze as though hypnotized. My fingers pleat my dress.

'A nurse – why should I need a nurse?'

Doris darts forward, her face not soft and flabby now, but peering earnestly. She gesticulates, as though she could convince me by this trembling of her hands.

'They're young and strong, and it's their business. They know how to lift a person. And all the other things – the beds –'

'What of the beds?' My voice is austere, but for some reason my hands are unsteady on the squeezed silk of the dress. Doris reddens, glances at Marvin. He shrugs, abandoning her to her own judgment.

'You've wet your sheets,' she says, 'nearly every night these past few months. It makes a lot of laundry, and we haven't been able to afford the automatic washer yet.'

Appalled, I search her face.

'That's a lie. I never did any such thing. You're making it up. I know your ways. Just so you'll have some reason for putting me away.'

She grimaces, an unappealing look, and I see that she is nearly in tears.

'I guess maybe I shouldn't have told you,' she says. 'It's not a nice thing to be told. But we're not blaming you. We never said it was your fault. You can't help –'

'Please!'

My head is lowered, as I flee their scrutiny, but I cannot

move, and now I see that in this entire house, mine, there is no concealment. How is it that all these years I fancied violation meant an attack upon the flesh?

How is it that I never knew about the sheets?

How could I not have noticed?

'I'm sorry,' Doris mumbles, perhaps wanting to make it totally unendurable, or perhaps only blundering, having to wait another thirty years or so before she can know.

'Mother –' Marvin's voice is deep and determined. 'All this is beside the point. The point is – at the nursing home you'd get the care you need, and the company of others your own age –'

He is repeating the advertisement. Despite myself, I have to smile. So unoriginal. And all at once the printed words are given back to me, as well, like a revelation.

'Yes – give Mother the care she deserves. Remember the Loving Care she lavished upon you.'

I throw back my head and laugh. Then I stop suddenly, wheeze and come to a halt, and see his face. Does it express a vulnerability, or do I only imagine it?

'You're making it very hard for me,' Marvin says. 'I wouldn't have thought you'd be so queer about it. I've seen the place. It's just as Doris says. It's comfortable and nice. It would be all for the best, believe me.'

'It's certainly not cheap,' Doris says. 'But you've got the money yourself, luckily, and it's only right it should be spent on you.'

'It's in the country,' Marvin says. 'Cedars and alders all around, and the garden's well kept.'

'Full of petunias, I suppose.'

'What?'

'Petunias. I said petunias.'

'We'd visit you every weekend,' Marvin says.

I gather myself, my strength, my forces. I intend to speak with dignity. No reproaches, only a firm clear word. But that's not what I find myself saying.

'If it were John, he'd not consign his mother to the poorhouse.'

'Poorhouse!' Doris cries. 'If you had the slightest notion what it costs –'

'You're thinking of years ago,' Marvin says. 'Those places aren't like that now. They're inspected, for heaven's sake. They're – more like hotels, I guess. And as for John –'

He stops speaking abruptly, biting off the words.

'What of him? What were you going to say?'

'I won't discuss it,' Marvin says. 'It's not the time.'

'No? Well, he wouldn't have done what you're trying to do, you can be sure of that.'

'You think not? He was marvellous with Dad, I suppose?'

'At least he was there,' I say. 'At least he went to him.'

'Oh God, yes,' Marvin says heavily. 'He went, all right.'

'Marv –' Doris puts in. 'Let's stick to the point, eh? It's hard enough, without bringing up all that ancient history.'

Ancient history indeed. 'You make me sick and tired. I won't go. I won't go to that place. You'll not get me to agree.'

'You've got an appointment with the doctor next week,' Marvin says. 'We don't want to force the issue, Mother, but if Doctor Corby thinks you should go –'

Can they force me? I glance from one to the other, and see they are united against me. Their faces are set, unyielding. I am no longer certain of my rights. What is right and what rights have I? Can I obtain legal advice against a son? How would I go about it? A name from the telephone directory? It has been so long since I dealt with that kind of thing.

'If you make me go there, you're only signing my death warrant, I hope that's clear to you. I'd not last a month, not a week, I tell you –'

They stand transfixed by my thundering voice. And then, just when I've gained this ground, I falter. My whole hulk shakes, the blubber prancing up and down upon my rib-cage, and I betray myself in shameful tears.

'How can I leave my house, my things? It's mean – it's mean of you – oh, what a thing to do.'

'Hush, hush,' says Marvin.

'There, there,' says Doris. 'Don't take on.'

I see, recovering myself a little and peeking through the fingers fanned before my face, that I have frightened them. Good. It serves them right. I hope they're scared to death.

'We won't say any more right now,' Marvin says. 'We'll see. Later on, we'll see. Now, don't you get all upset, Mother.'

'I'd hoped to settle it,' Doris bleats.

'It's damn near midnight,' Marvin says. 'I gotta go to work tomorrow.'

She sees the moment has passed, so she makes the best of it, becomes attentive, plumps the pillows on my bed.

'You get a good sleep, then,' she says to me. 'We'll discuss it when we're none of us worked up.'

Marvin goes. She helps me into my nightdress. How it irks me to have to take her hand, allow her to pull my dress over my head, undo my corsets and strip them off me, and have her see my blue-veined swollen flesh and the hairy triangle that still proclaims with lunatic insistence a nonexistent woman-hood.

'Good night,' she says. 'Sleep well.'

Sleep well. Sleep at all, after this evening? I turn from one side to the other. Nowhere is right, and my eyes remain open wide. Finally I sink as though into layers and deeper layers of mist or delirium, into a half awakeness. Then I am jerked alert by one of the strutting shadows inhabiting the grey region where I lie drearily begging the mercy of sleep. *The soaking smelly sheets*, the shadow insinuates, in Doris's voice.

Then, just when I am afraid to sleep, for what may possibly occur, sleep wants to overcome me. I tussle with it, bid it begone, fidget and fuss so I may not yield. The result – my feet get cramps, and my toes are drawn up into knots. I must get out of bed. I cannot find the bedside lamp. I explore cautiously with my fingers in the air beside my bed, but discover nothing. Frantic, I wave my hands in the dark, and then the lamp goes over and shatters like a dropped icicle.

Doris comes running. She switches on the hall light, and I see, propped on an elbow, that she's put her hair up in curlers and looks hideous.

'What on earth's the matter?'

'Nothing. For mercy's sake, don't shriek so, Doris. You hurt my eardrums. That voice goes through me like a knife. It's only the lamp.'

'You've broken it,' she moans.

'Well, buy another. Buy ten, for all I care. I'll pay, I'll pay – you needn't fret. Here – I must stand – I've got cramped feet. Give me a hand up, for pity's sake, can't you? Can't you see how it hurts? Oh – oh – there. That's better.'

We stand on the bedside mat like two portly wrestling ghosts, pink satin nightdresses shivering, as I stamp up and down to work the muscles straight. She tries to bundle me back to bed, and I resist, lurching against her in the gloom.

'Good glory, what's the matter now?' she sighs.

'Go back to bed, for goodness' sake. I'm only going to the bathroom.'

'I'll take you.'

'You'll do no such thing. Get away. Get away now. Leave me be.'

In a huff she goes, ostentatiously turning on all the upstairs lights, as though I didn't even know the way to the bathroom in my own house.

When I return, I do not go to bed immediately. I leave the ceiling light on, and sit down at my dressing-table. Black walnut, it is, not solid, of course, but a good thick veneer, not like the plywood things they turn out these days. I reach for my cologne, dab a little on wrists and throat. I light a cigarette. I must take care to put it out properly.

I give a sideways glance at the mirror, and see a puffed face purpled with veins as though someone had scribbled over the skin with an indelible pencil. The skin itself is the silverish white of the creatures one fancies must live under the sea where the sun never reaches. Below the eyes the shadows bloom as though two soft black petals had been stuck there. The hair which should by rights be black is yellowed white, like damask stored too long in a damp basement.

Well, Hagar Shipley, you are a sight for sore eyes, all right.

I remember a quarrel I had with Bram, once. Sometimes he used to blow his nose with his fingers, a not-unskilled performance. He'd grasp the bridge between thumb and forefinger, lean over, snort heftily, and there it'd be, bubbling down the couchgrass like snake spit, and he'd wipe his fingers on his overalls, just above the rump, the same spot always, as I saw when I did the week's wash. I spoke my disgust in no uncertain terms, not for the first time. It had gone on for years, but my words never altered him. He'd only say 'Quit yapping, Hagar – what makes me want to puke is a nagging woman.' He couldn't string two words together without some crudity, that man. He knew it riled me. That's why he kept it up so.

And yet – here's the joker in the pack – we'd each married for those qualities we later found we couldn't bear, he for my manners and speech, I for his flaunting of them. This one time, though, he didn't speak as usual. He only shrugged, wiping his mucoused hand, and grinned.

'You know something, Hagar? There's men in Manawaka call their wives "Mother" all the time. That's one thing I never done.'

It was true. He never did, not once. I was Hagar to him, and if he were alive, I'd be Hagar to him yet. And now I think he was the only person close to me who ever thought of me by my name, not daughter, nor sister, nor mother, nor even wife, but Hagar, always.

His banner over me was love. Where that line comes from, I can't now rightly say, or else for some reason it hurts me to remember. He had a banner over me for many years. I never thought it love, though, after we wed. Love, I fancied, must consist of words and deeds delicate as lavender sachets, not like the things he did sprawled on the high white bedstead that rattled like a train. That bed was covered with a lambswool comforter quilted by his first wife, the cotton flowered with pink gladioli, the sort of thing Clara would have considered quite elegant, no doubt. In one corner of the room was my black leather travelling trunk, my former name on it in neat white paint, *Miss H. Currie*. In another corner stood the washstand, a shaky metal frame with a china bowl on top and a thick white china jug below. The bedroom was uncarpeted until finally Bram bought a piece of worn linoleum secondhand at an auction sale, and then the floor was shiny and beige, patterned in parrots, of all things, and every time you stepped across it, you had to tread on those stiff unnatural feathers of paddy green, those sharp-beaked grins. The upstairs smelled of dust, however much I cleaned. In winter it was cold as charity, in summer hot as Hades. Outside the bedroom window a maple grew, the leaves a golden green as the sunlight seeped through them, and in the early mornings the sparrows congregated there to argue, splattering their insults in voices brassy as Mammon, and I'd hear them and laugh, liking their spit and fire.

His banner over me was only his own skin, and now I no longer know why it should have shamed me. People thought of things differently in those days. Perhaps some people didn't. I wouldn't know. I never spoke of it to anyone.

It was not so very long after we wed, when first I felt my blood and vitals rise to meet his. He never knew. I never let him know. I never spoke aloud, and I made certain that the trembling was all inner. He had an innocence about him, I guess, or he'd have known. How could he not have known? Didn't I betray myself in rising sap, like a heedless and compelled maple after a winter? But no. He never expected any such a thing, and so he never perceived it. I prided myself upon keeping my pride intact, like some maidenhead.

Now there is no one to speak to. It is late, late in the night. Carefully, I put out the cigarette. Doris has the room littered with ashtrays. I rise, turn off the light, grope for my sheets.

My bed is cold as winter, and now it seems to me that I am lying as the children used to do, on fields of snow, and they would spread their arms and sweep them down to their sides, and when they rose, there would be the outline of an angel with spread wings. The icy whiteness covers me, drifts over me, and I could drift to sleep in it, like someone caught in a blizzard, and freeze.

SUSAN A. KATZ

New Directions

Outside there is a thin
wind flirting with the trees
it has teased the curtains
into dancing; I keep time
in my head.

Memorizing the seasons, I touch
things as if my fingers
will learn them
again; weary of explanations,
at mid-life I am more comfortable
with the truth.

Outside, the mountain ash hangs
heavy with orange berries,
like overripe breasts they weight
the branches down; I feel
the tug, my flesh molding
itself to gravity; closer now
to the soil than ever
to the sky.

JULIA BIRLEY

Rage

'You're very quiet,' she said, driving home. 'Anyone would think it was you only had the one champagne. All those different wines, you should have more to say for yourself, this night of all nights.'

That was a bit rich, in view of the fact that she had never drawn breath, even with her head poked over the wheel and eyes screwed up against the splashing rain and queue of oncoming lights. But when he said: 'I knew we should have taken a minicab,' she replied that it was nothing. 'We've got to pull in our horns a bit, all we're going to spend on the cruise. But come on now, what did you reckon?'

'Good. They certainly went to a lot of trouble to dignify the Order of the Boot.'

'Yes, Solly did ring, did I ever tell you, to ask if we'd like the Waggoner, as it's nearer, but when I said the Rose & Crown, he was pleased, because it seems they've a very good cellar. What was it he gave you with the lobster, all so nicely served, with all those little whatdyoucallems –'

She was just through with the menu by the time they turned into their drive. He opened up the garage with his pocket switch for her to drive in, and they both clambered out. There was a pause while he held the umbrella for her to unlock the house door, then shook it out while she switched off the alarm. Then it was into the lounge. The antique presentation clock was chiming a quarter to ten. On the console table, as if they had just got married, were ranged at least twenty cards and all the other sweeteners, including a great tome: *Construct a Rockery*, with 400 illustrations. She had to bend over it to make that strange grimace, her mirror face, which had intrigued him all through their married life, then mop up a slight overflow of mascara. By now she was on to the speeches.

'– really appreciative, and I thought what you said was excellent.'

'Thank you –' he was beginning, but she was chuckling, facing round and opening her freshly scarlet mouth so wide that the sad pouches under her eyes disappeared in a nest of mirthful wrinkles. 'That Jack – what a devil!' You have to laugh, but I could see some of the wives thinking, *well*. Sexy stuff about the boardroom gorillas challenging the old dominant male – and then pretending to shed tears about exchanging your p.c. for a life support machine! What's the matter?' For he had closed his eyes a moment, there in the middle of the room.

'You feeling all right?'

'Of course. Jack. Yes. Well. I wasn't thinking about him just then. I was thinking about someone quite different.'

He came to stand beside her, facing the mirror. A white-haired old josser was watching him in there. One who had done well for himself, sharply dressed, a bit red in the face, trim about the eyebrows and nostrils. Only those lizard eyes flicked away on meeting his; patently they were strangers, or wanted to be.

The stranger's wife was prinking in her dress, all over diamanté, that she had bought for the Gala Evening on the cruise; her little mug was perky under a helmet of black wire wool, streaked with copper and set off with sparkly danglers. The stranger could still fancy her, but not 'this night of all nights'.

'So here we are, two old things together,' she said. 'We're not so bad, are we?'

'You look fine.' He put his hand out, gently massaging a

knob of shoulder behind the diamanté cuirass, then took it away again.

She purred: 'You too. That jacket always makes you look younger.' Then pounced: 'So who were you thinking of?'

'Oh – Douglas McCree, for some reason.'

'How strange, why him?'

She had never known Doug, who was killed in a car crash long before they met (both having been married before). For her he was a young man in a demob suit, popping up once or twice in old photo albums; the one who had helped to start the business, just after the war.

'Ah well, it's like they say: all life passes before a drowning man's eyes.'

'Come off it, you're not drowning. You've a home, a pension and a nice wife – me. Aren't I nice? Anyway, what about him?'

'Oh – wondering how it would have been, what he'd have said if he'd been sitting in my place tonight. As he should have been.'

She snorted. 'You mean to say that anyone else but you would have hung on till past seventy?' Then, drawing a careful breath, 'You'd never have gone till you were pushed, you know.'

'True. Though they need not have made it quite so obvious. What else was I to do? It's too late to start anything fresh, my memory's not reliable.'

'God bless the man, haven't you earned a rest?'

'I never wanted a rest.'

'Well, you'll have to learn to like it, won't you, like everyone else. It's a question of finding your feet. All the people we know say the same – they're retired, but they've never been busier.'

'Doing *what*?' He swallowed as if his mouth was full of something bitter, and bent to pick up a fallen card, which was inscribed, 'May halcyon days be yours'. 'Well – I think I'll watch "Sports Night".'

'And I'm going up. Oh dear, I hope I'm not going to have trouble with you.'

He saw the programme, then the late film, and drank two double whiskies. At two-thirty he went upstairs, to be greeted by a torrent of snores. At four he went down again to turn off those incarnadined chimes. He would have said he had not slept at all, but suddenly it was day, and he was sitting up, befuddled by a dream so vivid he could still feel and even smell it: he was going up in the office lift with little Wendy from Accounts standing beside him and holding – whatever for? – a great sheaf of suffocating white lilies. It was past nine, he had missed the alarm, what the hell was she thinking of not to wake him? He thrust both trembling legs out of bed; then remembered.

Ten minutes later he was downstairs, wearing slippers and his weekend cardigan. She was dressed ready for the street. 'Hullo there. You were dead to the world, so I thought you were best left. Not jogging today? It isn't actually raining.'

He said he would go after breakfast.

'You shouldn't do it on a full stomach. You're looking seedy – is it the hangover?'

'Seedy', he guessed, was a euphemism for 'a hundred and five'. He said coldly, 'I'll go after lunch.'

'Well – about lunch. I'm off to work, as you know.' (He'd forgotten: what she pleased to call work, two days a week making tea and keeping records at the Community Centre, hardly paid her hairdressing bills.) 'If you stop in, just help yourself from the fridge, what you fancy, and pop it in the microwave. We'd better always lunch independently, that will leave you more free.'

'You too, I imagine.'

'If you like, yes. It's really enough to cook one meal a day. So now, what are you going to do?'

'Have breakfast, read the paper.'

'I mean today, dear. I've got to go now. What I thought you might do for me is to go down to the travel agent and collect the tickets and the insurance forms. They should be there by today.'

'Won't he post them? I thought of sorting my books. After all, there's weeks in hand.'

'Three. I prefer to collect them, it's less of a risk.' She whipped her bag over the shoulder of a cinnamon coloured trouser suit, tucked in a bright scarf. 'Only three weeks and it's Abu Simbel here we come!'

'I know,' he said, picking up the paper.

She got back to find him watching 'Neighbours', so she parked herself on the sofa, her suit smelling of the bus, and described how irritating someone had been at the Centre. On such occasions the marital autopilot may take over the listening and answering. When she said: 'I see you've still got the old bags on – does that mean you've made a start on the rockery?' it retorted:

'Actually no. But there's all the time in the world.'

'I hope you managed some jogging, then. You mustn't let things slide. Did you remember the tickets when you were out?'

The autopilot stalled a bit. 'They hadn't come. Mr Jeavons said he'd slip them in the post for us.'

'But I expressly – oh well. What did you have for lunch, anyway? Did you cook something?'

His own voice cut in. 'I thought you were giving up all responsibility?'

'Bet you forgot.' She put her arms round him while he sat there stiff as a waxwork. 'This isn't treating me right,' she coaxed him. 'You're pressurising me to baby you, tell you I'm leaving you this or that and you've got to do so and so and eat it up and wash the dishes –'

'But if you don't want to be bothered, then don't bother. Good Lord, what does it matter?'

Later on he asked: 'Won't the Nile be very hot, even at this time of year?' and fell to remembering why they had never taken holidays in the autumn. He had been too busy organising his Promotion Week, with the reps calling in from all over, full of high spirits and good stories. Recession had put paid to those Weeks. The PR was too expensive, according to his colleagues.

'Are you listening? I said it won't be any hotter than Majorca that time, and you know you loved it then. Which reminds me, I bought you a little something.'

She fetched a bag and shook out of it a sky blue T shirt with the London Marathon logo. 'There wasn't a plain one anywhere to be found. I thought this was just right, after all you did qualify once upon a time.'

He thanked her, and some days later put it in another bag, then into the bin. If she found it, she said nothing; nor did she comment on the piles of books which remained on the floor in front of the dusted shelves. But tactfulness got them nowhere. It was just being so much together that was making him wilt like an overwatered plant; something was wilting, anyway, to judge by the result.

Worst was the grisly ritual imposed by the business of not sleeping. She would have loved an excuse to pack him off to that fulsome G.P. ('Magnificent blood pressure – well done you!') Then pills, drowsiness, dependency, a giant step towards 'sans everything'. So he had to lie all night, listening for snores, flexing what he called his 'bovver knee', until he could see to get up and into his tracksuit, and shuffle down to the kitchen to kill an hour or so. When she got down, he would be standing by the back door, waiting to say that he was just leaving. A slow jog to the end of the road, or sometimes not so far, then stay out as long as he could, chilled to the bone by the wretched weather. If she asked, he always lied about the direction he had taken.

Then there was the business of eating: an absolute bone of

contention. She was so uptight about it, he could only assume she must feel guilty. When they went for a pub lunch on the Saturday, after shopping, and he said: 'I'll have whatever you're having,' she snarled at him so that people actually turned their heads.

'Even here you refuse to – I hope you're not going to be like this on the cruise. It won't be worth going if you're not going to enjoy anything.'

'Why wouldn't I enjoy it?'

'Goodness knows.' She put on a face of despair, then exclaimed, 'It's odd those tickets never came.'

'They did. Sorry, I forgot to tell you.'

He believed he had put them just inside the bureau, but of course when they got home, there was no trace. They ransacked the house until it seemed he must have imagined the arrival on the mat of that thick envelope with an ibis in the corner, which he had excused himself from opening.

'We must just go down together and sort it out Monday first thing. What about your passport now, is that up to date?'

His secretary had always seen to those things, even though the work had not taken him abroad much lately. But she must have been negligent, for when prodded into checking, he found it was due to expire three days before the end of the trip. The ensuing ruckus was infinitely more exhausting than negotiating some large contract ahead of competition. He began to lose count of time in the second week. Neighbours dropped in, the autopilot talked to them, and afterwards he could not remember who had been there.

Then Solly called round to deliver a fancy goblet with an inscription which had not been ready in time for the Presentation. Suddenly the autopilot let him down. He had not wanted to see any of them from the office so soon. The relevant questions would not come, so he had to hear how they missed him and all the rest of it, from this nice fellow who had probably taken his part to some extent against Jack and the other gorillas. Solly looked at the rumpled cardigan and suggested it must be hard to learn to let go.

Let go the rope. Life passes before the drowning man's eyes.

'Well, of course if you don't, sooner or later they chop your hands off.'

The nice fellow left, looking pained.

Now all the clothes they would both be taking were laid out on the spare room beds, one for him and one for her. Glossy brochures proliferated in other rooms, so that he was always putting something down on a pyramid or a string of camels, or find himself gazing at a page which showed, in columns of figures ringed here and there in biro, the unheard of sums he was about to disgorge. She had left off talking of the cruise in his presence, but at any time of day or evening she would be on the telephone, regurgitating the details ad infinitum. Once he heard her confiding: 'No, I can't wait to get him away. He wants it badly – yes, obstinate as they come – Rockery? Don't make me laugh –'

On the Friday, after he had been for a very long walk, she asked quietly, 'Where *do* you go all the time?' And now he honestly could not remember. Then she said: 'Your daughter phoned, she wants to see you. I said you'll be over tomorrow. She'll close the shop at one.'

'Will you come?'

'No, I've plenty to do. And she doesn't want to see me.'

It was true that Mara had not taken kindly to a stepmother, more or less shutting them both out of her life. But the rare chance of seeing Zoe, his lovely granddaughter could give a small fillip to existence even now. As if in sympathy the rain held off and the leaden clouds were thinning as he started on the twenty mile drive. As usual it awakened thoughts of his only daughter and her wasted life. A single parent in her twenties, tied by the leg and missing all her chances: now she shared a crumby little house on the edge of a nondescript village, not even with a bloke, just with the hard-nosed woman she worked for in the Craft Shop.

Mara was actually waiting for him, perched on the low wall like a schoolgirl, and smoking. When she jumped down and came to help him out of the car, he saw what he expected to see. That she moved well on her skinny, jeans-clad legs, that with this and the everlasting pony-tail, there was little to show that she must be pushing forty, no, past it by golly. The trouble, he was sure, lay in her offhand, jocular manners, which never conveyed the least hint of sex. Though his own idea of her must always be connected with the toddler who fell over at every other step and then mutely pushed her leg or her head under his nose to be 'kissed better', it had to be admitted that he and certainly most men, wanted women to be openly pleased with themselves and their difference, with a shade of 'come hither', even as battered old scarecrows with one foot in the grave.

On the doorstep he asked: 'And where's my Zoe?'

Busy opening the door, Mara said in a scratchy voice: 'She's gone back-packing to Nepal. A sudden decision. I'm sorry, you won't see her this side of Christmas, longer if her money holds out.'

Then, leaving him to get out of his coat by himself, she sloped off into the kitchen, sank down at the table and muttered: 'Sorry!' while the tears came splashing down.

Sorry, was she? He could hardly speak. 'Well, I'm gobsmacked. And you let her? What about her college place?'

'Postponed till next year.' Already scrabbling for another cigarette, Mara paused to blow her nose. 'Thinks she'll never have another chance like this. She was unstoppable.'

'I'd have stopped her, by gum I would. All that way, and she's only eighteen. It's bloody dangerous, you know that? Is she going with a group, or what?'

'No group,' she sniffed, smoking wildly. 'It's the boyfriend, of course. They'll be all right, he's really quite mature, but oh god, how I hate it! It's just me all over again . . .'

'But you never –'

'I don't mean she'll be caught like I was, but she goes off and spends all that time alone with him, so then she's *his*. Just when she's changing so fast, life's opening up, all the friends she should be making. Ah, it's the end of her youth.'

Not wanting to hear any more, he only said: 'Isn't it about time you gave up smoking?'

'Why should you care?' And she looked at him with red, sunken eyes of absolute vulnerability, yearning to be kissed better. Bitter rage made his legs weak, so that he had to sit down at last.

'Of course I care. Granted that old age isn't much to look forward to, it will be worse if you ruin your health. Did you get me over just to tell me about all this? It's a bit late.'

'You couldn't have helped anyway,' she answered, in his own flat tone. 'As a matter of fact your wife's been on the phone to me, saying she can't do a thing with you. I won't repeat all she said, but she wanted to know if I thought she should give up the cruise. To think of her asking my opinion!'

He was equally struck. 'But that's just absurd. She's not only totally dead set on it, she's made it pretty plain it's all I'm useful for now. Why should I be bothered? One thing's much the same as another for me now.'

'So I gathered.' She waited, leaving the cigarette to fume in its saucer, and he found himself letting out a little more. 'Not that it doesn't seem ironical, shelling out of my lump sum to spend a fortnight in a floating geriatric centre! I know these cruises: everyone under sixty gets out of the way, there's always some disabled and one or two who've lost their marbles. There's a gala night, you all dress up, a couple of fifth-rate belly dancers jump up on the tables and exercise their flab, then all the most senile characters, half seas over, women as well as men, get up and try to wiggle their pectorals, the waiters cheer and stamp to get a bigger tip, and they block the exits so you can hardly get out to go to the john. It's not such a big deal, you must admit. Not if you reflect that I was in Cairo at the end of the war. I saw the Sphinx and all the rest of it with Doug McCree, under rather different circumstances.'

'Doug McCree? I remember him. He was fun, wasn't he?'

'Yes, I think a lot about Doug lately. You know, I was supposed to have gone instead of him, that day his car piled up on the motorway. Then of course I was with him when he died.'

'Were you? I never knew.'

'Yes, I got there just in time, but he didn't know me. He was delirious, kept muttering to himself, "These figures – I now have pleasure in presenting these figures." He must have thought he was addressing a shareholders' meeting or something.'

'I see – yes. You wish now you'd gone like that, in his place.'

'Well it does sometimes seem that he had the best of it. This retirement thing is a sick joke, Mara, as far as I'm concerned. Never mind, now I'm here, what are we going to do? Shall I take you over to that place Trelandon, where they do the cream teas? You always used to go for those.'

'Yes, I passed the other day, and they've still got the notice up. Perhaps we should. She says you're not eating properly.'

Less than enthusiastic, she hauled herself to her feet and untied the pony-tail, getting ready. Suddenly she paused, comb in hand.

'And is that all the message you've got for me?'

'Message, how do you mean?'

'I'm in the middle of it all and you're at the end, so you know. Is there nothing you learn? Nothing that helps you?'

Once again her eyes begged and challenged, but having begun to tell the truth, he would not lie. Instead his face reorganised itself into an odd, secretive smile. 'Is that what my life is for, according to you? To give you a message?'

'So?'

Still he smiled and even laughed a little, putting a hand to her wan cheek. 'You're a good girl, you know that? Are we starting?'

Curious how the body reacts instantly to a change in the weather, like the leaden pall that dissolves into dove-coloured bars and folds, over blues ranging from duck egg to lavender! His own was feeling no less stiff, but lighter, freed of the clogging pressure that resembled drowning. It was easier to talk too. He could have told her now that it was no use blaming anybody or anything: if you live, time takes away whatever matters most to you. You are left with just yourself and it's a nasty shock; only perhaps you can do something about it. But that would hardly be comforting to a distraught mother, and besides, he wanted more time to think it over for himself.

Beyond the village the road plunged into a remembered valley, above a long meadow. A river ran at the bottom, where in days made sunshiny by distance, they used to come for picnics. A small ecstatic Mara haunted the place; he could all but see her down there, waving a branch and shouting. When he turned his head, another Mara was throwing her cigarette out of the window.

'She'll be back, you know, pet. It's not so long. She'll be all the more pleased to be at home because you didn't stop her going.'

'I hope so. Do you remember the marvellous trees along here? They're just beginning to turn. Oh, look at that!'

The maple, forgotten until this moment, and twice the size it used to be, stood by itself, a crimson curtain, fifty feet high and almost as broad. Refracted from breaking clouds, the light made it appear transparent, as if a fire burned inside a vast ruby.

He stopped the car and they both got out to stare at it. She said: 'It's better than ever. I'd no idea . . .'

'I must get her up here one day before we go,' he said. 'There'll be nothing more worth seeing on the cruise, that's for sure. Really, just at this moment, you wonder if there could be anything more beautiful in the world.'

KATHLEEN DAYUS

·••·

from *Her People*

Each Friday night Liza, Frankie and I had to stay up later than usual. This was not a treat, far from it. We had to blacklead the grate and the big, iron kettle that stood on the hob, as well as rub off any soot on the enamel teapot that stood beside it. On the other hob was a battered copper kettle which had a hole in the bottom; Mum never threw anything away. She said Dad would mend it one day, but he never did, and we still had to polish it. Jutting out from the top of the grate was a large meat jack which always held our stewpot. I called it a witch's cauldron. We had to scrub the deal-topped table, the stairs, chairs and the broken flag-stones, brown as they were from years of hard wear. The soda we used hardly touched them, the only things that were cleaned were our hands.

Standing each side of the fireplace were two wooden arm-chairs, one for Mum and one for Dad. We children were never allowed to sit in these unless given permission to do so, but we did make good use of them when Mum and Dad were out at the pub. Our usual seat was the old horsehair sofa under the window. Someone had given this to Dad in return for doing odd jobs. It replaced the old wooden one which was chopped up for firewood. Only the legs were spared because Dad said they might come in handy for something one day. Every corner of the house was cluttered up with odds and ends. Our sofa was moulting badly and had bare patches all over. We nicknamed it 'Neddy'.

66

Beside the table were two ladder-backed chairs, one for my brother Jack and the other for Mary. There had been three but after Charlie and Dad had a row over money, Charlie left home, and Dad burnt the chair. There was also a three-legged stool under the table; on its top stood our large, tin washing bowl. Set into the wall beside the fireplace was a long, shallow, brown earthenware sink. We only used this for putting dirty crocks in because we had no running water indoors. On the other side of the fireplace was an alcove behind the stairs door where the old, rotten mangle was kept; this was a permanent fixture. We had orders that if anyone called we had to leave the stairs door open to hide our laundry from view.

The fireguard, round the fireplace, was always covered with things airing or drying, especially when the lines across the room were full. Around the mantel-shelf was a string fringe with faded, coloured bobbles and on the shelf were two white, cracked Staffordshire dogs and several odd vases which contained paper flowers and pawn tickets. Hanging high on the wall above was a large photograph of our granny. We'd have loved to have got rid of it, but didn't dare. When you stared at it, the eyes seemed to follow you round the room. The effect was heightened at night when the paraffin lamp was lit. This was the only picture in the room with the glass intact. Mum in particular objected to it.

'I carn't see why yer don't 'ave a smaller picture of 'er. It takes up too much room.'

'No!' Dad would reply. 'Nothing's big enough for my mother. It stays where it is.'

'It'll fall down, you'll see, one of these days!' Mum replied.

'Not if you don't intend it to. But I'm warning you, Polly!' He wagged his finger at her in admonishment. So there the picture stayed.

We also had to dust all the pictures and knick-knacks that hung over the walls. There were three pictures, 'Faith', 'Hope' and 'Charity', as well as a print of 'Bubbles' – the advertisement for Pear's soap – and many photographs of Mum's first-, second- and third-born, all dead and gone. Underneath these were the death cards and birth certificates of the others, and photographs of relatives framed in red and green plush. They were so faded you had to squint to recognise who they were. There were even paper mottoes stuck to the wall which announced such sentiments as 'God Bless This House' and 'Home Sweet Home'. I could never understand why they were there, our house or home was far from happy. They were supposed to be Christmas decorations but they were not taken down until Easter, when Mum folded them up and put them away for next year.

On the wall opposite was a picture of Mum and Dad taken years ago on their wedding day. Mum looked happy, wearing leg o' mutton sleeves with her hair parted in the middle. Dad had one hand on her shoulder and was standing erect like a regimental sergeant-major. His hair was dark like Mum's and was also parted in the middle, with a kiss-curl flat in the middle of his forehead. His moustache was waxed into curls at each end. He held a bowler across his chest. Now as it happened this was the very same hat which had pride of place on the wall, just low enough for me to dust. One night I happened to knock this hat on the floor just as Mary entered. As I stooped to retrieve it she said, 'You'd better put that back on its nail before Mum comes in.'

So I snatched it up and, as I put it back, I replied, 'It's no good. It's going green. About time Mum got rid of it, like most of the relics here.'

'You'd better not let Mum hear you. She happens to be proud of that. It has a lot of memories for her.'

I went on working round the room; then I noticed that Mary was smiling. 'What are you smiling at, Mary?'

'Come and sit down and I'll tell you about it.'

I sat on 'Neddy', but before Mary sat down she peeped

round the curtain to see if anyone was coming. Then she began her story.

'Now that billy-cock –' she pointed towards Dad's delapidated hat, '– that hat has sentimental value for Mum. About the time when she started having the family . . . I'll tell you all about it, but only if you don't laugh and can keep a secret. Every twelve months Mum gave birth to a baby and when it was a few weeks old Mum and Dad went to church to have it christened. They thought they'd gone on their own. They never saw me watching them. I used to hide behind the pillar.'

Her face was beaming and I was intrigued to hear what was coming next.

'Now when the parson took the child off Mum he'd sprinkle water on its forehead and then it would cry and water would come out the other end. When the parson had finished the christening and handed Mum the baby she'd sit down in her pew and change its nappy. Well, it was then that Dad was at the ready. Taking off his billy-cock he'd take out a dry nappy and put the wet one inside the hat and then when he replaced it on his head, they'd leave the church and go in the pub to celebrate. You see I always followed them, just like you do.'

She gave me a sly wink and we both burst out laughing.

'Phew!' I cried, holding my nose.

Then she left and I finished my chores and although the house looked and smelt better it was not fresh air, it was carbolic soap and Keating's Powder. In the end I was almost too tired to crawl up the attic stairs and fall into bed. I just peeled off my clothes and was asleep immediately. I didn't even say my prayers.

Friday wasn't the only day I had chores to do. Saturday mornings was my day to get up early and be down to riddle the overnight ashes and place the embers in the steel fender ready to place on the back of the fire when it was lit. It was also my job to make a pot of tea and take a mug for Mum and Dad.

Now as the reader can imagine, Mum's temper wasn't always at its longest first thing in the morning. She'd yell at me, 'The tea's too 'ot!' or 'It's too cold!' or 'Not enough sugar in it. You ain't stirred it up!' She'd find fault with anything. This particular morning I was saved from her nagging, but only for a short time. Just as I was about to take the mug of hot tea upstairs, a loud knock sounded on the door. I lifted the corner of the curtain and peeped out. It was only the postman, who was a cheery man with a smile for everyone he met.

'Good morning, Katie, and how are you this bright, cheery morning?'

'Very well, thank you, Mr Postman,' I replied.

If only everybody in our district was as pleasant, life would have been much happier. He asked me to give a letter to Dad and returned down the yard. He'd only just stepped down from our door when Mum shouted, 'Who's that bangin' on the dower this time of the mornin'? Carn't we get any sleep around 'ere?'

She'd forgotten that she woke everybody, singing and banging at the maiding-tub at six o'clock every Monday morning.

'It's the postman, Mum. He's brought a letter for Dad,' I called back from the foot of the stairs.

I put the letter between my lips and turned to get the mugs of tea. It was then that I saw the postman standing under the window, shaking his head from side to side. I heard him tutting to himself as he walked down the yard. Mum shouted down again for the letter, so I hurried up to the bedroom where I found her sitting up in bed. I put the mugs down on the cracked, marble-topped washstand and had the letter snatched from my lips.

'An' about time too!'

'It's for Dad,' I said, loud enough to wake him.

'I know, I know,' she repeated. 'An' where's me tea?'

'On the table,' I answered timidly.

I made to go downstairs, but she called me back to read
the letter. Mum couldn't read or write. She couldn't even
count, except on her fingers and then it always took a pain-
fully long struggle. I always did any reading or writing when
Dad wasn't about. Dad could correct my spelling because he
was more literate than Mum and he spoke better too.
I watched him stir and yawn as I fumbled with the envelope.
I was glad he was awake; it was his letter anyway. But he
waved me away.

'Oh, read it, Katie, and let's get back to sleep.'

I was anxious myself now to find out what the letter con-
tained but when I'd opened it and read it there was no extra
rest for anyone that morning. It was from Granny and
although her spelling was bad I managed to read it out.

'"Sam an Polly,"' I read aloud, '"I'm not well in elth me
ouse as got ter be fumigated The Mans bin an ses Ive gotter
move for two weeks so Im coming ter you Ill bring wot bitta
money I got an Im goin ter joyn the salvashun army an Ill
bring me rockin chare an me trunk so Ill see yer all tomorra
so be up early. Hannah."'

She didn't ask if she could come, she just assumed she
could. When I'd finished reading the jumbled and nearly illeg-
ible writing, Mum jumped up with a start.

'Good God above!' she cried, waving her arms about. 'We
ain't 'avin 'er nuisance agen, are we?'

She glared at Dad, who was still lying on his back. He
wasn't asleep. Who could be, the way Mum was raving? But
he did have his eyes closed. He was thinking about how to deal
with Mum.

'Yow asleep, Sam? Dain't yer 'ear wot I said?'

'I heard yer,' he shouted back and opened his eyes wide.
'The whole bloody town can hear when you start.'

'Well, what can we do?'

'It's only for two weeks. Nobody will take her, so we'll have
to do the best we can,' Dad replied.

They must have forgotten that I was still standing at the foot of the bed. I watched them both lay back again and stare up at the ceiling deep in thought. Then suddenly Mum shot up out of bed. I'd never seen her move so quickly, nor look so misshapen as she did then, standing beside the bed in her calico chemise all twisted up in the front. I'd never seen her undressed before, or without her whale-bone stays. She used to have them laced so tightly she used to look like a pouter pigeon with her heavy breasts pushed up high. I never knew how she got all that flabby flesh inside those stays. She looked so comical that I had to put my hand over my mouth to keep from laughing out loud. As she leant over the bed and shook Dad, her belly wobbled and her bare breasts flopped out of the top of her chemise.

'Sam!' she shrieked. 'Wake up!'

'Stop bawling. I'm not deaf.'

'I wanta knoo where 'er's gonna sleep.'

I thought it was about time to go downstairs before they noticed me giggling.

'Shall I go and make some more hot tea, Mum?' I managed to say.

Suddenly she realised that I was still there and she yelled at me to shut up and clear off as she tried to cover herself with her shift. This was the chance I'd been waiting for, so I fled downstairs, but still strained to hear what was being said.

'Now listen, Polly, and calm down. You know she'll help. She'll bring you some money for her keep and if you don't tell the relief officer we'll be all right.'

'But where d'yer think she's gonna sleep? She carn't sleep with us. It ain't decent.'

'I'll sleep on "Neddy" for the time being so don't worry about me.'

This arrangement must have pleased her because I heard a change in her voice.

'Orl right, just as yer like, Sam.'

Now the shouting had died down, I took two mugs of tea up to find that they were still discussing Granny. I stood the mugs on the table and stood anticipating the usual grumbles from Mum but she and Dad just lay there looking snug and warm. She pulled the clothes around her and turned to Dad.

'Do yer think the bed'll 'old us two? She's sixteen stone. I'm sixteen stone an' that meks us . . . er . . . er . . .'

I could see she was trying to puzzle out how many stones they would both be. Suddenly she sat up in bed. Sticking her two hands in front of her face and spreading her fingers apart she began to count. 'I'm sixteen and sixteen makes seventeen, eighteen, nineteen . . .'

'Sixteen and sixteen makes thirty-two,' I said, trying to help.

'I count my way then I know I'm right,' she snapped.

Dad lay back smiling and let her get on with it. Up went the fingers again and she counted on each finger again and again until eventually she yelled, 'The bed'll never 'old us!'

Dad and I collapsed in laughter as she tried with her hands to demonstrate the combined weight.

'Well,' Dad replied, still smiling, 'if you both come through the ceiling we'll have to do a moonlight flit.'

This was not the first time a flit was threatened, but we never did.

'Well, we'd better get up an' goo downstairs an' 'ave an 'ot cuppa. This is stone cold.' She handed me the mugs of tea which they'd forgotten to drink.

I found Frankie and Liza washed and dressed when I got downstairs. I was pleased because I could see that my brother had lit the fire and had put the kettle on to boil. Mum and Dad were not long following. We pulled our chairs up to the table and waited for our breakfast which turned out to be a burnt offering of toast; however, the tea was fresh, as I'd just made some more. Usually the leaves were used over and over again until they were too · weak to stand the strain, then they were thrown on the back of the fire. Nothing was ever wasted if it could be reused, not even water or paper. We seldom had enough to eat. Sometimes we sat like three Oliver Twists, although we didn't dare ask for more. In fact, if we ever refused to eat anything that was placed in front of us, it was taken away and we had to eat it next mealtime, by which time we'd be so hungry we'd be glad of it. After our burnt toast, Dad told Mum to get the bedroom ready and he pinched her bottom as she rose from the table. She waved his hand away and warned him not to do it in front of us children. They both seemed happier. He pushed her gently up the stairs and turned to wink at us. I thought, if only they were always smiling or acting this way our lives would be much happier.

As we stood washing up the mugs and enamel plates we could hear the iron bedsteads being dragged along the bare floorboards towards the wall so that Granny wouldn't fall out of bed. This was only the preliminary to a hectic tidying up operation and although we'd cleaned the night before, we had to get out the carbolic soap and begin again. Mum was always one for making an impression when Granny called, but I couldn't see why because Granny's house was far more cluttered than ours. Dad cleared out and Frankie and I were left singing as we dusted and scrubbed. When Liza joined in Mum yelled at her to stop her 'cat warlin'. I think she was expecting another gob-stopper but if so she was unlucky. We all fell silent and I thought maybe Granny would bring a little cheerfulness into our home now she was going to join the Salvation Army.

Very early next morning, before anyone was awake, I heard a loud knock on the downstairs door and before I could get out of bed a louder knock and three taps on the window pane. I woke Frankie and Liza with a good hard shake and told them what was happening. We three got out of bed and dressed quickly. Then we lifted the window to see what the racket was all about. As we leant over the window sill to look down into the yard below we saw Granny at the door, calling and waving her arms in all directions.

'Ain't nobody awake yet! 'Ave I gotta stand 'ere all day? I'm freezin' an' if nobody lets me in I'm comin' through the winda.'

She sounds just like Mum, I thought. Then, before anyone could get down to let her in, she tried to push up the window. Turning to the little man who'd brought her things on a hand cart, she shouted for assistance. He looked too scared to move. Then Granny saw the bucket of rainwater that Mum kept for washing her hair. She promptly tipped the water away and turned the bucket upside down. Then she pushed the window up and stepped on to the bucket to aid her entry. The reader can imagine what a funny sight sixteen stone Granny was, standing on a rusty old bucket. We were not used to the capers that Granny cut. Suddenly, just as she was halfway through, disaster struck. The sash cord broke and the bucket slipped leaving Granny pinned half in, half out, by the window frame. She began to kick her legs in a vain attempt to free herself but she only succeeded in showing the neighbours her pantaloons. For the first time we experienced a temper worse than Mum's. She swore till the air was blue. Proof, I thought, that she needed to join the Salvation Army. Then Dad popped his head out of the window and called down angrily, 'You'll have to wait, Mother, while I slip me trousers on.'

When he came downstairs and saw the plight she was in, he lifted the window but he was too quick. Granny fell out backwards, rolled over the bucket and landed in a puddle of rainwater.

'An' about time too,' she bawled while he struggled to pick her off the floor.

'I'll get meself up,' she muttered.

By this time Mum's head had appeared at the window and the neighbours too were peering down at the commotion.

"Annah!' Mum shouted. 'Yer'll wake up all the neighbours.'

'Wake 'em up! Wake 'em up!' she shrieked, struggling to her feet.

She turned round and waved her fist at the amused onlookers and bellowed at them, getting redder and redder in the process.

'Look at 'em! The nosy lot of idle sods.'

All the time she'd been carrying on, the little old chap was standing still, waiting to be paid for his labours. Suddenly she turned on him, leaned against the cart and sniffed.

'Don't stand there all day. 'Elp me off with me trunk an' me rockin'-chair. An' mind 'ow yer 'andle me aspidistra.'

He couldn't manage the trunk nor the rocking-chair, but Dad soon came to the rescue. Meantime Granny felt inside the bosom of her frock, sniffed a couple of times and pushed a silver sixpence into his outstretched hand. He looked down at it disdainfully and mumbled a barely audible 'Skinny old Jew'.

'What did yer say?'

'I said, "Thank you",' he answered meekly.

'Dain't sound much like "thank yer" ter me,' she retorted.

Scratching his head, he wheeled his empty cart away and said to Dad in a louder voice, 'I feel sorry for yow, mate,' but Dad ignored him.

The neighbours closed their windows. The fun was over for them but for us the trouble was only just beginning. We dressed hurriedly and dashed down to see Granny. She looked huge standing beside the trunk. We hadn't seen her for some time and it was easy to forget her size. She wore a black taffeta frock almost to her feet, black elastic-sided boots and a battered black woollen shawl. Her lace bonnet, also black, was hanging from ribbons on the back of her neck where it had slipped while she'd been trying to climb through the window.

Her hair, too, was dishevelled, but what I noticed most was the large raised lump on her behind. I poked Frankie and he whispered, 'Ain't she got a big bum.'

'That ain't her bum. It's a bustle,' I replied as he started to snigger.

Liza too stared at Granny, but Granny paid us no attention until she suddenly straightened herself up to her full height of six feet, pulled her shawl around her and addressed us. 'Don't just stand theea gorpin'. Come an give yer ol' gran a kiss.'

I closed my eyes and lifted my face up sideways for her to kiss my cheek. She must have read my thoughts because she just pushed me roughly away, with a slap and bent to peck Liza and Frankie's cheeks. As I walked off clutching Topsey she asked what I was holding.

'It's the golly you made me, Granny,' I replied.

'I don't remember mekin' that.' She shrugged her shoulders and dismissed me.

'Now, now, Mother. You gave it to her last Christmas. You must have forgotten.' Dad attempted to pacify her.

'Er's always forgettin',' Mum piped up from putting Granny's plant away.

'Put the kettle on Polly, and we'll all sit down and have a cup of tea.'

This was Dad's favourite tactic when he saw a quarrel brewing. He drew Gran's rocking-chair towards the fire. Granny sat down and rocked in the creaking chair. With hers in the middle and Mum's and Dad's chairs on either side of the fireplace no one else could feel or see the flames. I picked up Topsey and sat with Frankie on 'Neddy' to await my tea. When it was made, Granny's was the first cup to be filled. Then she took a sip and without warning spat it back out.

'What yer call this?' she spluttered, pulling a face at Mum.

'It's yer tea. Like it or lump it.' This was a favourite retort.

'Tastes like maid's water ter me.' Granny could give as good as she got.

We looked at each other; we all knew what Mum's tea was like. The pot had been stewing all morning. Dad told me to make a fresh pot. As I squeezed past Mum to empty the tea leaves into the spare bucket, I heard her whisper to Dad, 'Thank the Lord we've only got 'er fer two weeks.'

COLETTE

In the Flower of Age

'Thursday . . . Thursday is the cocktail party at the
Schlumbergers', a little six to nine affair . . . Friday we're
taking a picnic to Thoronet. I'm preparing one of those warm
breads for them, stuffed with crushed anchovies in oil and
sweet red peppers, with a pinch of thyme . . .'

Madame Vasco pressed her lips together in greedy antici-
pation, half closing her eyes.

'Sunday, of course, we're giving the whole house the night
off. Martine and Marinette want to go to the movies with the
valet. Teobaldo will stay with the dogs . . . Oh, and about
tonight . . . Shall we accept the invitation to the artists'
impromptu? You know, everyone dresses up in costumes made
exclusively out of whatever's lying around, old newspapers,
kitchen aprons, wrapping paper, and towels . . . You already
stood us up the day before yesterday, you bad boy. And last
Wednesday it was the Simonis who brought me home. You
don't have to worry about being bored tonight . . . Henri
Simoni is making his costume out of discarded postal parcels,
all corrugated cardboard and string, it'll be smashing!'

Paul Vasco did not answer right away. He lay stretched out
on his back on the wide conjugal bed, his outspread arms
bronze against the pink batiste and russet lace. A hand, whose
firmness he knew well, ran like a stiff comb through the dis-
order of his damp, blond hair, and he decided it was time he
opened his eyes.

'Ah, there you are, my two periwinkles!' said his wife in a softer voice.

Sitting up beside him, she held on her lap the small lemon-wood breakfast tray laden with pink china. The Paris morning papers were strewn across the pink bed, soiling it with their ink; a branch of pale blue plumbago, brought back by Paul from the path that led down to the sea, was being used by the white cat, which was deaf, as a toy. The sun had just entered the room and was making its way across the black rug. The bougainvillea hung slightly over the edge of the balcony. A pale sky, the sky of summer mornings on the Mediterranean, filled the window. Paul Vasco resigned himself, as he did every morning, to looking up at his wife, and every morning he was amazed.

Tall, careful of her weight, strong and healthy, she didn't hesitate to tie her hair, thrown back and dyed a golden chestnut, with a little ribbon whose color changed with that of her dressing gown, and in the summer she tanned like a young woman. But her tan refused to penetrate certain creases, fine as incisions, forming at the corners of her eyes and around her neck, despite surgical intervention. Madeleine Vasco smiled down at her young husband, showing her teeth looked after and corrected by a master. Between her ear and her hairline, between the hair at her temples and the corner of her eye, Paul could make out the thin, scarred folds, looking mauve beneath the ochered powder. 'She's amazing,' he thought. 'Even I would never imagine she was sixty-two years old. Besides, even if I did, she'd tell me it was all in my imagination.'

He closed his eyes again with the irresistible laziness that followed his morning swim and a run on the beach.

'You haven't answered me about tonight. Sleepyhead, oh, my beautiful sleepyhead . . .'

For him it was not a question of answering but of stalling for time, of holding out, by lying motionless, until the moment when his wife, summoned by the need to oblige her stubborn beauty, would leave him for an hour and a half.

'Whatever you like,' he sighed at last.

With a snap of his fingers he called for a cigarette, which Madeleine put, already lit, between his lips.

'You could say,' he joked, 'that the only thing I brought here was a mouth to smoke with . . .'

'And who's asking you for anything else?' she countered.

With a penetrating and bold gaze, she caressed that mouth, whose smile and firm freshness had persuaded her into the foolishness of remarrying, ten months after the death of her first husband, thus snatching, from a minor office position, a poor, handsome, and by chance honest young man. For Paul Vasco she had given up her widow's weeds and her semi-mourning, dyed her gray hair, and from her widow's chrysalis had emerged a tall, strong woman in love, so set on happiness that she dazzled her young spouse, thirty years her junior. For two years now, from January to May, they had been coming 'to the Riviera,' as Paul naively put it, he as yet not having grown tired of the luxury of an estate in the south, with its paths of pink sand, its wisteria, and its marble terraces. The smiles around them were discreet, for Madame Paul Vasco, shaded by large hats, wearing simple makeup, had a rather flashy way of refusing her husband's arm when climbing the stairs of the casinos. He followed her, served her, and found her young. However, he could never overcome his apprehension when she was dancing with him. 'I've got a strong heart, you know . . .' she would say. 'I'll give you a few pointers when they play the hesitation waltz.' In fact, she waltzed with long, gliding, somewhat masculine steps, and she never had to stop to catch her breath, holding her hand to her flat, jewel-clad breast. It was Paul who while dancing would experience a certain anguish, grow pale, and say softly, 'Enough . . .' He could not hold up next to his wife's stamina, her bony and mechanical lightness. He had a childish fear of a sudden creaking of hinges, a squeaking of springs. She never seemed less alive than when she was proving her agility, and as they danced he would press his temple against hers, trying not to notice that as she waltzed she stared wildly, straight ahead, and breathed through her painted, half-open mouth.

But once he was back at the estate, life again became sweet and easy. He felt at home there, and quickly developed a taste for laying out gardens and plotting the best colors for the flower beds with the head gardener.

'Shall we go somewhere?' Madeleine asked him after their siesta.

'Yes!' exclaimed Paul enthusiastically. 'Let's go to Fréjus. I need seven hundred geranium-ivy cuttings!'

'Teobaldo will pick them up in the station wagon, don't bother.'

He pouted, and Madeleine looked at the pouting mouth.

'What a child! You really want to go? Have them bring the car around . . .'

For she gave in whenever she feared he might be getting bored. Somewhat distracted, and vain about his physical beauty, he was never bored when he was parading around half naked in the sun or tossing the medicine ball with the trainer who came down from Cannes.

One evening as Madeleine Vasco was calling her husband and fidgeting with impatience in a long black velvet dress trimmed with monkey fur, and shouting, 'We'll be late! The ballet starts at nine in Monte Carlo!' she was stupefied to see Paul emerge from the cellar, whitened ever so slightly by spider webs and saltpeter, with a venerable old bottle under each arm.

'Where have you been?'

'Can't you tell?' he said. 'We absolutely have to put the wine book back in order and the vintages in the racks have to be reclassified. It's a shambles down there!'

Madeleine raised her plucked eyebrows and the wrinkles on her forehead all the way up to her hairline.

'What can that possibly have to do with us, my darling?'

'Why,' said Vasco, 'it's the man's job to keep the cellar in order.'

'Does it amuse you?'

He smiled a competent smile. 'Very much.'

'And that's why you're going to make us miss *Les Sylphides*?'

He seemed to wake up suddenly, looked at the dress, the woman, and the dazzling new jewel she was wearing on her bodice, next to skin which had lost its smoothness, its soft and supple mystery. He offered no protest and dashed off to get dressed.

'Give me five minutes!'

She remained alone, waiting for him on the lower terrace, walking in the wind which was ruffling the water and bringing the day to an end. She yawned and admitted to herself that she had no less of an appetite for delicate fish and champagne than for lights, music, new faces . . .

As soon as his wife had closed the door to her bathroom, Paul Vasco sat up on the rumpled bed and let out a gentle sigh. He was not a cynical man and he accepted kindness in a spirit of resignation. His wife's frivolous energy did not frighten him unduly, for she did not bring to her way of leading the life of a young socialite the insane bitterness of aged bacchantes, but rather the determination of an ex-bourgeoise who remembered what it was like to have a dotty old home-body for a first husband. Paul learned how to escape, every fifth time, then every third time, from the dinners, the suppers, the automobile races, and the rallies. 'Banner of Honor to the red-and-white sedan of Madame Paul Vasco . . . '

He slid down to the foot of the pink bed and swore to himself that he would not go to the artists' costume party. 'Those clowns of all ages can get themselves up in old newspapers, grocery bags, straw wigs, curtains, and straw mats without me.' There was sure to be a painful moment when he would say to Madeleine, 'I'm not going.' There would be that look in his wife's eyes, as if they were lying in ambush between the lashes of a starlet, and the silent disdain inflicted on a stay-at-home young man by an indomitable sixty-year-old scatter-brain . . . But what a reward it was, afterward, to savor an evening devoted to filing away bills and reading a manual dealing with the rejuvenation of trees by frequent injections into the root cap!

He managed his day as carefully as an adolescent wanting to spend the night at a friend's, a soldier hoping to slip over the wall . . . While she was having a light dinner across from him, he asked his wife what sort of costume she was planning. Excitedly, she confided to him that, for herself, she was counting on using a crocheted bedspread lent her by Luc-Albert Moreau, and for Paul, a big lampshade tied around his waist, or else a woven straw seat cover.

'But we go in evening clothes, and put our costumes on there,' she added.

He made no objection, but as soon as he was alone, he put on a comfortable robe and his slippers, sat down in front of a blazing fire which made his cheeks glow, and, while waiting for the conjugal onslaught, read the evening edition of *L'Eclaireur de Nice et du Sud-Est*, over which he fell asleep.

Toward midnight, a sequined train slithered down the stairs with a delicate, snake-like sound. But the heavy tapping of heels, on each step, made it known that Madeleine's knees were struggling against the onset of anchylosis. She came to the bottom of the stairs followed by her obedient, steel-gray, and glittering train. A scarlet cape, thrown over her shoulders, left only her bedecked, golden, proud head showing. Walking toward a mirror, she caught sight of her young sleeping husband and stopped. He was asleep with his head drooping to one side, with the light from the fire caressing his plump, dimpled chin, and two clearly drawn frown marks framing his childishly pouting mouth. An empty cup was proof that he had had some verbena tea, and the deaf cat slept at his feet on the open newspaper. Leaning over, Madeleine Vasco pressed her bracelets to her side to keep them from jingling. Where had she seen that robe and those slippers before, and the hermetic cat, the medicinal cup, and above all this sudden sleepiness which betrays a man's weakness? . . . The image of the late Monsieur Perrin, her first husband, rose up between her and Paul Vasco, and she drew back. Facing her in the mirror, a tall woman, scarlet and gray, thin because she had to be, erect because she wanted to be, matched her glance for glance, and her mouth, smothered with lipstick, smiled. Madame Vasco took a last look at the sleeping man, muttered gruffly, 'Just another old man!' and with two fingers picked up her train and left without looking back.

Translated by Matthew Ward

MARI BEINSET WAAGAARD

The Sweet Old Lady
Who Cried Wolf

One day the sweet old lady came into the police station and said, 'Forgive my disturbing you again, Inspector, but you see, there's a dead body in my garden in Grefsen Alleen.'

She leaned confidentially across the desk and whispered, 'He's such a nice elderly gentleman. He's lying in my poppy bed in such a peculiar, twisted attitude. And there's a knife in his back too. I'm certain this must be foul play, Inspector; wilful and cold blooded murder, don't you think?'

Chief Constable Ole Gregersen looked at Thea Dahl, his new assistant, and made a sign to her. Then he bent down and patted the sweet little old lady on the arm and said reassuringly, 'Come now, Mrs Werle. Are you quite sure you saw a body? You may be mistaken, you know. Have another look. And promise me,' he pointed a mock-threatening finger, 'promise me you'll stop reading all that nonsense you're filling your pretty little head with. All those detective stories aren't good for you, you're much too sensitive and imaginative. Promise, Mrs Werle! Now, you be a good girl . . .'

The sweet old lady blushed, looked reproachfully at the policeman and muttered under her breath as she turned to leave the station, 'My, oh my, Inspector, you're incorrigible – and a great tease too. But I'll do as I'm told. I'll walk straight home and have another look. But I'm sure the gentleman with the knife will still be there. It's a shame. Anyway . . . Good day to you, Inspector, and to you too, Miss.'

Thea Dahl gazed appalled at her superior. 'For heavens' sake, Mr Gregersen, what if the woman's telling the truth? There *might* be a dead man in her garden. You really shouldn't snub her like that, Sir, a sweet old lady like her!'

Mr Gregersen grinned then sighed and said musingly, 'You're new here. If you weren't, you'd know that this little old lady, Agnete Werle, pops in every month or so to report crimes. Crimes which only exist in her imagination, that is. A murder, a theft, a swindle. You remember when Edward Munch's "Vampire" was stolen from the Munch Museum? She turned up regularly once a week and told us where we could find the painting. It was even hanging in her sitting-room! As we didn't know her then we sent a couple of the boys to check, just in case, but of course it was sheer non-sense. Actually we checked her false reports of thefts and murders on several occasions and gave her quite a talking-to. She just looked at us with those innocent blue eyes and said she was sorry! She is very sweet but more than a bit eccentric and I think a little bit soft in the head too. But don't worry, I won't offend her or hurt her. After all, she wouldn't hurt a fly.'

Gregersen paused and thought for a while, then went on, 'I feel sorry for her, in a way, although she seems happy enough. She's rich, mind you – rolling in money and she lives in a beautiful house, all inherited from her husband. He was a war hero – fought in the resistance against the Nazis.'

Thea Dahl listened attentively. 'Does she really live by herself? She must be quite an age.'

'As a matter of fact she's in her eighties but she's fit as a fiddle. Alone, yes, but there's a woman who comes in to clean the house once a week and I think she rents out a room to a female student just to have a young person around, not for the cash of course; and she certainly is generous with her money . . .'

Meanwhile the young tenant in Mrs Werle's house, Ellida Wang, was deep in conversation with her boyfriend, Jorgen. Both 'students', both unemployed, both very broke, both obsessed with the idea of getting hold of money, lots of money, in the easiest way possible. They had tried burglary and the like without success and had so far avoided the police.

But now there was a chance of realising their dreams. Money, exciting journeys, *la dolce vita* . . . Let us listen for a moment to their interesting conversation.

Jorgen: To hell with your crappy sentimentality. It's settled now. The old bat has absolutely no use for all that cash. Damn Amnesty or Save the Children or whatever she gives it to. It's you and me who need to be saved – before we die of boredom and poverty.

Ellida: Okay, okay. But I can't help feeling a bit sorry for the old girl. I mean, she is sweet in a way. And she relies on me. She's even told me she'll give me some money when I've graduated.

Jorgen: Shut up, idiot! When did you manage to pass an exam in your life? No, we've got to do the job. Remember, she's worth two million. It'll be like taking a lollipop from a baby.

Ellida: She's cleverer than you think, hides her dough pretty cunningly . . . Hey, look out of the window! Here she comes, toddling along. Look at her smile and that white hair – and look at that crazy hat!

Jorgen: Don't go all soft on her now. You weren't all that soft when we did over that old couple, remember? You laughed your head off when the old bloke saw his pension disappear . . . Well, I'd better make myself scarce before the old lady catches me.

Ellida was sitting with Ibsen's 'The Doll's House' propped in front of her when Mrs Werle entered, flushed and breathless after her quick walk.

She beamed when she saw Ellida studying so diligently in the huge library.

'That's right, my dear. I see you're working hard and using

my library as I told you to do. You'll find all the books you'll need here, classics and the moderns. But isn't it time you were off, Ellida? It's Wednesday: there's that lecture in old Norwegian literature this afternoon, the one you told me about, remember?'

When the young woman was out of sight Mrs Werle went straight to one of the shelves. She pulled out a couple of books. Between Doyle's "A Study in Scarlet" and Chesterton's "The Innocence of Father Brown" was a small tape recorder neatly hidden away.

It *had* to succeed this time.

Agnete Werle sat down in her best chair, rewound the tape and listened. She heard it all. 'To hell with your crappy sentimentality . . . we've got to do the job . . . worth two million . . . like taking a lollipop from a baby.'

Mrs Werle listened very carefully. She didn't miss a word. Then she played the whole conversation from the beginning again.

Oh yes, oh yes, she said and nodded repeatedly.

Then she took out a book by one of her favourite writers, Patricia Highsmith. But she had not read more than a few pages of *The Talented Mr Ripley* when she lowered the book and began to hum softly.

She always did, when she was planning something.

'Hi, Mrs Werle! I've come straight from the lecture and I hope you don't mind my friend, he's a student too. Jorgen, meet Mrs Werle. Mrs Werle, this is Jorgen Thomassen, my – er – fiancé.'

Agnete started. She must have dozed off in her best chair with the book lying in her lap. Fortunately she had hidden the little tape recorder. She looked at her visitors; slim bodies dressed in almost similar sweaters, jeans and sneakers. Two quite good looking youngsters if it hadn't been for that watchful greedy look on their faces – oh yes – even on Ellida's, that was quite obvious now.

She said slowly, 'Any friend of Ellida's is a friend of mine. Glad to meet you, young man. You go to medical school, is that so? You'll end up as a surgeon, then – and Ellida studies art and she'll be a teacher in grammar school. Oh, you'll be successful, the two of you! Have you got far in your studies, Mr Thomassen?'

'Just a year or two left. But call me Jorgen, please. Ellida's your good friend and –'

'We have grown quite close, that's right. But do sit down, I'll make you a meal. You young people must be hungry.'

The old lady went off towards the kitchen, beaming and talking. 'I'll make you a really nice snack. Tea and sandwiches – relax, both of you! – make yourself at home, Jorgen, the way Ellida does. Oh, it's so lovely to have young people in the house.'

There was a pause. The boy and girl looked at each other. Jorgen tapped one finger against his head in a meaningful way.

'My young friends, I have a splendid idea!' Agnete almost ran into the sitting room again, clapping her hands in joy. 'Now listen. Ellida, I'm sure you remember that I've shown you all the rooms in the house *except* one. The secret room – the exciting room, Ellida!'

'Do you mean the bomb-proof room your husband built just before the second world war, is that the one?'

'Exactly, my dear,' cried Agnete, as if inspired. 'My husband had a very important and trusted position in the resistance movement during the German occupation. He was helping people escape to Sweden and Britain. That special room was so well hidden it was a marvellous place for anyone who had to hide from the Nazis, and for other people too . . . It's under the cellar, beautifully furnished with a thick carpet on the floor and book shelves and expensive paintings – it's the most exciting, most bomb-proof and best secret room in

Oslo, maybe in the whole of Norway! To show you how much I appreciate having you here I want us to celebrate in what is, for me, the most sacred room in the whole world. But now, I must finish in the kitchen. It won't take a minute.'

She disappeared again. Jorgen grinned at Ellida. He was holding a heavy silver candlestick in his hand, examining it.

Agnete reappeared out of breath, her cheeks rosy.

'Oh, I'm so looking forward to celebrating in there with you. Jorgen, you take this – oh, please don't fiddle with that candlestick, my cleaner isn't too fond of polishing silver and neither am I. By the way, there are two marvellous candelabra in the secret room, pure gold, you'll see. If you want something stronger than tea there's plenty to drink down there . . . Here we go. I'll lead the way.' Agnete smiled at them. She was all joy and enthusiasm.

'Watch it now, Ellida, here comes our chance,' whispered Jorgen as they followed the old lady down the cellar stairs and beyond, along a corridor lit by a faint bulb in the ceiling.

Eventually Agnete stopped in front of a massive half-open door. She turned to the young couple, extending her arms invitingly.

'Here we are. Please go in – and put the tea things on the little table over there in the corner. We'll have a grand time, the three of us! There's plenty of wine and sherry in the corner cupboard. Now, in you go.'

'Oh, Mrs Werle, it's awfully dark in here. Can you put on the light? We can't see a thing.'

'Just a second, dear. There's a switch here in the corridor, here it is. Oh, my, the door's shutting! And it's so heavy, impossible to open from this side . . . ! Well, well, well – it can't be helped. You'll have to celebrate alone in there, my dears. Take your time.'

And Agnete Werle bolted the heavy door with great care.

Standing for a moment outside, listening, she could scarcely hear their shouts. Faint, oh so faint were the voices heard here in the corridor. And nothing at all could be heard from any-where else in the house. Nothing at all. This she knew for certain. Not even the screaming and shouting of that traitor, the Norwegian Nazi, himself a torturer, had been heard in that autumn of 1943. Served him right, the rough treatment he'd got.

No room in the world could be more soundproof. And no room could be more hermetically sealed – when the valves in the ventilator were closed. They were now. They could be reg-ulated from the corridor.

'I hope they drink their tea first. It will put them to sleep quite gently,' murmured the old lady on her way upstairs. Ever so gently she chuckled as she sat down in her favourite chair with *The Talented Mr Ripley*.

She looked forward to reading it, then to watching a 'Poirot' film on the telly at ten o'clock sharp.

'*Carpe diem*, that's a good maxim,' said Agnete Werle, pleased.

'Excuse me, Inspector, I've got something very important to tell you today.'

Chief Constable Ole Gregersen looked at the old lady with a resigned expression. There was a troubled look in her bright blue eyes. Her hat was askew on her snow-white hair and her small thin fingers were clasping her handbag. No way could he be angry with her, she was such a sweet pathetic creature.

'What extraordinary things have happened now, Mrs Werle?' he asked patiently, far more patiently than he felt.

'I think something really peculiar and sinister has happened in my house, Mr Gregersen. There are actually *two* bodies, in my cellar. A young man and woman.'

'With knives in their backs, I presume?'

He winked mischievously and made a face at his assistant, Thea Dahl.

'No, no, Inspector, nothing of the sort! Would you imagine it, they're strangled, *choked*, both of them. Anyway, their faces are quite blue. Isn't it terrible? Do you think the murderer will be caught, Mr Gregersen?'

The policeman gave a sigh.

'You just go home to that nice house of yours and have another look and you'll find that everything's all right . . . But mind you, no more mystery books from now on. Why don't you read something nice, something edifying and uplifting for a change? Well, goodbye to you.'

The old lady walked slowly to the door, then abruptly turned round with a stern look at the policeman, cocking her head.

'What if I told you, Inspector, that I was the culprit – that it was I who killed the two poor creatures? Then you'd have to arrest me, wouldn't you, Mr Gregersen?'

'Shame on you, Mrs Werle! You are a wicked old lady, aren't you, in spite of being so sweet.' He took her gently by the arm and escorted her to the door.

'And now, Mrs Werle, please don't bother us again with that vivid imagination of yours.'

'All right, Inspector, I'll do as I'm told. But listen, shall I let the couple stay in the locked room in the cellar and never go into the room again as long as I live?'

'That's right, madam. Now off you go, have a nice walk home, and remember if someone is ever really unkind to you or tries to be violent – you know how young people can behave these days – you come straight here to us. It's lucky you don't live very far away.'

'Very well, Inspector. I'm glad to know there is some goodness in this cruel world. Goodbye, Mr Gregersen, and good day to you, Miss. And *thank you* with all my heart.'

The sweet old lady gave them a friendly nod and tripped out of the office.

Thea Dahl looked inquiringly at her superior.

'What on earth did she thank us like that for?'

'Hard to tell. She's very polite and well-bred, so why not? Well, she *is*, in spite of her crazy ideas.'

'Eccentric but harmless, isn't that how you put it, sir?'

'That's right, Miss Dahl. Eccentric but harmless.' The Chief Constable nodded, pleased with this apt description.

Translated from the Norwegian
by the author

MARY COWAN

Sonnet, Consolation

Do you think now, my friends, that it is time
   To look at little things, as long ago
We studied life as children in our prime,
   To look at insects, feathers, grass . . . to watch things grow,

Find tiny treasures, try to enjoy once more
   The savoury smells of matches, leaves and stones,
Try to regard the large things as a bore.
   Forget the newspapers and telephones,

Reports of agonies where once we dreamed
   A springing hope, a glorious time to come.
Nothing is anymore what once it seemed
   Evil triumphant beats its bloody drum.

With courage once we strove the world to free,
Now we'll be glad to help one bumble-bee.

Elizabeth Taylor

Mice and Birds and Boy

'Was this when you were pretty?' William asked, holding the photograph in both hands and raising his eyes to the old lady's with a look of near certainty.

'I was thought to be beautiful,' she said; and she wondered: How long ago was that? Who had been the last person to comment upon her beauty, and how many years ago? She thought that it might have been her husband, from loyalty or from still seeing what was no longer there. He had been dead for over twenty years and her beauty had not, by any means, been the burden of his dying words.

The photograph had faded to a pale coffee-colour, but William could distinguish a cloud of fair hair, a rounded face with lace to the chin, and the drooping, sad expression so many beautiful women have. Poor Mrs May, he thought.

The photographs were all jumbled up in a carved sandal-wood box lined with dusty felt. There was a large one mounted on stiff cardboard, of the big house where Mrs May had lived as a child. It had been pulled down between the wars and in its grounds was built a housing estate, a row of small shops by the bus stop and a children's playground, with swings and slides. William could look out of the narrow window of the old gardener's lodge where Mrs May lived now and watch the shrieking toddlers climbing the frames, swinging on the swings. He never went to the playground himself now that he was six.

'It was all fields,' Mrs May would often say, following his glance. 'All fields and parkland. I used to ride my pony over it. It was a different world. We had two grooms and seven indoor servants and four gardeners. Yet we were just ordinary people. Everybody had such things in those days.'

'Did every child have a pony?' William asked.

'All *country* children had one,' she said firmly.

His curiosity endeared him to her. It was so long since any-one had asked her a question and been interested in the answer. His curiosity had been the beginning of their friend-ship. Going out into her overgrown little garden one after-noon, she had found him leaning against the rickety fence staring at her house, which was round in shape and had attracted his attention. It was made of dark flint and had narrow, arched windows and an arched door studded with big square-headed nails. A high twisted chimney-stack rose from the centre of the roof. Surrounded by the looped and tangled growth of the garden – rusty, black-leaved briers and crooked apple trees – the place reminded the boy of a menacing-looking illustration by Arthur Rackham in a book he had at home. Then the door had opened and the witch herself had come out, leaning on a stick. She had untidy white hair and a face cross-hatched with wrinkles; but her eyes weren't witch-like, not black and beady and evil, but large and milky blue and kind, though crows had trodden about them.

'How can your house be round inside?' William asked, in his high, clear voice. She looked about her and then saw his red jersey through the fence and, above it, his bright face with its straight fringe of hair. 'How can rooms be round?' he asked. He came up to the broken gate and stood there.

Beyond a row of old elm trees which hid the lodge from the main road, a double-decker bus went by, taking the women from the estate to Market Swanford for their afternoon's shopping. When it had gone, William turned back to the old lady and said: 'Or are they like this shape?' He made a wedge with his hands.

'You had better come and see,' she said. He opened the gate at once and went in. 'She might pop me into the oven,' he thought.

One room was half a circle, the other two were quarters. All three were dark and crammed with furniture. A mouse streaked across the kitchen floor. The sink was stacked with dirty china, the table littered with odds and ends of food in torn paper wrappings.

'Do you live here alone?' he asked.

'Except for the mice; but I should prefer to be alone.'

'You are more like a hermit than a witch.'

'And would rather be,' she said.

He examined a dish of stewed fruit which had a greenish-grey mantling of mould.

'Pooh! It smells like beer,' he said.

'I meant to throw it away, but it seemed such a criminal waste when the natives are starving everywhere.'

In the sitting-room, with frail and shaking hands, she offered him a chocolate box; there was one chocolate left in it. It was stale and had a bloom on it, and might be poisoned, he thought; but he took it politely and turned it about in his mouth. It was very hard and tasted musty. 'Curiosity killed the cat,' his mother would say, when his body was discovered.

Mrs May began then to tell him about the fields and park and her pony. He felt drowsy and wondered if the poison were taking effect. She had such a beautiful voice – wavering, floating – that he could not believe in his heart that she would do him any harm. The room was airless and he sat in a little spoon-shaped velvet chair and stared up at her, listening to a little of her story, here and there. Living alone, except for the mice, she had no one to blame her when she spilt egg and tea down her front, he supposed; and she had taken full advantage of her freedom. She was really very dirty, he decided dispassionately. But smelt nice. She had the cosy smell that he liked so much about his guinea-pigs – a warm, stuffy, old smell.

'I'd better go,' he said suddenly. 'I might come back again tomorrow.'

She seemed to understand at once, but like all grown-up people was compelled to prolong the leave-taking a little. He answered her questions briefly, anxious to be off once he had made up his mind to go.

'There,' he said, pointing up the hill. 'My house is there.' The gilt weather-vane, veering round, glittered in the sun above the slate roofs.

'Our old stables,' Mrs May said quite excitedly. 'Oh, the memories.'

He shut the gate and sauntered off, between piles of bricks and tiles on the site where more houses were being built. Trees had been left standing here and there, looking strange upon the scarred, untidy landscape. William walked round the foundations of a little house, stood in the middle of a rectangle and tried to imagine a family sitting at a table in the middle of it, but it seemed far too small. The walls were only three bricks high. He walked round them, one foot before the other, his arms lifted to keep his balance. Some workmen shouted at him. They were tiling the roof of a nearby house. He took no notice, made a completed round of the walls and then walked off across the rough grass, where Mrs May had ridden her pony when she was a little girl.

'Do you *hear* me?' his mother said again, her voice shrill, with anxiety and vexation. She even took William's shoulder and shook him. 'You are *not* to talk to strangers.'

His sister, Jennifer, who was ballet-mad, practised an arabesque, and watched the scene without interest, her mind on her own schemes.

William looked gravely at his mother, rubbing his shoulder. 'Do you understand?'

He nodded.

'That's right, remember what your mother told you,' his father said, for the sake of peace.

The next morning, William took a piece of cheese from the larder and a pen-knife and went to the building-site. His mother was having an Italian lesson. Some of the workmen were sitting against a wall in the sun, drinking tea and eating bread and cheese, and William sat down amongst them, settling himself comfortably with his back against the wall. He cut pieces of cheese against his thumb as the others did and popped them neatly into his mouth. They drew him into solemn conversation, winking at one another above his head. He answered them politely, but knew that they were making fun of him. One wag, going too far, grimacing too obviously, asked: 'And what is your considered opinion of the present emergency?'

'I don't know,' William replied, and he got up and walked away – more in sorrow than in anger, he tried to convey.

He lingered for a while, watching a bulldozer going over the uneven ground, opening wounds in the fields where Mrs May had ridden her pony; then he wandered on towards the main road. Mrs May came out to her front doorstep and dropped an apronful of crumbs on to the path. Thrushes and starlings descended about her.

'So you're back again,' she called. 'I am shortly off to the shops. It will be nice to have a boy go with me.' She went inside, untying her apron.

He tried to swing on the gate, but it was lopsided. When she came out after a long time, she was wearing a torn raincoat, although it was quite hot already. It had no buttons and hung open. Her dirty jersey was held to her flat chest with rows of jet beads.

William noted that they were much stared at as they passed the bus queue and, in the butcher's shop, Mrs May was the subject of the same knowing looks and gravely-kept straight faces that he himself had suffered from the builders. He felt, uncomfortably, that this behaviour was something that children came to expect, but that an older person should neither expect nor tolerate. He could not find words to explain his keen uneasiness on Mrs May's account.

He watched the butcher unhook a drab piece of liver, slap it on the counter and cut off a slice.

'When I think of the saddles of mutton, the sucking pigs . . .' said Mrs May vaguely, counting out coppers.

'Yes, I expect so,' said the butcher's wife, with a straight face turned towards her husband.

Outside the shop, Mrs May continued the list. 'And ribs of beef, green goose at Michaelmas,' she chattered on to herself, going past the dairy, the grocer's, the draper's, with quick, herringbone steps. William caught glimpses of themselves reflected in the shop windows, against a pyramid of syrup tins, then a bolt of sprigged cotton.

'And what are *you* going to tell *me*?' Mrs May suddenly asked. 'I can't do all the entertaining, you know. Are you quite warm up there in the stables? Have you beds and chairs and all you need?'

'We have even more beds than we need.'

'Well, don't ask me to imagine it, because I can't. Shall we turn back? I'll buy an egg at the dairy and I might get some stale bread for the birds. "My only friends," I say to them, as they come to greet me.'

'You have the mice as well.'

'I can't make friends with mice. The mice get on my nerves, as a matter of fact.'

'You could get a cat,' he suggested.

'And seem more like a witch than ever?'

There appeared to be no stale bread at the baker's. At sight of Mrs May, the woman behind the counter seemed to shutter her face; stood waiting with lowered eyes for them to go.

When they reached Mrs May's broken gate – with only the slice of meat and the egg – William would not go in. He ran home as fast as he could over the uneven ground, his heart banging, his throat aching.

When he reached it, the house was quiet and a strange, spicy smell he could not identify came from the kitchen. His mother, as well as her Italian lessons, had taken up Japanese cooking. His sister, returning from ballet class, with her shoes hanging from her neck by their ribbons, found him lying on the floor pushing a toy car back and forth. Her suspicions were roused; for he was pretending to be playing, she was convinced, with an almost cross-eyed effort at concentration. He began to hum unconcernedly. Jennifer's nose wrinkled. 'It smells as if we're going to have that horrid soup with stalks in it.'

'I like it,' he murmured.

'You would. What have you been doing, anyway?'

Still wearing her coat, she practised a few pliés.

Never waste a moment, he thought.

'Nothing.'

But she was not interested in him; had been once – long ago, it seemed to her, when his birth she hoped would brighten up the house. The novelty of him had soon worn off.

'The death duties,' Mrs May explained. Because of them, she could not light a fire until the really chilly days and sometimes had only an egg to eat all day. These death duties William thought of as moral obligations upon which both her father and husband had insisted on discharging while dying – some charitable undertakings, plainly not approved of by Mrs May. He was only puzzled by the varying effect of this upon her day-to-day life; sometimes she was miserably conscious of her poverty, but at other times she bought peppermint creams for herself and William and digestive biscuits for the birds.

Every time she opened or shut the garden gate, she explained how she would have had it mended if it were not for the death duties. *The* death duties made them sound a normal sort of procedure, a fairly usual change of heart brought about perhaps by the approach of death and clearly happening only in Mrs May's family.

The days were beginning to grow chilly, too chilly to be without a fire. The leaves on the great chestnut trees about the building site turned yellow and fell. William went back to school and called on Mrs May only on Saturday mornings. He did not miss her. His life was suddenly very full and some weeks he did not go at all and she fretted for him, watching from a window like a love-sick girl, postponing her visit to the shops. She missed not only him, but her glimpses – from his conversation – of the strange life going on up in the old stables. His descriptions – in answer to her questions – and what she read into them formed a bewildering picture. She imagined the family sitting round the bench in the old harness room, drinking a thin soup with blades of grass in it – the brisk mother, the gentle, dreamy father and an objectionable little girl who kept getting down from the frugal meal to practise pas-de-chats across the old, broken brick floor. She had built the scene from his phrases – 'My mother will be cross if I'm late' (more polite he thought, than, 'My mother will be cross if she knows I came to see you'), and 'My father wouldn't mind.' His sister, it seemed, complained about the soup; apart from this, she only talked of Margot Fonteyn. But confusions came into it – in William's helping to clean silver for a dinner-party and having been sent to bed early for spilling ink on a carpet. Silver and carpets were hard to imagine as part of the old stables.

She had forgotten what a family was like, and had never had much chance of learning – only child and childless wife. William was too young to be a satisfactory informant. He was haphazardly selective, interested too much in his own separate affairs, unobservant and forgetful of the adult world; yet she managed to piece something together and it had slowly grown – a continuous story, without direction or catharsis – but could no longer grow if he were not to visit her.

Holding the curtains, her frail hands shook. When he did come, he was enticed to return. On those mornings now, there were always sweets. But her questions tired him, as they tire and antagonise all children, who begin to feel uneasily in the wrong role. He had by now satisfied his curiosity about her and was content to let what he did not understand – the death duties, for instance – lie at peace.

'You shall have this when I'm gone,' she began to say, closing the lid of the sandalwood box in which she kept the old photographs. Also promised was her father's sword and scabbard, in which William was more interested, and a stuffed parrot called Bertha – once a childhood pet and still talked to as if no change had taken place.

One morning, she saw him playing on the building-site and went out to the gate and called to him, lured him into the garden and then the house with witch-like tactics, sat him down on the spoon-shaped chair and gave him a bag of sweets.

'And how is your mother?' she enquired. She had a feeling that she detested the woman. William nodded absent-mindedly, poking about in the sweet bag. His hair was like gold silk, she thought.

'People have always lost patience with me,' she said, feeling his attention wandering from her. 'I only had my beauty.'

She was going on to describe how her husband's attention had also wandered, then thought it perhaps an unsuitable sub-ject to discuss with a child. She had never discussed it with anyone else. Such a vague marriage, and her memories of it were vague, too – seemed farther away than her childhood.

A mouse gnawed with a delicate sound in the wainscot and William turned his gaze towards it, waiting for the minutes to pass until the time when he could rise politely from the dusty chair and say good-bye.

If only he would tell me! Mrs May thought in despair. Tell me what there was for breakfast, for instance, and who said what and who went where, so that I could have something to think about in the evening.

'Oh, well, the winter will come if it means to,' she said aloud. Rain had swept in a gust upon the window, as if cast upon the little panes in spite. 'Nothing we can do can stop it. Only dig in and make ourselves comfortable – roast chestnuts on my little coal shovel.' William glanced from the wainscot to the empty grate, but Mrs May seemed not to see its emptiness. 'Once when I had a *nice* governess, we roasted some over the school-room fire. But the next governess would never let me do anything that pleased me. 'Want must be your master,' she said. She had many low phrases of that kind. 'Yes, want must be your master,' she said again, and sighed.

The visit was running down and her visitor simply sitting there until he could go. Courageously, when he had refused another peppermint cream and showed that he did not want to see again the photograph of her home, she released him, she even urged him to go, speeding him on his way, and watched him from the open door, her hands clasped close to her flat chest. He was like a most beloved caged bird that she had set at liberty. She felt regret and yet a sense of triumph, seeing him go.

She returned to the room and looked dully at the stuffed parrot, feeling a little like crying, but she had been brought up not to do so. 'Yes, want must be your master, Bertha,' she said in a soft but serene voice.

'I can't see harm in it,' William's father told his wife. Jennifer had seen William leaving Mrs May's and hurried to tell her mother, who began complaining the moment her husband returned for lunch.

'She's stark, staring mad and the place is filthy, everybody says so.'

'Children sometimes see what we can't.'

'I don't know what you mean by that. I forbade him to go there and he repeatedly disobeyed me. You should speak to him.'

So his father spoke to William – rather off-handedly, over his shoulder, while hanging his coat up in the hall, as William passed through.

To be reprimanded for what he had not wanted to do, for what he looked on as a duty, did not vex William. It was the kind of thing that happened to him a great deal and he let it go rather than tie himself up in explanations.

'You did hear what I said?' his father asked.

'Yes, I heard.'

'Your mother has her reasons. You can leave it at that.'

It happened that he obeyed his parents. His father one day passing Mrs May's garden came on her feeding her birds there. He raised his hat and saw, as she glanced up, her ruined face, bewildered eyes, and was stirred by pity as he walked on.

As the nights grew colder, Mrs May was forced to light a fire and she wandered about the building site collecting sawn off pieces of batten and wood-shavings. She met William there once, playing with another boy. He returned her greeting, answered her questions unwillingly, knowing that his companion had ducked his head, trying to hide a smile. When she had wandered on at last, there were more questions from his friend. 'Oh, she's only an old witch I know,' he replied.

The truth was that he could hardly remember how once he had liked to go to see her. Then he had tired of her stories about her childhood, grew bored with her photographs, became embarrassed by her and realised, in an adult way, that the little house was filthy. One afternoon, on his way home from school, he had seen her coming out of the butcher's shop ahead of him and had slackened his pace, almost walked backwards not to overtake her.

She was alone again, except for the birds in the daytime, the mice at night. The deep winter came and the birds grew fewer and the mice increased. The cold weather birds, double their summer size, hopped dottily about the crisp, rimed grass, jabbing their beaks into frozen puddles, bewildered as refugees. Out she hurried, first thing in the mornings, to break the ice and scatter crumbs. She found a dead thrush and grieved over it. 'Oh, Bertha, one of ours,' she mourned.

Deep snow came and she was quite cut off – the garden was full of strange shapes, as if heaped with pillows and bolsters, and the birds made their dagger tracks across the drifts. She could not open her door.

Seeing the untrodden path, William's father, passing by, went to borrow a spade from the nearest house and cleared the snow from the gateway to the door. He saw her watching from a window and, when at last she could, she opened the door to thank him.

'I'm afraid I don't know who you are,' she began.

'I live in the old stables up on the hill.'

'Then I know your little boy. He used to visit me. It was very kind of you to come to my rescue.'

William's father returned the spade and then walked home, feeling sad and ashamed. 'Oh, dear, that house,' he said to his wife. 'It is quite filthy – what I glimpsed of it. You were perfectly right. Someone ought to do something to help her.'

'She should help herself. She must have plenty of money – All this building land.'

'I think she misses William.'

'It was just a passing thing,' said his wife, who was a great one herself for passing things. 'He simply lost interest.'

'Lost innocence, perhaps. The truth is, I suppose, that children grow up and begin to lose their simple vision.'

'The truth is,' she said tartly, 'that if people don't wash

themselves they go unloved.' Her voice was cold and disdainful. She had summed up many other lives than Mrs May's and knew the tone to use.

The thaw began, then froze in buds upon the red twigs of the dog-wood in Mrs May's untidy hedge. The hardening snow was pitted with drips from the branches.

Mrs May was afraid to venture on her frozen path beyond her doorway, and threw her remaining bits of bread from there. There was no one to run an errand for her. The cold drove her inside, but she kept going to the window to see if the ice were melting. Instead, the sky darkened. Both sky and earth were iron.

'It's my old bones,' she said to Bertha. 'I'm afraid for my old bones.'

Then she saw William running and sliding on the ice, his red scarf flying, his cheeks bright. He fell, and scrambled up, laughing.

'It's falling I'm afraid of,' Mrs May whispered to the window pane. 'My old bones are too brittle.'

She went to the front door and opened it. Standing shivering on the step, she called to William. He seemed not to hear and she tried to raise her voice. He took a run and, with his arms flung up above his head, slithered across a patch of ice. He shouted to someone out of sight and dashed forward.

Mrs May shut the door again. 'Someone will come,' she told Bertha briskly. She straightened her father's sword suspended above the fireplace and bustled about, trying to tidy the room ready for an unknown visitor. 'There's no knowing what might happen. Anyone might call,' she murmured.

PAM GIDNEY

Time Travel

Fifty years of time travel
Have left their mark on me.
The weightlessness
Of the constant journeying
In the capsule of my mind
Has made my features sag
A little.
My path in time
Has reached its apogee
And the way from now on can only be downward,
But I am not dismayed.
The ascent has been joyous –
Why then should the rest be different?
My craft leads me on,
Is equidistant in all directions
From the farthest stars the eye can see.
In this alone I have location.
This is the pinpointing of my identity.
I gaze out through the portholes of my craft
And hope
Splashdown's light years away.

SUSAN HILL

A Bit of Singing and Dancing

There was no one else on the beach so late in the afternoon.
She walked very close to the water, where there was a rim of
hard, flat sand, easier on her feet than the loose shelves of
shingle, which folded one on top of the other, up to the storm
wall. She thought, I can stay out here just as long as I like, I
can do anything I choose, anything at all, for now I am
answerable only to myself.

But it was an unpromising afternoon, already half dark, an
afternoon for early tea and banked-up fires and entertainment
on television. And a small thrill went through her as she
realized that that, too, was entirely up to her, she could
watch whichever programme she chose, or not watch any
at all. There had not been an evening for the past eleven
years when the television had stayed off and there was
silence to hear the ticking of the clock and the central heating
pipes.

'It is her only pleasure,' she used to say, 'She sees things she
would otherwise be quite unable to see, the television has
given her a new lease of life. You're never too old to learn.'
But in truth her mother had watched variety shows,
Morecambe and Wise and the Black and White Minstrels,
whereas she herself would have chosen BBC 2 and something
cultural or educational.

'I like a bit of singing and dancing, it cheers you up, Esme,
it takes you out of yourself. I like a bit of spectacular.'

But tonight there might be a play or a film about Arabia or the Archipelagoes, or a master class for cellists, tonight she would please herself, for the first time. Because it was two weeks now, since her mother's death, a decent interval.

It was February. It was a cold evening. As far as she could see, the beach and the sea and the sky were all grey, merging into one another in the distance. On the day of her mother's funeral it had been blowing a gale, with sleet, she had looked round at all their lifeless, pinched faces under the black hats and thought, this is right, this is fitting, that we should all of us seem bowed and old and disconsolate. Her mother had a right to a proper grief, a proper mourning.

She had wanted to leave the beach and walk back, her hands were stiff with cold inside the pockets of her navy-blue coat – navy, she thought, was the correct first step away from black. She wanted to go back and toast scones and eat them with too much butter, of which her mother would have strongly disapproved. '*We* never had it, *we* were never allowed to indulge ourselves in rich foods, and besides, they've been discovering more about heart disease in relation to butter, haven't you read that in the newspapers, Esme? I'm surprised you don't pay attention to these things. I pay attention. I don't believe in butter at every meal – butter on this, butter with that.'

Every morning, her mother had read two newspapers from cover to cover – the *Daily Telegraph* and the *Daily Mirror*, and marked out with a green ball point pen news items in which she thought that her daughter ought to take an interest. She said, 'I like to see both sides of every question.' And so, whichever side her daughter or some visitor took, on some issue of the day, she was informed enough by both her newspapers to take the opposing view. An argument, she had said, sharpened the mind.

'I do not intend to become a cabbage, Esme, just because I am forced to be bedridden.'

She had reached the breakwater. A few gulls circled, bleating, in the gunmetal sky, and the waterline was strewn with fish-heads, the flesh all picked away. She thought, I am free, I may go on or go back, or else stand here for an hour, I am mistress of myself. It was a long time since she had been out for so long, she could not quite get used to it, this absence of the need to look at her watch, to scurry home. But after a while, because it was really very damp and there was so little to see, she did turn, and then the thought of tomorrow, and the out-ing she had promised herself to buy new clothes. It would take some months for her mother's will to be proven, the solicitor had explained to her, things were generally delayed, but there was no doubt that they would be settled to her advantage and really, Mrs Fanshaw had been very careful, very prudent, and so she would not be in want. Meanwhile, perhaps an advance for immediate expenses? Perhaps a hundred pounds?

When the will was read, her first reaction had been one of admiration, she had said, 'The cunning old woman' under her breath, and then put her hand up to her mouth, afraid of being overheard. 'The cunning old woman.' For Mildred Fanshaw had saved up £6,000, scattered about in bank and savings accounts. Yet they had always apparently depended upon Esme's salary and the old age pension, they had had to be careful, she said, about electricity and extra cream and joints of beef. 'Extravagance,' Mrs Fanshaw said, 'it is a cardinal sin. That is where all other evils stem from, Esme. Extravagance. We should all live within our means.'

And now here was £6,000. For a moment or two it had gone to her head, she had been quite giddy with plans, she would buy a car and learn to drive, buy a washing machine and a television set, she would have a holiday abroad and get properly fitting underwear and eat out in a restaurant now and again, she would . . .

But she was over fifty, she should be putting money on one side herself now, saving for her own old age, and besides, even the idea of spending made her feel guilty, as though her mother could hear, now, what was going on inside her head, just as, in life, she had known her thoughts from the expression on her face.

She had reached the steps leading up from the beach. It was almost dark.

She shivered, then, in a moment of fear and bewilderment at her new freedom, for there was nothing she had to do, she could please herself about everything, anything, and this she could not get used to. Perhaps she ought not to stay here, perhaps she could try and sell the house, which was really far too big for her, perhaps she ought to get a job and a small flat in London. London was the city of opportunity . . .

She felt flushed and a little drunk then, she felt that all things were possible, the future was in her power, and she wanted to shout and sing and dance, standing alone in the February twilight, looking at the deserted beach. All the houses along the seafront promenade had blank, black windows, for this was a summer place, in February it was only half alive.

She said, 'And that is what I have been. But I am fifty-one years old and look at the chances before me.'

Far out on the shingle bank the green warning light flashed on-on-off, on-on-off. It had been flashing the night of her mother's stroke, she had gone to the window and watched it and felt comforted at three a.m. in the aftermath of death. Now, the shock of that death came to her again like a hand slapped across her face, she thought, my mother is not here, my mother is in a box in the earth, and she began to shiver violently, her mind crawling with images of corruption, she started to walk very quickly along the promenade and up the hill towards home.

When she opened the front door she listened, and everything was quite silent, quite still. There had always been the voice from upstairs, 'Esme?' and each time she had wanted to say, 'Who else would it be?' and bitten back the words, only said, 'Hello, it's me.' Now, again, she called, 'It's me. Hello,' and her voice echoed softly up the dark stair well, when she heard it, it was a shock, for what kind of woman was it who talked to herself and was afraid of an empty house? What kind of woman?

She went quickly into the sitting-room and drew the curtains and then poured herself a small glass of sherry, the kind her mother had preferred. It was shock, of course, they had told her, all of them, her brother-in-law and her Uncle Cecil and cousin George Golightly, when they had come back for tea and ham sandwiches after the funeral.

'You will feel the real shock later. Shock is always delayed.' Because she had been so calm and self-possessed, she had made all the arrangements so neatly, they were very surprised.

'If you ever feel the need of company, Esme – and you will – of course you must come to us. Just a telephone call, that's all we need, just a little warning in advance. You are sure to feel strange.'

Strange. Yes. She sat by the electric fire. Well, the truth was she had got herself thoroughly chilled, walking on the beach like that, so late in the afternoon. It had been her own fault.

After a while, the silence of the house oppressed her, so that when she had taken a second glass of sherry and made herself a poached egg on toast, she turned on the television and watched a variety show, because it was something cheerful, and she needed taking out of herself. There would be time enough for the educational programmes when she was used to this new life. But a thought went through her head, backwards and forwards, backwards and forwards, it was as though she were reading from a tape.

'She is upstairs. She is still in her room. If you go upstairs you will see her. Your mother.' The words danced across the television screen, intermingling with the limbs of dancers, issuing like spume out of the mouths of comedians and crooners, they took on the rhythm of the drums and the double basses.

'Upstairs. In her room. Upstairs. In her room.

Your mother. Your mother. Your mother.

Upstairs . . .'

She jabbed at the push button on top of the set and the picture shrank and died, there was silence, and then she heard her own heart beating and the breath coming out of her in little gasps. She scolded herself for being morbid, neurotic. Very well then, she said, go upstairs and see for yourself.

Very deliberately and calmly she went out of the room and climbed the stairs, and went into her mother's bedroom. The light from the street lamp immediately outside the window shone a pale triangle of light down onto the white runner on the dressing table, the white lining of the curtains and the smooth white cover of the bed. Everything had gone. Her mother might never have been here. Esme had been very anxious not to hoard reminders and so, the very day after the funeral, she had cleared out and packed up clothes, linen, medicine, papers, spectacles, she had ruthlessly emptied the room of her mother.

Now, standing in the doorway, smelling lavender polish and dust, she felt ashamed, as though she wanted to be rid of all memory, as though she had wanted her mother to die. She said, but that is what I did want, to be rid of the person who bound me to her for fifty years. She spoke aloud into the bedroom, 'I wanted you dead.' She felt her hands trembling and held them tightly together, she thought, I am a wicked woman. But the sherry she had drunk began to have some effect now, her heart was beating more quietly, and she was able to walk out into the room and draw the curtains, even though it was now unnecessary to scold herself for being so hysterical.

In the living room, she sat beside the fire reading a historical biography until eleven o'clock – when her mother was alive she had always been in bed by ten – and the fears had quite left her, she felt entirely calm. She thought, it is only natural, you have had a shock, you are bound to be affected. That night she slept extremely well.

When she answered the front doorbell at eleven fifteen the following morning and found Mr Amos Curry, hat in hand, upon the step, inquiring about a room, she remembered a remark her Uncle Cecil had made to her on the day of the funeral. 'You will surely not want to be here all on your own, Esme, in this great house. You should take a lodger.'

Mr Amos Curry rubbed his left eyebrow with a nervous finger, a gesture of his because he was habitually shy. 'A room to let,' he said, and she noticed that he wore gold cuff links and very well-polished shoes. 'I understand from the agency . . . a room to let with breakfast.'

'I know nothing of any agency. I think you have the wrong address.'

He took out a small loose-leaf notebook. 'Number 23, Park Close.'

'Oh no, I'm so sorry, we are . . .' she corrected herself, 'I am twenty-three Park *Walk*.'

A flush of embarrassment began to seep up over his face and neck like an ink stain, he loosened his collar a little until she felt quite sorry for him, quite upset.

'An easy mistake, a perfectly understandable mistake. Mr . . . Please do not feel at all . . .'

'. . . Curry. Amos Curry.'

'. . . embarrassed.'

'I am looking for a quiet room with breakfast. It seemed so hopeful. Park Close. Such a comfortable address.'

She thought, he is a very clean man, very neat and spruce, he has a gold incisor tooth and he wears gloves. Her mother had always approved of men who wore gloves. 'So few do, nowadays. Gloves and hats. It is easy to pick out a gentleman.'

Mr Curry also wore a hat.

'I do apologize, Madam, I feel so . . . I would not have troubled . . .'

'No . . . no, please . . .'

'I must look for Park Close, Number 23.'

'It is just around the bend, to the left, a few hundred yards. A very secluded road.'

'Like this. This road is secluded. I thought as I approached this house, how suitable, I should . . . I feel one can tell, a house has a certain . . . But I am so sorry.'

He settled his hat upon his neat grey hair, and then raised it again politely, turning away.

She took in a quick breath. She said, 'What exactly . . . that is to say, if you are looking for a room with breakfast, I wonder if I . . .'

Mr Amos Curry turned back.

He held a small pickled onion delicately on the end of his fork. 'There is,' he said, 'the question of my equipment.'

Esme Fanshaw heard his voice as though it issued from the wireless – there was a distortion about it, a curious echo. She shook her head. He is not real, she thought . . . But he was here, Mr Amos Curry, in a navy-blue pin stripe suit and with a small neat darn just below his shirt collar. He was sitting at her kitchen table – for she had hesitated to ask him into the dining room, which in any case was rarely used, the kitchen had seemed a proper compromise. He was here. She had made a pot of coffee, and then, after an hour, a cold snack of beef and pickles, bread and butter, her hands were a little moist with excitement. She thought again how rash she had been, she said, he is a total stranger, someone from the street, a casual caller, I know nothing at all about him. But she recognized the voice of her mother, then, and rebelled against it. Besides, it was not true, for Mr Curry had told her a great deal. She thought, this is how life should be, I should be daring, I should allow myself to be constantly surprised. Each day I should be ready for some new encounter. That is how to stay young. She was most anxious to stay young.

In his youth, Mr Curry had been abroad a great deal, had lived, he said, in Ceylon, Singapore and India. 'I always keep an open mind, Miss Fanshaw, I believe in the principle of tolerance, live and let live. Nation shall speak peace unto nation.'

'Oh, I do agree.'

'I have seen the world and its ways. I have no prejudices. The customs of others may be quite different from our own but human beings are human beings the world over. We learn from one another every day. By keeping an open mind, Miss Fanshaw.'

'Oh yes.'

'You have travelled?'

'I - I have visited Europe. Not too far afield, I'm afraid.'

'I have journeyed on foot through most of the European countries, I have earned my passage at all times.'

She did not like to ask how, but she was impressed, having only been abroad once herself, to France.

Mr Curry had been an orphan, he said, life for him had begun in a children's home. 'But it was a more than adequate start, Miss Fanshaw, we were all happy together. I do not think memory deceives me. We were one big family. Never let it be said that the Society did not do its best by me. I see how lucky I am. Well, you have only to look about you, Miss Fanshaw – how many people do you see from broken families, unhappy homes? I know nothing of that: I count myself fortunate. I like to think I have made the best of my circumstances.'

His education, he said, had been rather elementary, he had a good brain which had never been taxed to the full.

'Untapped resources,' he said, pointing to his forehead.

They talked so easily, she thought she had never found conversation flowing along with any other stranger, any other man. Mr Curry had exactly the right amount of formal politeness, mixed with informal ease, and she decided that he was destined to live here, he had style and he seemed so much at home.

He had an ordinary face, for which she was grateful, but there was something slightly unreal about it, as though she were seeing it on a cinema screen. All the same, it was very easy to picture him sitting in this kitchen, eating breakfast, before putting on his hat, which had a small feather in the band, each morning and going off to work.

'I do have some rather bulky equipment.'

'What exactly . . .'

'I have two jobs, Miss Fanshaw, two strings to my bow, as it were. That surprises you? But I have always been anxious to fill up every hour of the day, I have boundless energy.'

She noticed that he had some tufts of pepper coloured hair sprouting from his ears and nostrils and wondered if, when he visited the barber for a haircut, he also had these trimmed. She knew nothing about the habits of men.

'Of course, it is to some extent seasonal work.'

'Seasonal?'

'Yes. For those odd wet and windy days which always come upon us at the English seaside, and of course during the winter, I travel in cleaning utensils.'

He looked around him quickly, as though to see where she kept her polish and dusters and brooms, to make note of any requirements.

'Perhaps you would require some extra storage space? Other than the room itself.'

Mr Curry got up from the table and began to clear away dishes, she watched him in astonishment. The man on the doorstep with a note of the wrong address had become the luncheon visitor, the friend who helped with the washing up.

'There is quite a large loft.'

'Inaccessible.'

'Oh.'

'And I do have to be a little careful. No strain on the back. Not that I am a sick man, Miss Fanshaw, I hasten to reassure you, you will not have an invalid on your hands. Oh no. I am extremely healthy for my age. It is because I lead such an active life.'

She thought of him, knocking upon all the doors, walking back down so many front paths. Though this was not what he did in the summer.

'Sound in wind and limb, as you might say.'

She thought of racehorses, and tried to decide whether he had ever been married. She said, 'Or else, perhaps, the large cupboard under the stairs, where the gas meter . . .'

'Perfect.'

He poured just the right amount of washing up liquid into the bowl; his sleeves were already unbuttoned and rolled up to the elbows, his jacket hung on the hook behind the back door. She saw the hairs lying like thatch on his sinewy arms, and a dozen questions sprang up into her mind, then, for although he seemed to have told her a great deal about himself, there were many gaps.

He had visited the town previously, he told her, in the course of his work, and fell for it. 'I never forgot it, Miss Fanshaw. I should be very happy here, I told myself. It is my kind of place. Do you see?'

'And so you came back.'

'Certainly. I know when I am meant to do something. I never ignore that feeling. I was intended to return here.'

'It is rather a small town.'

'But select.'

'I was only wondering – we do have a very short season, really only July and August . . .'

'Yes?'

'Perhaps it would not be suitable for your – er – summer work?'

'Oh, I think it would, Miss Fanshaw, I think so, I size these things up rather carefully, you know, rather carefully.'

She did not question him further, only said, 'Well, it is winter now.'

'Indeed. I shall, to coin a phrase, be plying my other trade. In a town like this, full of ladies such as yourself, in nice houses with comfortable circumstances, the possibilities are endless, endless.'

'For – er – cleaning materials?'

'Quite so.'

'I do see that.'

'Now you take a pride, don't you? Anyone can see that for himself.'

He waved a hand around the small kitchen, scattering little drops of foamy water, and she saw the room through his eyes, the clean windows, the shining taps, the immaculate sinks. Yes, she took a pride, that was true. Her mother had insisted upon it. Now, she heard herself saying, 'My mother died only a fortnight ago,' forgetting that she had told him already and the shock of the fact overcame her again, she could not believe in the empty room, which she was planning to give to Mr Curry, and her eyes filled up with tears of guilt. And what would her mother have said about a strange man washing up in their kitchen, about this new, daring friendship.

'You should have consulted me, Esme, you take far too much on trust. You never think. You should have consulted me.'

Two days after her mother's funeral, Mrs Bickerdike, from The Lilacs, had met her in the pharmacy, and mentioned, in lowered voice, that she 'did work for the bereaved', which, Esme gathered, meant that she conducted seances. She implied that contact might be established with the deceased

Mrs Fanshaw. Esme had been shocked, most of all by the thought of that contact, and a continuing relationship with her mother, though she had only said that she believed in letting the dead have their rest. 'I think, if you will forgive me, and with respect, that we are not meant to inquire about them, or to follow them on.'

Now, she heard her mother talking about Mr Curry. 'You should always take particular notice of the eyes, Esme, never trust anyone with eyes set too closely together.'

She tried to see his eyes, but he was turned sideways to her.

'Or else too widely apart. That indicates idleness.'

She was ashamed of what she had just said about her mother's recent death, for she did not at all wish to embarrass him, or to appear hysterical. Mr Curry had finished washing up and was resting his reddened wet hands upon the rim of the sink. When he spoke, his voice was a little changed and rather solemn. 'I do not believe in shutting away the dead, Miss Fanshaw, I believe in the sacredness of memory. I am only glad that you feel able to talk to me about the good lady.'

She felt suddenly glad to have him here in the kitchen, for his presence took the edge off the emptiness and silence which lately had seemed to fill up every corner of the house.

She said, 'It was not always easy . . . My mother was a very . . . forthright woman.'

'Say no more. I understand only too well. The older generation believed in speaking their minds.'

She thought, he is obviously a very sensitive man, he can read between the lines: and she wanted to laugh with relief, for there was no need to go into details about how dominating her mother had been and how taxing were the last years of her illness – he knew, he understood.

Mr Curry dried his hands, smoothing the towel down one finger at a time, as though he were drawing on gloves. He rolled down his shirt-sleeves and fastened them and put on his jacket. His movements were neat and deliberate. He coughed.

'Regarding the room – there is just the question of payment, Miss Fanshaw, I believe in having these matters out at once. There is nothing to be embarrassed about in speaking of money, I hope you agree.'

'Oh no, certainly, I . . .'

'Shall we say four pounds a week?'

Her head swam. She had no idea at all how much a lodger should pay, how much his breakfasts would cost, and she was anxious to be both business-like and fair. Well, he had suggested what seemed to him a most suitable sum, he was more experienced in these matters than herself.

'For the time being I am staying at a commercial guest house in Cedars Road. I have only linoleum covering the floor of my room, there is nothing cooked at breakfast. I am not accustomed to luxury, Miss Fanshaw, you will understand that from what I have told you of my life, but I think I am entitled to comfort at the end of the working day.'

'Oh, you will be more than comfortable here, I shall see to that, I shall do my very best. I feel . . .'

'Yes?'

She was suddenly nervous of how she appeared in his eyes.

'I do feel that the mistake you made in the address was somehow . . .'

'Fortuitous.'

'Yes, oh yes.'

Mr Curry gave a little bow.

'When would you wish to move in, Mr Curry? There are one or two things . . .'

'Tomorrow evening, say?'

'Tomorrow is Friday.'

'Perhaps that is inconvenient.'

'No . . . no . . . certainly . . . our week could begin on a Friday, as it were.'

'I shall greatly look forward to having you as a landlady. Miss Fanshaw.'

Landlady. She wanted to say, 'I hope I shall be a friend, Mr Curry,' but it sounded presumptuous.

When he had gone she made herself a pot of tea, and sat quietly at the kitchen table, a little dazed. She thought, this is a new phase of my life. But she was still a little alarmed. She had acted out of character and against what she would normally have called her better judgement. Her mother would have warned her against inviting strangers into the house, just as, when she was a child, she had warned her about speaking to them in the street. 'You can never be sure, Esme, there are some very peculiar people about.' For she was a great reader of the crime reports in her newspapers, and of books about famous trials. The life of Doctor Crippen had particularly impressed her.

Esme shook her head. Now, all the plans she had made for selling the house and moving to London and going abroad were necessarily curtailed, and for the moment she felt depressed, as though the old life were going to continue, and she wondered, too, what neighbours and friends might say, and whether anyone had seen Mr Curry standing on her doorstep, paper in hand, whether, when he went from house to house selling cleaning utensils, they would recognize him as Miss Fanshaw's lodger and disapprove. There was no doubt that her mother would have disapproved, and not only because he was a 'stranger off the streets'.

'He is a salesman, Esme, a doorstep pedlar, and you do not *know* what his employment in the summer months may turn out to be.'

'He has impeccable manners, mother, quite old-fashioned ones, and a most genteel way of speaking.' She remembered the gloves and the raised hat, the little bow, and also the way he had quietly and confidently done the washing up, as though he were already living here.

'How do you know where things will lead, Esme?'

'I am prepared to take a risk. I have taken too few risks in my life so far.'

She saw her mother purse her lips and fold her hands together, refusing to argue further, only certain that she was in the right. Well, it was her own life now, and she was mistress of it, she would follow her instincts for once. And she went and got a sheet of paper, on which to write a list of things that were needed to make her mother's old bedroom quite comfortable for him. After that, she would buy cereal and bacon and kidneys for the week's breakfasts.

She was surprised at how little time it took for her to grow quite accustomed to having Mr Curry in the house. It helped, of course, that he was a man of very regular habits and neat, too, when she had first gone into his room to clean it, she could have believed that no one was using it at all. The bed was neatly made, clothes hung out of sight or in drawers – he had locked the wardrobe, she discovered, and taken away the key. Only two pairs of shoes side by side, below the washbasin, and a shaving brush and razor on the shelf above it, gave the lodger away.

Mr Curry got up promptly at eight – she heard his alarm clock and then the pips of the radio news. At eight twenty he came down to the kitchen for his breakfast, smelling of shaving soap and shoe polish. Always, he said, 'Ah, good morning, Miss Fanshaw, good morning to you,' and then commented briefly upon the weather. It was 'a bit nippy' or 'a touch of sunshine, I see' or 'bleak'. He ate a cooked breakfast, followed by toast and two cups of strong tea.

Esme took a pride in her breakfasts, in the neat way she laid the table and the freshness of the cloth, she warmed his plate under the grill and waited until the last minute before doing the toast so that it should still be crisp and hot. She thought, it is a very bad thing for a woman such as myself to live alone and become entirely selfish. I am the sort of person who needs to give service.

At ten minutes to nine, Mr Curry got his suitcase from the

downstairs cupboard, wished her good morning again, and left the house. After that she was free for the rest of the day, to live as she had always lived, or else to make changes – though much of her time was taken up with cleaning the house and especially Mr Curry's room, and shopping for something unusual for Mr Curry's breakfasts.

She had hoped to enrol for lampshade-making classes at the evening institute but it was too late for that year, they had told her she must apply again after the summer, so she borrowed a book upon the subject from the public library and bought frames and card and fringing, and taught herself. She went to one or two bring-and-buy sales and planned to hold a coffee morning and do a little voluntary work for old people. Her life was full. She enjoyed having Mr Curry in the house. Easter came, and she began to wonder when he would change to his summer work, and what that work might be. He never spoke of it.

To begin with he had come in between five thirty and six every evening, and gone straight to his room. Sometimes he went out again for an hour, she presumed to buy a meal somewhere and perhaps drink a glass of beer, but more often he stayed in, and Esme did not see him again until the following morning. Once or twice she heard music coming from his room – presumably from the radio, and she thought how nice it was to hear that the house was alive, a home for someone else.

One Friday evening, Mr Curry came down into the kitchen to give her the four pounds rent, just as she was serving up lamb casserole, and when she invited him to stay and share it with her, he accepted so quickly that she felt guilty, for perhaps, he went without an evening meal altogether. She decided to offer him the use of the kitchen, when a moment should arise which seemed suitable.

But a moment did not arise. Instead, Mr Curry came down two or three evenings a week and shared her meal, she got used to shopping for two, and when he offered her an extra pound a week, she accepted, it was so nice to have company, though she felt a little daring, a little carefree. She heard her mother telling her that the meals cost more than a pound a week. 'Well, I do not mind, they give me pleasure, it is worth it for that.'

One evening, Mr Curry asked her if she were good at figures, and when she told him that she had studied book-keeping, asked her help with the accounts for the kitchen utensil customers. After that, two or three times a month, she helped him regularly, they set up a temporary office on the dining-room table, and she remembered how good she had been at this kind of work, she began to feel useful, to enjoy herself.

He said, 'Well, it will not be for much longer, Miss Fanshaw, the summer is almost upon us, and in the summer, of course, I am self-employed.'

But when she opened her mouth to question him more closely, he changed the subject. Nor did she like to inquire whether the firm who supplied him with the cleaning utensils to sell, objected to the dearth of summer orders.

Mr Curry was an avid reader, 'in the winter', he said, when he had the time. He read not novels or biographies or war memoirs, but his encyclopedia, of which he had a handsome set, bound in cream mock-leather and paid for by monthly instalments. In the evenings, he took to bringing a volume down to the sitting-room, at her invitation, and keeping her company, she grew used to the sight of him in the opposite armchair. From time to time he would read out to her some curious or entertaining piece of information. His mind soaked up everything, but particularly of a zoological, geographical or anthropological nature, he said that he never forgot a fact, and that you never knew when something might prove of use. And Esme Fanshaw listened, her hands deftly fringing a lampshade – it was a skill she had acquired easily – and continued her education.

'One is never too old to learn, Mr Curry.'

'How splendid that we are of like mind! How nice!'

She thought, yes, it is nice, as she was washing up the dishes the next morning, and she flushed a little with pleasure and a curious kind of excitement. She wished that she had some woman friend whom she could telephone and invite round for coffee, in order to say, 'How nice it is to have a man about the house, really, I had no idea what a difference it could make.' But she had no close friends, she and her mother had always kept themselves to themselves. She would have said, 'I feel younger, and it is all thanks to Mr Curry. I see now that I was only half-alive.'

Then, it was summer. Mr Curry was out until half past nine or ten o'clock at night, the suitcase full of brooms and brushes and polish was put away under the stairs and he had changed his clothing. He wore a cream linen jacket and a straw hat with a black band, a rose or carnation in his button hole. He looked very dapper, very smart, and she had no idea at all what work he was doing. Each morning he left the house carrying a black case, quite large and square. She thought, I shall follow him. But she did not do so. Then, one evening in July, she decided to explore, to discover what she could from other people in the town, for someone must know Mr Curry, he was a distinctive sight, now, in the fresh summer clothes. She had, at the back of her mind, some idea that he might be a beach photographer.

She herself put on a quite different outfit – a white piqué dress she had bought fifteen years ago, but which still not only fitted, but suited her, and a straw boater, edged with ribbon, not unlike Mr Curry's own hat. When she went smartly down the front path, she hardly dared to look about her, certain that she was observed and spoken about by the neighbours. For it was well known now that Miss Fanshaw had a lodger.

She almost never went on to the promenade in the summer. She had told Mr Curry so. 'I keep to the residential streets, to the shops near home, I do so dislike the summer crowds.' And besides, her mother had impressed on her that the summer visitors were 'quite common'. But tonight walking along in the warm evening air, smelling the sea, she felt ashamed of that opinion, she would not like anyone to think that she had been brought up a snob – live and let live, as Mr Curry would tell her. And the people sitting in the deckchairs and walking in couples along the seafront looked perfectly nice, perfectly respectable, there were a number of older women and families with well-behaved children, this was a small, select resort, and charabancs were discouraged.

But Mr Curry was not to be seen. There were no beach photographers. She walked quite slowly along the promenade, looking all about her. There was a pool, in which children could sail boats, beside the War Memorial, and a putting green alongside the gardens of the Raincliffe Hotel. Really, she thought, I should come out more often, really it is very pleasant here in the summer, I have been missing a good deal.

When she reached the putting green she paused, not wanting to go back, for her sitting-room was rather dark, and she had no real inclination to make lampshades in the middle of July. She was going to sit down, next to an elderly couple on one of the green benches, she was going to enjoy the balm of the evening. Then, she heard music. After a moment, she recognized it. The tune had come quite often through the closed door of Mr Curry's bedroom.

And there, on a corner opposite the hotel, and the putting green, she saw Mr Curry. The black case contained a portable gramophone, the old-fashioned kind, with a horn, and this was set on the pavement. Beside it was Mr Curry, straw hat tipped a little to one side, cane beneath his arm, buttonhole in place. He was singing, in a tuneful, but rather cracked voice, and doing an elaborate little tap dance on the spot, his rather small feet moving swiftly and daintily in time with the music.

Esme Fanshaw put her hand to her face, feeling herself

flush, and wishing to conceal herself from him: she turned her head away and looked out to sea, her ears full of the sentimental music. But Mr Curry was paying attention only to the small crowd which had gathered about him. One or two passers by, on the opposite side of the road, crossed over to watch, as Mr Curry danced, a fixed smile on his elderly face. At his feet was an upturned bowler hat, into which people dropped coins, and when the record ended, he bent down, turned it over neatly, and began to dance again. At the end of the second tune, he packed the gramophone up and moved on, farther down the promenade, to begin his performance all over again.

She sat on the green bench feeling a little faint and giddy, her heart pounding. She thought of her mother, and what she would have said, she thought of how foolish she had been made to look, for surely someone knew, surely half the town had seen Mr Curry? The strains of his music drifted up the promenade on the evening air. It was almost dark now, the sea was creeping back up the shingle.

She thought of going home, of turning the contents of Mr Curry's room out onto the pavement and locking the front door, she thought of calling the police, or her Uncle Cecil, of going to a neighbour. She had been humiliated, taken in, disgraced, and almost wept for the shame of it.

And then, presently, she wondered what it was she had meant by 'shame'. Mr Curry was not dishonest. He had not told her what he did in the summer months, he had not lied. Perhaps he had simply kept it from her because she might disapprove. It was his own business. And certainly there was no doubt at all that in the winter months he sold cleaning utensils from door to door. He paid his rent. He was neat and tidy and a pleasant companion. What was there to fear?

All at once, then, she felt sorry for him, and at the same time, he became a romantic figure in her eyes, for he had danced well and his singing had not been without a certain

style, perhaps he had a fascinating past as a music hall per-
former, and who was she, Esme Fanshaw, to despise him,
what talent had she? Did she earn her living by giving enter-
tainment to others?

'I told you so, Esme. What did I tell you?'

'Told me what, mother? What is it you have to say to me?
Why do you not leave me alone?'

Her mother was silent.

Quietly then, she picked up her handbag and left the green
bench and the promenade and walked up through the dark
residential streets, past the gardens sweet with stocks and
roses, past open windows, towards Park Walk, and when she
reached her own house, she put away the straw hat, though
she kept on the dress of white piqué, because it was such a
warm night. She went down into the kitchen and made coffee
and set it, with a plate of sandwiches and a plate of biscuits,
on a tray, and presently Mr Curry came in, and she called out
to him, she said, 'Do come and have a little snack with me, I
am quite sure you can do with it, I'm quite sure you are tired.'

And she saw from his face that he knew that she knew.

But nothing was said that evening, or until some weeks lat-
er, when Mr Curry was sitting opposite her, on a cold, windy
August night, reading from the volume cow to DIN. Esme
Fanshaw said, looking at him, 'My mother used to say,
Mr Curry, "I always like a bit of singing and dancing, some
variety. It takes you out of yourself, singing and dancing."'

Mr Curry gave a little bow.

ISMAT CHUGTAI

Tiny's Granny

God knows what her real name was. No one had ever called
her by it. When she was a little snotty-nosed girl roaming
about the alleys, people used to call her 'Bafatan's kid.' Then
she was 'Bashira's daughter-in-law,' and then 'Bismillah's
mother'; and when Bismillah died in childbirth leaving Tiny
an orphan, she became 'Tiny's Granny' to her dying day.

There was no occupation which Tiny's Granny had not
tried at some stage of her life. From the time she was old
enough to hold her own cup she had started working at odd
jobs in people's houses in return for her two meals a day and
cast off clothes. Exactly what the words 'odd jobs' mean, only
those know who have been kept at them at an age when they
ought to have been laughing and playing with other children.
Anything from the uninteresting duty of shaking the baby's
rattle to massaging the master's head comes under the cate-
gory of 'odd jobs.' As she grew older she learnt to do a bit of
cooking, and she spent some years of her life as a cook. But
when her sight began to fail and she began to cook lizards in
the lentils and knead flies into the bread, she had to retire. All
she was fit for after that was gossiping and tale-bearing. But
that also was a fairly paying trade. In every muhalla* there is
always some quarrel going on, and one who has the wit to
carry information to the enemy camp can be sure of a

* A ward or quarter of a city.

hospitable reception. But it's a game that doesn't last. People began to call her tell-tale, and when she saw that there was no future there, she took up her last and most profitable profession: she became a polished and accomplished beggar.

At meal times Granny would dilate her nostrils to smell what was cooking, single out the smell she liked best and be set off on its track until she reached the house it was coming from.

'Lady, are you cooking aravi with the meat?' she would ask with a disinterested air.

'No, Granny. The aravi you get these days doesn't get soft. I'm cooking potatoes with it.'

'Potatoes! What a lovely smell! Bismillah's father, God rest him, used to love meat and potatoes.' Every day it was the same thing: 'Let's have meat and potatoes, and now' (she would heave a sigh), 'I don't see meat and potatoes for months together.' Then, suddenly getting anxious, 'Lady, have you put any coriander leaf in the meat?'

'No, Granny. All our coriander was ruined. The confounded water carrier's dog got into the garden and rolled all over it.'

'That's a pity. A bit of coriander leaf in with the meat and potatoes makes all the difference. Hakimji's got any amount in his garden.'

'That's no good to me, Granny. Yesterday his boy cut Shabban Mian's [Shabban Mian is the son of the lady speaking] kite string and I told him that if he showed his face again he'd better look out for himself.'

'Good heavens, I shan't say it's for you.' And Granny would gather her burqa* around her and be off with slippers clacking to Hakimji's. She'd get into the garden on the plea of wanting to sit in the sun, and then edge towards the coriander

* A loose flowing garment worn by Muslim women who observe purdah, competely enveloping them from head to foot.

bed. Then she'd pluck a leaf and crush it between her finger and thumb and savour the pleasant smell and as soon as the Hakimji's daughter-in-law turned her back, Granny would make a grab. And obviously, when she had provided the coriander leaf, she could hardly be refused a bite to eat.

Granny was famed throughout the muhalla for her sleight of hand. You couldn't leave food and drink lying unwatched when Granny was about. She would pick the children's milk and drink it straight from the pan: two swallows and it would be gone. She'd put a little sugar in the palm of her hand and toss it straight into her mouth. Or press a lump of gur to her palate, and sit in the sun sucking it at her ease. She made good use of her waist band too. She would whip up an areca nut and tuck it in. Or stuff in a couple of chapatis, half in and half out, but with her thick kurta* concealing them from view, and hobble away, groaning and grunting in her usual style. Everyone knew all about these things, but no one had the courage to say anything, firstly because her old hands were as quick as lightning, and moreover when in a tight corner she had no objection to swallowing whole whatever was in her mouth; and secondly, because if anyone expressed the slightest suspicion of her she made such a fuss that they soon thought better of it. She would swear her innocence by all that was sacred, and threaten to take an oath on the Holy Quran. And who would disgrace himself in the next world by directly inviting her to swear a false oath on the Quran?

Granny was not only a tale-bearer, thief, and cheat. She was also a first-rate liar. And her biggest lie was her burqa which she always wore.

At one time it had had a veil, but when one by one the old men of the muhalla died off, or their eyesight failed, Granny said goodbye to her veil. But you never saw her without the cap of her burqa, with its fashionably serrated pattern on her

* A shirt-like garment worn outside the trousers.

head, as though it were stuck to her skull, and though she might leave it open down the front (even when she was wearing a transparent kurta with no vest underneath) it would billow out behind her like a king's robe. This burqa was not simply for keeping her head modestly covered. She put it to every possible and impossible use. It served her as bedclothes: bundled up, it became a pillow. On the rare occasions when she bathed, she used it as a towel. At the five times of prayer, it was her prayer mat. When the local dogs bared their teeth at her, it became a serviceable shield for her protection. As the dog leapt at her calves it would find the voluminous folds of Granny's burqa hissing in its face. Granny was exceedingly fond of her burqa, and in her spare moments would sit and lament with the keenest regret over its advancing old age. To forestall further wear and tear, she would patch it with any scrap of cloth that came her way, and she trembled at the very thought of the day when it would be no more. Where would she get eight yards of white cloth to make another one? She would be lucky if she could get as much together for her shroud.

Granny had no permanent headquarters. Like a soldier, she was always on the march – today in someone's verandah, tomorrow in someone else's back yard. Wherever she spied a suitable site she would pitch camp and, when they turned her out, would move on. With half her burqa laid out under her and the other half wrapped over her, she would lie down and take her ease.

But even more than she worried about her burqa, she worried about her only grand-daughter Tiny. Like a broody old hen, she would always have her safe under her sheltering wing, and never let her out of her sight. But a time came when Granny could no longer get about, and when the people of the muhalla had got wise to her ways – as soon as they heard the shuffle of her slippers approaching they sounded the alert and took up positions of defense: and then all Granny's broad hints and suggestions would fall on deaf ears. So there was nothing that Granny could do except put Tiny to her ancestral trade, doing odd jobs in people's houses. She thought about it for a long time, and then got her a job at the Deputy Sahib's for her food, clothing, and one and a half rupees a month. She was never far away though, and stuck to Tiny like a shadow. The moment Tiny was out of sight she would set up a hullabaloo.

But a pair of old hands cannot wipe out what is inscribed in a person's fate. It was midday. The deputy's wife had gone off to her brother's to discuss the possibility of marrying her son to his daughter. Granny was sitting at the edge of the garden taking a nap under the shade of a tree. The lord and master was taking his siesta in a room enclosed by water-cooled screens. And Tiny, who was supposed to be pulling the rope of the ceiling fan, was dozing with the rope in her hand. The fan stopped moving, the lord and master woke up, his animality was aroused, and Tiny's fate was sealed.

They say that to ward off the failing powers of old age the hakims and vaids, besides all the medicines and ointments which they employ, also prescribe chicken broth – well, the nine-year-old Tiny was no more than a chicken herself.

When Tiny's Granny awoke from her nap, Tiny had disappeared. She searched the whole muhalla, but there was no sign of her anywhere. But when she returned tired out to her room at night, there was Tiny in a corner leaning up against the wall, staring about her with listless eyes like a wounded bird. Granny was almost too terrified to speak, but to conceal the weakness she felt she began swearing at Tiny. 'You little whore, so this is where you've got to! And I've been all over the place looking for you until my poor old legs are all swollen. Just wait till I tell the Master. I'll get you thrashed within an inch of your life!'

But Tiny couldn't conceal what had happened to her for long, and when Granny found out, she beat her head and shrieked. When the woman next door was told, she clutched her head in horror. If the deputy's son had done it, then perhaps something might have been said. But the deputy himself . . . one of the leading men in the muhalla, grandfather to three grandchildren, a religious man who regularly said his five daily prayers and had only recently provided mats and water-vessels to the local mosque – how could anyone raise a voice against him?

So Granny, who was used to being at the mercy of others, swallowed her sorrow, applied warm cloths to Tiny's back, gave her sweets to comfort her, and bore her trouble as best she might. Tiny spent a day or two in bed, and then was up and about again. And in a few days she had forgotten all about it.

Not so the gentlewomen of the muhalla! They would send for her on the quiet and ask her all about it.

'No, Granny will smack me,' Tiny would try to get out of it.

'Here take these bangles . . . Granny won't know anything about it.' The eager ladies would coax her.

'What happened? How did it happen?' They would ask for all the details, and Tiny who was too young and innocent to understand entirely what it all meant, would tell them as well as she could and they would cover their faces and laugh delightedly.

Tiny might forget, but nature cannot. If you pluck a flower in the bud and make it bloom before it is ready, its petals fall and only the stump is left. Who knows how many innocent petals Tiny's face had shed? It acquired a forward, brazen look, a look older than its years. Tiny did not grow from a child into girl, but at one leap became a woman, and not a fully-fashioned woman moulded by nature's skilled and practiced hands, but one like a figure on whom some giant with feet two yards long had trodden – squat, fat, puffy, like a clay toy which the potter had knelt on before it had hardened.

When a rag is all dirty and greasy, no one minds too much if someone wipes his nose on it. The boys would pinch her play-fully in the open street, and give her sweets to eat. Tiny's eyes began to dance with an evil light . . . And now Granny no longer stuffed her with sweets: she beat her black and blue instead. But you can't shake the dust off a greasy cloth. Tiny was like a rubber ball: hit it and it comes bouncing back at you.

Within a few years Tiny's promiscuity had made her the pest of the whole muhalla. It was rumored that the Deputy Sahib and his son had quarreled over her . . . then that Rajva the palanquin-bearer had given the mulla a thorough thrash-ing . . . then that she had taken up regularly with the nephew of Siddiq the wrestler. Every day Tiny came near to losing her nose,★ and there was fighting and brawling in the alleys.

The place became too hot to hold her. There was nowhere she could safely set foot anymore. Thanks to Tiny's youthful charms and Siddiq's nephew's youthful strength, life in the muhalla became intolerable. They say that in places like Delhi and Bombay there is an abundant demand for their kind of commodity. Perhaps the two of them migrated there. The day Tiny ran away, Granny had not the slightest suspicion of what was afoot. For several days the little wretch had been unusu-ally quiet. She hadn't sworn at Granny, but had spent a lot of time sitting quietly on her own, staring into space.

'Come and get your dinner, Tiny,' Granny would say.

'I'm not hungry, Granny.'

'Tiny, it's getting late. Go to bed.'

'I don't feel sleepy, Granny.'

That night she began to massage Granny's feet for her. 'Granny . . . Granny; just hear me recite the "Subhanakal-lahumma," and see if I have got it right.' Granny heard it: Tiny had it off pat.

★ Cutting off the nose was the traditional punishment inflicted on a loose woman. In this context, it would be the act of a jealous lover, punishing her for her promiscuity.

'All right, dear. Off you go now. It's time you were asleep.'
And Granny turned over and tried to sleep.

A little later she could hear Tiny moving about in the yard.

'What the devil is she up to now?' she muttered. 'What b—
has she brought home now? Little whore. She's got to use
even the back yard now!' But when she peered down into the
yard, Granny was filled with awe. Tiny was saying her isha
prayer. And in the morning she was gone.

People who return to this place from journeyings far afield
sometimes bring news of her. One says that a great lord has
made her his mistress and that she is living in fine style like a
lady, with a carriage and any amount of gold. Another says she
has seen her in the diamond market . . . others say she has
been seen in Faras Road or in Sona Gachi.*

But Granny's story is that Tiny had had a sudden attack of
cholera and was dead before anyone knew it.

After her period of mourning for Tiny, Granny's mind
started to wander. People passing her in the street would tease
her and make jokes at her expense.

'Granny, why don't you get married?' my sister would say.

Granny would get annoyed. 'Who to? Your husband?'

'Why not marry the mullah? I tell you he is crazy about you.
By God he is!'

Then the swearing would begin, and Granny's swearing was
so novel and colorful that people could only stare aghast.

'That pimp! Just see what happens if I get hold of him! If I
don't pull his beard out, you can call me what you like.' But
whenever she met the mullah at the corner of the street, then,
believe it or not, she would go all shy.

Apart from the urchins of the muhalla, Granny's lifelong
enemies were the monkeys – 'the confounded, blasted mon-
keys.' They had been settled in the muhalla for generations
and knew all about everyone who lived there. They knew that

* Prostitutes' quarters in various big Indian cities.

men were dangerous and children mischievous, but that women were only afraid of them. But then Granny too had spent all her life among them. She'd got hold of some child's catapult to frighten them with, and when she wound her burqa round her head like a great turban and pounced upon them with her catapult at the ready, the monkeys really did panic for a moment before returning to their usual attitude of indifference towards her.

Day in and day out, Granny and the monkeys used to fight over her bits and pieces of stale food. Whenever there was a wedding in the muhalla, or a funeral feast, or the celebrations that mark the fortieth day after childbirth, Granny would be there, gathering up the scraps left over as though she were under contract to do so. Where free food was being distributed she would contrive to come up for her share four times over. In this way she would pile up a regular stack of food, and then she would gaze at it regretfully, wishing that God had arranged her stomach like the camel's so that she could tuck away four days' supply. Why should He be so utterly haphazard? Why had He provided her with a machine for eating so defective that if she had more than two meals' supply at any one time, it simply couldn't cope with it? So what she used to do was to spread out the food to dry on bits of sacking and then put them in a pitcher. When she felt hungry she would take some out and crumble it up, add a dash of water and a pinch of chillies and salt, and there was a tasty mash all ready to eat. But during the summer and during the rains this recipe had often given her severe diarrhoea. So when her bits of food got stale and began to smell she would with the greatest reluctance sell them to people for whatever price she could get to feed to their dogs and goats. The trouble was that generally the stomachs of the dogs and the goats proved less brazen than Granny's and people would not take her dainties as a gift, let alone buy them. All this notwithstanding that these bits and pieces were dearer to

Granny than life itself, that she put up with countless kicks
and curses to get them, and that to dry them in the sun meant
waging holy war against the whole monkey race. She would no
sooner spread them out than the news would, as though by
wireless, reach the monkey tribes, and band upon band of
them would come and take up their positions on the wall or
frisk about on the tiles raising a din. They would pull out the
straws from the thatch and chatter and scold the passers-by.
Granny would take the field against them. Swathing her burqa
round her head and taking her catapult in her hand, she would
take her stand. The battle would rage all day, Granny scaring
the monkeys off again and again. And when evening came she
would gather up what was left after their depredations, and
cursing them from the bottom of her heart, creep exhausted
into her little room to sleep.

The monkeys must have acquired a personal grudge against
Granny. How else can you explain the fact that they turned
their backs on everything else the world had to offer and con-
centrated all their attacks on Granny's scraps of food? And
how else can you explain the fact that a big rascally, red-
behinded monkey ran off with her pillow, which she loved
more than her life? Once Tiny had gone, this pillow was the
only thing left in the world that was near and dear to her. She
fussed and worried over it as much as she did over her burqa.
She was forever repairing its seams with stout stitches. Time
and again she would sit herself down in some secluded corner
and start playing with it as if it were a doll. She had none but
the pillow now to tell all her troubles to and so lighten her
burden. And the greater the love she felt for her pillow, the
more stout stitches she would put into it to strengthen its
seams.

And now see what trick Fate played on her. She was
sitting leaning against the parapet with her burqa wrapped
around her, picking the lice out of her waist-band, when
suddenly a monkey flopped down, whipped up her pillow,

and was off. You would have thought that someone had plucked Granny's heart out of her breast. She wept and screamed and carried on so much that the whole muhalla came flocking.

You know what monkeys are like. They wait until no one is looking and then run off with a glass or a katora, go and sit on the parapet, and taking it in both hands start rubbing it against the wall. The person it belongs to stands there looking up and making coaxing noises, and holding out bread, or an onion: but the monkey takes his time, and when he has had his bellyful of fun, throws the thing down and goes his own way. Granny poured out the whole contents of a pitcher, but the b— monkey had set his heart on the pillow, and that was that. She did all she could to coax him, but his heart would not melt and he proceeded with the greatest enjoyment to peel the manifold coverings off the pillow as though he were peeling the successive skins off an onion – those same coverings over which Granny had pored with her weak and watering eyes, trying to hold them together with stitching. As every fresh cover came off, Granny's hysterical wailing grew louder. And now the last covering was off, and the monkey began bit by bit to throw down the contents . . . not cotton wadding but . . . Shabban's quilted jacket . . . Bannu the water carrier's waist-cloth . . . Hasina's bodice . . . the baggy trousers belonging to little Munni's doll . . . Rahmat's little dupatta . . . and Khairati's knickers . . . Khairan's little boy's pistol . . . Munshiji's muffler . . . the sleeve (with cuff) of Ibrahim's shirt . . . a piece of Siddiq's loin cloth . . . Amina's collyrium bottle and Batafan's kajal-box . . . Sakina's box of tinsel clippings . . . the big bead of Mullan's rosary and Baqir Mian's prayer board . . . Bismillah's dried navel string, the knob of turmeric in its sachet from Tiny's first birthday, some lucky grass, and a silver ring . . . and Bashir Khan's gilt medal conferred on him by the government for having returned safe and sound from the war.

But it was not these trinkets that interested the onlookers. What they had their eyes on was the precious stock of stolen goods which Granny had got together by years of raiding.

'Thief! . . . Swindler! . . . Old hag! . . . Turn the old devil out! . . . Hand her over to the police! Search her bedding: you might find a lot more stuff in it!' In short, they all came straight out with anything they felt like saying.

Granny's shrieking suddenly stopped. Her tears dried up, her head drooped, and she stood there stunned and speechless . . . She passed that night sitting on her haunches, her hands grasping her knees, rocking backwards and forwards, her body shaken by dry sobbing, lamenting and calling the names of now her mother and father, now her husband, now her daughter, Bismillah, and her granddaughter, Tiny. Every now and then, just for a moment, she would doze, then wake with a cry, as though ants were stinging an old sore. At times she would laugh and cry hysterically, at times talk to herself, then suddenly, for no reason, break into a smile. Then out of the darkness some old recollection would hurl its spear at her, and like a sick dog howling in a half human voice, she would rouse the whole muhalla with her cries. Two days passed in this way, and the people of the muhalla gradually began to feel sorry for what they had done. After all, no one had the slightest need of any of these things. They had disappeared years ago, and though there had been weeping and wailing over them at the time, they had long since been forgotten. It was just that they themselves were no millionaires, and sometimes on such occasions a mere straw weighs down upon you like a great beam. But the loss of these things had not killed them. Shabban's quilted jacket had long since lost any ability to grapple with the cold, and he couldn't stop himself growing up while he waited for it to be found. Hasina had long felt she was past the age for wearing a bodice. Of what use to Munni were her doll's baggy trousers? She had long passed the stage of playing with dolls and graduated to toy cooking pots. And none of the people of the muhalla were out for Granny's blood.

In olden days there lived a giant. This giant's life was in a big black bee. Across the seven seas in a cave there was a big chest, and in it another chest, and inside that was a little box, in which there was a big black bee. A brave prince came . . . and first he tore off the bee's legs and, by the power of the spell, one of the giant's legs broke. Then the prince broke another leg, and the giant's other leg broke. And then he crushed the bee, and the giant died.

Granny's life was in the pillow, and the monkey had torn the enchanted pillow with his teeth, and so thrust a red hot iron bar into Granny's heart.

There was no sorrow in the world, no humiliation, no disgrace, which Fate had not brought to Granny. When her husband died and her bangles were broken,* Granny had thought she had not many more days to live; when Bismillah was wrapped in her shroud, she felt certain that this was the last straw on the camel's back. And when Tiny brought disgrace upon her and ran away, Granny had thought that this was the death-blow.

From the day of her birth onwards, every conceivable illness had assailed her. Small pox had left its marks upon her face. Every year at some festival she would contract severe diarrhoea.

Her fingers were worn to the bone by years of cleaning up other people's filth, and she had scoured pots and pans until her hands were all pitted and marked. Some time every year she would fall down the stairs in the dark, take to bed for a

* A sign of widowhood.

day or two and then start dragging herself about again. In her last birth Granny surely must have been a dog-tick; that's why she was so hard to kill. It seemed as though death always gave her a wide berth. She'd wander about with her clothes hanging in tatters, but she would never accept the clothes of anyone who had died, nor even let them come into contact with her. The dead person might have hidden death in the seams to jump out and grab the delicately nurtured Granny. Who could have imagined that in the end it would be the monkeys who would settle her account? Early in the morning, when the water carrier came with his water skin, he saw that Granny was sitting on her haunches on the stairs. Her mouth was open and flies were crawling in the corners of her half-closed eyes.

People had often seen Granny asleep just like this, and had feared she was dead. But Granny had always started up, cleared her throat and spat out the phlegm, and poured out a shower of abuse on the person who had disturbed her. But that day Granny remained sitting on her haunches on the stairs. Fixed in death, she showered continuous abuse upon the world. Her whole life through she had never known a moment's ease and wherever she had laid herself down there had been thorns. Granny was shrouded just as she was, squatting on her haunches. Her body had set fast, and no amount of pulling and tugging could straighten it.

On Judgment Day the trumpet sounded, and Granny woke with a start and got up coughing and clearing her throat, as though her ears had caught the sound of free food being doled out . . . Cursing and swearing at the angels, she dragged herself somehow or other doubled up as she was over the Bridge of Sirat and burst into the presence of God the All Powerful and All Kind . . . And God, beholding the degradation of humanity, bowed his head in shame and wept tears and those divine tears of blood fell upon Granny's rough grave, and bright red poppies sprang up there and began to dance in the breeze.

Translated from the Urdu
by Dr Ralph Russell

MURIEL SPARK

from *Memento Mori*

Lisa Brooke died in her seventy-third year after her second stroke. She had taken nine months to die, and in fact it was only a year before her death that, feeling rather ill, she had decided to reform her life, and reminding herself how attractive she still was, offered up the new idea, her celibacy to the Lord to whom no gift whatsoever is unacceptable.

It did not occur to Godfrey as he marched into a pew in the crematorium chapel that anyone else present had ever been Lisa's lover except himself. It did not even come to mind that he had been Lisa's lover, for he had never been her lover in any part of England, only Spain and Belgium, and at the moment he was busy with statistics. There were sixteen people present. On first analysis it emerged that five were relatives of Lisa. Next, among the remaining eleven, Godfrey elicited Lisa's lawyer, her housekeeper, the bank manager. Lettie had just arrived. Then there was himself. That left six, only one of whom he recognized, but all of whom were presumably Lisa's hangers-on, and he was glad their fountain of ready cash had dried up. All those years of daylight robbery; and many a time he had told Lisa, 'A child of six could do better than that,' when she displayed one of the paintings, outrages, committed by one of her pets. 'If he hasn't made his way in the world by now,' he had said, time and again, of old Percy Mannering the poet, 'he never will. You are a fool, Lisa, letting him drink your gin and shout his poetry in your ears.'

Percy Mannering, almost eighty, stood with his lean stoop as the coffin was borne up the aisle. Godfrey stared hard at the poet's red-veined hatchet cheek-bones and thin nose. He thought, 'I bet he's regretting the termination of his income. They've all bled poor Lisa white . . .' The poet was, in fact, in a state of excitement. Lisa's death had filled him with thrilling awe, for though he knew the general axiom that death was everyone's lot he could never realize the particular case; each new death gave him something fresh to feel. It came to him as the service began that within a few minutes Lisa's coffin would start sliding down into the furnace, and he saw as in a fiery vision her flame-tinted hair aglow as always, competing with the angry tresses of the fire below. He grinned like an elated wolf and shed tears of human grief as if he were half-beast, half-man, instead of half-poet, half-man. Godfrey watched him and thought, 'He must be senile. He has probably lost his faculties.'

The coffin began to slide slowly down the slope towards a gap in the wall while the organ played something soft and religious. Godfrey, who was not a believer, was profoundly touched by this ensemble, and decided once and for all to be cremated when his time came. 'There goes Lisa Brooke,' he said to himself as he saw the last tilt of the coffin. The prow, thought the poet, lifts, and the ship goes under with the skipper on board . . . No, that's too banal, Lisa herself as the ship is a better idea. Godfrey looked round him and thought, 'She should have been good for another ten years, but what can you expect with all that drink and all these spongers?' So furiously did he glare about him that he startled the faces which caught his eye.

Tubby Dame Lettie caught up with her brother in the aisle as he moved with the others to the porch. 'What's the matter with you, Godfrey?' Lettie breathed.

The chaplain was shaking doleful hands with everyone at the door. As Godfrey gave his hand he said over his shoulder to Lettie, 'The matter with *me*? What d'you mean what's the matter with me? What's the matter with *you*?'

Lettie, as she dabbed her eyes, whispered, 'Don't talk so loud. Don't glare so. Everyone's looking at you.'

On the floor of the long porch was a muster of flowers done up, some in tasteful bunches, one or two in old-fashioned wreaths. These were being inspected by Lisa's relatives, her middle-aged nephew and his wife, her parched elder sister Janet Sidebottome who had been a missionary in India at a time when it *was* India, her brother Ronald Sidebottome who had long since retired from the City, and Ronald's Australian wife who had been christened Tempest. Godfrey did not immediately identify them, for he saw only the row of their several behinds as they stooped to examine the cards attached to each tribute.

'Look, Ronald, isn't this sweet? A tiny bunch of violets – oh, see, it says, "Thank you, Lisa dear, for all those wonderful times, with love from Tony."'

'Rather odd words. Are you sure –'

'Who's Tony, I wonder?'

'See, Janet, this huge yellow rose wreath here from Mrs Pettigrew. It must have cost her a fortune.'

'What did you say?' said Janet who did not hear well.

'A wreath from Mrs Pettigrew. It must have cost a fortune.'

'Sh-sh-sh,' said Janet, looking round. True enough, Mrs Pettigrew, Lisa's old housekeeper, was approaching in her well-dressed confident manner. Janet, cramped from the card-inspection, straightened painfully and turned to meet Mrs Pettigrew. She let the woman grip her hand.

'Thank you for all you have done for my sister,' said Janet sternly.

'It was a pleasure.' Mrs Pettigrew spoke in a surprisingly soft voice. It was understood Janet was thinking of the will. 'I loved Mrs Brooke, poor soul.'

Janet inclined her head graciously, firmly withdrew her hand and rudely turned her back.

'Can we see the ashes?' loudly inquired Percy Mannering as he emerged from the chapel. 'Is there any hope of *seeing* them? At the noise he made, Lisa's nephew and his wife jumped nervily and looked round.

'I want to see those ashes if possible.' The poet had cornered Dame Lettie, pressing his hungry demand. Lettie felt there was something unhealthy about the man. She moved away.

'That's one of Lisa's artists,' she whispered to John Sidebottome, not meaning to prompt him to say 'Oh!' and lift his hat in Percy's direction, as he did.

Godfrey stepped backwards and stood on a spray of pink carnations. 'Oh – sorry,' he said to the carnations, stepping off them quickly, and then was vexed at his folly, and knew that in any case no one had seen him after all. He ambled away from the trampled flowers.

'What's that fellow want with the ashes?' he said to Lettie.

'He wants to see them. Wants to see if they've gone grey. He is quite disgusting.'

'Of course they will be grey. The fellow must have lost his faculties. *If* he ever had any.'

'I don't know about faculties,' said Lettie. 'Certainly he has no feelings.'

Tempest Sidebottome, blue-haired and well corseted, was saying in a voice which carried away out to the Garden of Remembrance, 'To some people there's just nothing that's sacred.'

'Madam,' said Percy, baring his sparse green teeth in a smile, 'the ashes of Lisa Brooke will always be sacred to me. I desire to see them, kiss them if they are cool enough. Where's that cleric? – He'll have the ashes.'

'Do you see over there – Lisa's housekeeper?' Lettie said to Godfrey.

'Yes, yes, I wonder –'

'That's what *I'm* wondering,' said Lettie, who was wondering if Mrs Pettigrew wanted a job, and if so would agree to undertake the personal care of Charmian.

'But I think we would need a younger woman. That one must be getting on,' said Godfrey, 'if I remember aright.'

'Mrs Pettigrew has a constitution like a horse,' said Dame Lettie, casting a horse-dealer's glance over Mrs Pettigrew's upright form. 'And it is impossible to get younger women.'

'Has she got all her faculties?'

'Of course. She had poor Lisa right under her thumb.'

'I hardly think Charmian would want —'

'Charmian needs to be bullied. What Charmian needs is a firm hand. She will simply go to pieces if you don't keep at her. Charmian needs a firm hand. It's the only way.'

'But what about Mrs Anthony?' said Godfrey. 'The woman might not get on with Mrs Anthony. It would be tragic if we lost her.'

'If you don't find someone soon to look after Charmian you will certainly lose Mrs Anthony. Charmian is too much of a handful for Mrs Anthony. You will lose Mrs Anthony. Charmian keeps calling her Taylor. She is bound to resent it. Who are you staring at?'

Godfrey was staring at a short bent man walking with the aid of two sticks round a corner of the chapel. 'Who is that man?' said Godfrey. 'He looks familiar.'

Tempest Sidebottome fussed over to the little man who beamed up at her with a fresh face under his wide black hat. He spoke in a shrill boyish tone. 'Afraid I'm late,' he said. 'Is the party over? Are you all Lisa's sinisters and bothers?'

'That's Guy Leet,' said Godfrey, at once recognizing him, for Guy had always used to call sisters and brothers sinisters and bothers. 'The little rotter,' said Godfrey, 'he used to be after Charmian. It must be thirty-odd years since last I saw him. He can't be more than seventy-five and just see what he's come to.'

Tables at a tea-shop near Golders Green had been reserved for Lisa's post-crematorial party. Godfrey had intended to miss the tea party but the arrival of Guy Leet had changed his mind. He was magnetized by the sight of the clever little man doubled over his sticks, and could not keep his eyes off the arthritic hobbling of Guy making his way among the funeral flowers.

'Better join them for tea,' he said to Lettie, 'hadn't we?'

'What for?' said Lettie, looking round the company. 'We can have tea at home. Come back with me for tea, we can have it at home.'

'I think we'd better join them,' said Godfrey. 'We might have a word with Mrs Pettigrew about her taking on Charmian.'

Lettie saw Godfrey's gaze following the hunched figure of Guy Leet who, on his sticks, had now reached the door of his taxi. Several of the party helped Guy inside, then joined him. As they drove off, Godfrey said, 'Little rotter. Supposed to be a critic. Tried to take liberties with all the lady novelists, and then he was a theatre critic and he was after the actresses. You'll remember him, I dare say.'

'Vaguely,' said Lettie. 'He never got much change out of *me*.'

'He was never after you,' said Godfrey.

At the tea-shop Dame Lettie and Godfrey found the mourners being organized into their places by Tempest Sidebottome, big and firm in her corsets, aged seventy-five, with that accumulated energy which strikes despair in the hearts of jaded youth, and which now fairly intimidated even the two comparative youngsters in the group, Lisa's nephew and his wife who were not long past fifty.

'Ronald, sit down here and stay put,' Tempest said to her husband, who put on his glasses and sat down.

Godfrey was casting about for Guy Leet, but in the course of doing so his sight was waylaid by the tables on which were set silver-plate cakestands with thin bread and butter on the bottom tier, cut fruit cake above that, and on the top, a pile of iced cakes wrapped in Cellophane paper. Godfrey began to feel a passionate longing for his tea, and he pushed past Dame Lettie to stand conspicuously near the organizer, Tempest. She did notice him right away and allotted him a seat at a table. 'Lettie,' he called then, 'come over here. We're sitting here.'

'Dame Lettie,' said Tempest over his head, 'you must come and sit with us, my dear. Over here beside Ronald.'

'Damned snob,' thought Godfrey. 'I suppose she thinks Lettie is somebody.'

Someone leant over to offer him a cigarette which was a filter-tip. However, he said, 'Thanks, I'll keep it for after tea.' Then looking up, he saw the wolf grin on the face of the man who was offering him the packet with a trembling hand. Godfrey plucked out a cigarette and placed it beside his plate. He was angry at being put beside Percy Mannering, not only because Percy had been one of Lisa's spongers, but also because he must surely be senile with that grin and frightful teeth, and Godfrey felt the poet would not be able to manage his teacup with those shaking hands.

He was right, for Percy spilled a lot of his tea on the cloth. 'He ought to be in a home,' thought Godfrey. Tempest glanced at their table every now and then and tut-tutted a lot, but she did this all round, as if it were a children's beanfeast; Percy was oblivious of the mess he was making or of anyone's disapproval. Two others sat at their table, Janet Sidebottome and Mrs Pettigrew. The poet had taken it for granted that he was the most distinguished and therefore the leader of conversation.

'One time I fell out with Lisa,' he roared, 'was when she took up Dylan Thomas.' He pronounced the first name Dyelan. 'Dylan Thomas,' he said, 'and Lisa was good to him. Do you know, if I was to go to Heaven and find Dylan Thomas there, I'd prefer to go to HELL. *And* I wouldn't be surprised if Lisa hasn't gone to Hell for aiding and abetting him in his poetry so-called.'

Janet Sidebottome bent her ear closer to Percy. 'What did you say about poor Lisa? I don't hear well.'

'I say,' he said, 'I wonder if Lisa's gone to Hell because of her –'

'From respect to my dear sister,' said Janet with a hostile look, 'I don't think we will discuss –'

'Dye-lan Thomas died from D.T.' said the old poet, becoming gleeful. 'You see the coincidence? – His initials were D.T. and he *died* from D.T. Hah!'

'In respect for my late sister –'

'Poetry!' said Percy. 'Dylan Thomas didn't know the meaning of the word. As I said to Lisa, I said, "You're making a bloody fool of yourself supporting that charlatan. It isn't poetry, it's a leg-pull." She didn't see it, nobody saw it, but I'm telling you his verse was all a HOAX.'

Tempest turned round in her chair. 'Hush, Mr Mannering,' she said, tapping Percy on the shoulder.

Percy looked at her and roared, 'Ha! Do you know what you can tell Satan to do with Dye-lan Thomas's poetry?' He sat back to observe, with his two-fanged gloat, the effect of this question, which he next answered in unprintable terms, causing Mrs Pettigrew to say, 'Gracious!' and to wipe the corners of her mouth with her handkerchief. Meanwhile various commotions arose at the other tables and the senior waitress said, 'Not in *here*, sir!'

Godfrey's disgust was arrested by fear that the party might now break up. While everyone's attention was still on Percy he hastily took up a couple of the Cellophane-wrapped cakes from the top tier of the cakestand, and stuffed them into his pocket. He looked round and felt sure no one had noticed the action.

Janet Sidebottome leaned over to Mrs Pettigrew. 'What did he say?' she said.

'Well, Miss Sidebottome,' said Mrs Pettigrew, meanwhile glancing at herself sideways in a glass on the wall, 'as far as I could comprehend, he was talking about some gentleman indelicately.'

'Poor Lisa,' said Janet. Tears came to her eyes. She kissed her relatives and departed. Lisa's nephew and his wife sidled away, though before they had reached the door they were summoned back by Tempest because the nephew had left his scarf. Eventually, the couple were permitted to go. Percy Mannering remained grinning in his seat.

To Godfrey's relief Mrs Pettigrew refilled his cup. She also poured one for herself, but when Percy passed his shaking cup she ignored it. Percy said, 'Hah! That was strong meat for you ladies, wasn't it?' He reached for the teapot. 'I hope it wasn't me made Lisa's sister cry,' he said solemnly. 'I'd be sorry to have made her cry.' The teapot was too heavy for his quivering fingers and fell from them on to its side, while a leafy brown sea spread from the open lid over the tablecloth and on to Godfrey's trousers.

Tempest rose, pushing back her chair as if she meant business. She was followed to the calamitous table by Dame Lettie and a waitress. While Godfrey was being sponged, Lettie took the poet by the arm and said, 'Please go.' Tempest, busy with Godfrey's trousers, called over her shoulder to her husband, 'Ronald, you're a man. Give Dame Lettie a hand.'

'What? Who?' said Ronald.

'Wake up, Ronald. Can't you see what has to be done? Help Dame Lettie to take Mr Mannering outside.'

'Oh,' said Ronald, 'why, someone's spilt their tea!' He ogled the swimming tablecloth.

Percy shook off Dame Lettie's hand from his arm, and grinning to right and left, buttoning up his thin coat, departed.

A place was made for Godfrey and Mrs Pettigrew at the Sidebottomes' table. 'Now we shall have a fresh pot of tea,' said Tempest. Everyone gave deep sighs. The waitresses cleaned up the mess. The room was noticeably quiet.

Dame Lettie started to question Mrs Pettigrew about her future plans. Godfrey was anxious to overhear this conversation. He was not sure that he wanted Lisa Brooke's housekeeper to look after Charmian. She might be too old or too expensive. She looked a smart woman, she might have expensive ideas. And he was not sure that Charmian would not have to go into a home.

'There's no definite offer, of course,' he interposed.

'Well, Mr Colston, as I was saying,' said Mrs Pettigrew, 'I can't make any plans, myself, until things are settled.'

'What things?' said Godfrey.

'Godfrey, please,' said Lettie, 'Mrs Pettigrew and I are having a chat.' She slumped her elbow on the table and turned to Mrs Pettigrew, cutting off her brother from view.

'What is your feeling about the service?' said Tempest.

Godfrey looked round at the waitresses. 'Very satisfactory,' he said. 'That older one handled that Mannering very well, I thought.'

Tempest closed her eyes as one who prays for grace. 'I mean,' she said, 'poor Lisa's last rites at the crematorium.'

'Oh,' said Godfrey, 'you should have said funeral service. When you said the service, naturally I thought –'

'What do you feel about the cremation service?'

'First rate,' said Godfrey. 'I've quite decided to be cremated when my time comes. Cleanest way. Dead bodies under the ground only contaminate our water supplies. You should have said cremation service in the first place.'

'I thought it was cold,' said Tempest. 'I do wish the minister had read out poor Lisa's obituary. The last cremation I was at – that was Ronald's poor brother Henry – they read out his obituary from the *Nottingham Guardian*, all about his war service and his work for SSAFA and Road Safety. It was so very moving. Now why couldn't they have read out Lisa's? All that in the papers about what she did for the

Arts, he should have read it out to us.'

'I quite agree,' said Godfrey. 'It was the least he could have done. Did you make a special request for it?'

'No,' she sighed. 'I left the arrangements to Ronald. Unless you do everything yourself . . .'

'They always get very violent about other poets,' said Ronald. 'You see, they feel very personal about poetry.'

'Whatever is he talking about?' said Tempest. 'He's talking about Mr Mannering, that's what he's on about. We aren't talking about Mr Mannering, Ronald. Mr Mannering's left, it's a thing of the past. We've gone on to something else.'

As they rose to leave Godfrey felt a touch on his arm. Turning round he saw Guy Leet behind him, his body crouched over his sticks and his baby face raised askew to Godfrey's.

'Got your funeral baked meats all right?' said Guy.

'What?' said Godfrey.

Guy nodded his head towards Godfrey's pocket which bulged with the cakes. 'Taking them home to Charmian?'

'Yes,' said Godfrey.

'And how is Charmian?'

Godfrey had partly regained his poise. 'She's in wonderful form,' he said. 'I'm sorry,' he said, 'to see you having such a difficult time. Must be terrible not being able to get about on your own pins.'

Guy gave a high laugh. He came close to Godfrey and breathed into his waistcoat, 'But I *did* get about, dear fellow. At least I did.'

On the way home Godfrey threw the cakes out of his car window. Why did one pocket those damned things? he thought. One doesn't need them, one could buy up every cake-shop in London and never miss the money. Why did one do it? It doesn't make sense.

'I have been to Lisa Brooke's funeral,' he said to Charmian when he got home, 'or rather, cremation.'

Charmian remembered Lisa Brooke, she had cause to remember her. 'Personally, I'm afraid,' said Charmian, 'that Lisa was a little spiteful to me sometimes, but she had her better side. A generous nature when dealing with the right person, but –'

'Guy Leet was there,' said Godfrey. 'He's nearly finished now, bent over two sticks.'

Charmian said, 'Oh, and what a clever man he was!'

'Clever?' said Godfrey.

Charmian, when she saw Godfrey's face, giggled squeakily through her nose.

'I have quite decided to be cremated when my time comes,' said Godfrey. 'It is the cleanest way. The cemeteries only pollute our water supplies. Cremation is best.'

'I do so agree with you,' said Charmian sleepily.

'No, you do *not* agree with me,' he said. 'R.C.s are not allowed to be cremated.'

'I mean, I'm sure you are right, Eric dear.'

'I am not Eric,' said Godfrey. 'You are not sure I'm right. Ask Mrs Anthony, she'll tell you that R.C.s are against cremation.' He opened the door and bawled for Mrs Anthony. She came in with a sigh.

'Mrs Anthony, you're a Roman Catholic, aren't you?' said Godfrey.

'That's right. I've got something on the stove.'

'Do you believe in cremation?'

'Well,' she said, 'I don't really much like the idea of being shoved away quick like that. I feel somehow it's sort of –'

'It isn't a matter of how you feel, it's a question of what your Church says you've not got to do. Your Church says you must not be cremated, that's the point.'

'Well, as I say, Mr Colston, I don't really fancy the idea –'

'*Fancy the idea* . . . It is not a question of what you fancy. You have no choice in the matter, do you see?'

'Well, I always like to see a proper burial, I always like –'

'It's a point of discipline in your Church,' he said, 'that you mustn't be cremated. You women don't know your own system.'

'I see, Mr Colston. I've got something on the stove.'

'*I* believe in cremation, but you don't – Charmian, you disapprove of cremation, you understand.'

'Very well, Godfrey.'

'And you too, Mrs Anthony.'

'O.K., Mr Colston.'

'On principle,' said Godfrey.

'That's right,' said Mrs Anthony and disappeared.

Godfrey poured himself a stout whisky and soda. He took from a drawer a box of matches and a razor blade and set to work, carefully splitting the slim length of each match, so that from one box of matches he would eventually make two boxfuls. And while he worked he sipped his drink with satisfaction.

SARAH BARNHILL

Near Places, Far Places

We are both widows, Momma and me, and we live together under the same roof. When my husband died it seemed the right thing to do for me to move back home, so my boy Cleeve and me did, did move in with Momma, since she didn't have nobody and I didn't have nobody. Then Cleeve went and got hisself in trouble and had to leave home and now there's just Momma and me. Two women in a big old white house on the Asheville highway. We got a good view though, of the river and the valley and the mountains all around. And a good view is more than a lot of people got.

I was already living there with Momma when Mr Van Fleet showed up. He came from Delray Beach, Florida, and drove up here every year to escape the heat. Sometimes his wife came with him, but she didn't like the mountains. She got carsick, and it rained too much to suit her. She was with him that year he stopped the first time though, and when she got out of the car, she stretched to get the kinks out and stood by the car door with her hands on her back. She had on dark glasses as big as beer mats, and she said nothing about the quilts.

Mr Van Fleet had seen the quilts hanging on the clothes-line, six of them stretched out in the sun to dry. We watched him stop in the middle of the highway, back his car up, and drive up to the house. He told us he was Mr Van Fleet from Delray Beach, Florida, and offered to buy every last quilt.

Momma likes her quilts but Momma also likes making a

dollar, so I wasn't too surprised when she agreed to sell all but one. She let him have Double Wedding Ring, Drunkard's Path, Goose in the Pond, and Steps to the Altar and Rob Peter, Pay Paul. But when it come to Widow's Mite she put on the brakes.

'It's got bullion stitching in it,' she said. 'And a piece from my momma's wedding dress.'

'But you know there's pieces of Grannie's wedding dress in nearly every quilt you got,' I told her.

'I know. But this one's different. Each of them gold coins stitched into every square's different. Just look at that work. And see here,' she poked the quilt up at me, 'this one's got Momma's initials stitched into it.'

And there it was – ARC, for Addie Rae Case, stitched into the little yellow circle made out to look like a coin that was supposed to be part of the widow's mite.

'He'd give you a good price for it.'

'I know. But this one's different.'

'You are a stubborn soul, Momma.'

'I know that too,' she said.

Mr Van Fleet came back the next summer and the summer after that and bought more quilts. French Bouquet and Burgoyne's Quilt and Noonday Lily. Others too, but I can't remember them all. And every summer he asked Momma would she part with Widow's Mite and every summer Momma said no.

Last August we were sitting on the porch shucking corn, working our way through half a dozen ears Moon had brought in early that morning before me or her was out of bed. Moon is my oldest boy and him and another man worked sixteen acres of bottom land near the International plant they'd been renting for the last seven years. This was the last summer for the corn though, and for everything – the tobacco and the beans and the tomatoes. International bought the land for a new extension and a parking lot, and as soon as Moon harvested the last ear of corn they started to break ground.

The phone rang. I had so much corn silk stuck all over me that Momma went to get it. She was gone a long time for her since she doesn't like talking on the phone, and when she came back she said it was Mr Van Fleet and that he was heading back to Florida day after tomorrow.

'That's early,' I said. 'He usually stays till after the leaves turn.'

'He says his wife wants him to get home.'

'Something's not right here. When the man likes quilts and the wife tells him to get hisself home,' I said. 'But I reckon that's Florida for you.'

'He's still going on about Widow's Mite. He offered me three hundred and fifty dollars for it this time.'

'Take it,' I said. 'When Moon loses this land we're all going to need every little bit we can get.'

'What's anybody need a quilt in Delray Beach, Florida, for anyway?'

'This corn is full of cut worms. Moon says rain early in the summer brings them on.' This green worm stuck its head up at me and waved back and forth like someone's finger coaxing me on – to trouble, no doubt. I flicked it down onto the newspaper where all the shucks and silks was piled up.

'You reckon he's making something for hisself out of this?' Momma said.

'He's lucky to clear a dollar a bushel.'

'Not Moon. Mr Van Fleet.'

I sat there looking down at the rows of pyramids we'd stacked the corn into. Most of the ears we froze just as they were. Some of it I made into creamed corn and filled enough quart bags for Moon and his family when they came for Sunday dinner. The rest I just put into little pint bags for me and Momma. I sat there looking down at those ears of corn wondering what to say about Mr Van Fleet from Delray Beach, Florida.

Finally I said, 'He doesn't need money, Momma. He's got two houses we know of, and you seen his car and his clothes.'

I didn't tell Momma, but the thing I liked best – the only thing I reckon – about Mr Van Fleet was looking at him. I don't mean he was handsome, because he weren't. He was bald on top and had a thin face and wore funny little glasses that pinched his nose. But he was about the cleanest man I have ever seen and his clothes always looked like he'd just got them out the dry cleaners. Sometimes he wore a gold chain around his neck, and once he had on a shiny blue, zip-up boiler suit. But he didn't look like a mechanic. He looked like an astronaut. Moon and Cleeve are the best boys in the world, even if Cleeve did get in trouble and get sent down to Raleigh, but I know that they'll never look like Mr Van Fleet. It isn't in their nature.

'He collects them, Momma. Just like Moon and Cleeve collected all those license plates they tacked up inside the shed. He's retired and he's got money and he likes to collect things. And,' I stopped and looked straight at Momma because I wanted her to take this last point in, 'he wants Widow's Mite bad enough to give you three hundred and fifty dollars for it.'

Momma set her jaw the way she does when something doesn't please her, and she looked out across the valley, past the sourwoods that were beginning to turn red and their feathery blossoms that hung down like peacock tails, past the smoke stacks of the International plant, past the old quarry cut at Bledsoe, and on to the mountains that circle the whole valley.

'Esther,' she finally said to me, 'you and me are both old women. A person would think you'd know by now that there's some things you don't never get back once you let them get away.'

'Don't talk mopey, Momma.'

'This ain't mopey. This is facts.'

No use saying any more when Momma was like this, so we picked up the corn mess and went inside to start supper.

That evening we were setting on the porch when I saw his car between the gaps in the althea hedge that lines the driveway up to the house. It was creeping along, trying not to hit the ruts and potholes we hadn't gotten around to fixing since all the rain in July. Blue car, althea, blue car, althea, it went.

'You didn't tell me he was coming,' I said to Momma.

'He said he might. I didn't say not to.'

That gave me hope. Maybe she'd changed her mind about Widow's Mite.

Whenever Mr Van Fleet came to visit he put me in a strange way. From everything he said I figured he was four or five years younger than me, but he always made me feel like I was younger, and not in the good sense that old women like to feel younger. It was more like him and Momma was the grown-ups and I was just the little kid who didn't know nothing. So when he came I usually just sat on my hands and didn't say much. They mostly talked about quilts anyway.

I watched him get out the car and thought he looked like something from TV. He had on white tennis shoes and white socks with a word stitched into the top that I couldn't see so clear. In fact, he had writing on everything, on his shirt and his short pants that had big deep pockets in them. I had never seen his bare legs before and I hadn't expected them to have such muscles in them. He was trim, I'll have to admit, no rolls on his waist like even Moon and Cleeve have. Brown, too, brown like all those folks from Florida. Like burnt biscuits, Momma said once.

'So how's tricks?' he said as he came up the porch steps. He was always saying things like that – 'How's tricks?' and 'Hang in there' and 'Have a good one.' I don't care for such talk, personally.

But Momma seemed to pay no attention, just got up from her chair and said, 'Evening.'

Momma told me to get some tomato juice I had just made and when everybody got all settled down, talk turned to what it always turned to: quilts.

'I tell you, Molly, this morning in that shop in Biltmore Forest I saw in their window a Widow's Mite for three hundred dollars. God's truth. That's why I upped my offer to three fifty.'

'Whyn't you go ahead and buy that one?' Momma said.

'No antique value. And the filler was cheap. Probably just an old blanket.' He drank some of his tomato juice but you could tell he paid no attention to what he was drinking. 'And – this is the clincher – the blocks were quilted separately. The piecing gave it all away.'

Momma said, 'That's like plucking a chicken after it's baked.'

They kept up such talk for a good thirty minutes while I just sat there and watched the dusk come in.

After a while, I began to think about all those quilts Mr Van Fleet had bought. Wondering where Steps to the Altar and Drunkard's Path were, if they lay folded over a bed in a bright white bedroom that looked out over the blue ocean, or if Rob Peter, Pay Paul was draped over one of those rope hammocks you could lay down in and see palm trees and flowers that bloom the whole year long. It wasn't that I missed the quilts or put much more store by them. There was just too many of them squirreled away in Momma's old trunks or stacked up to the ceiling in closets for a dozen or so to make any difference. And I've never been much for sewing or darning. My hands are just too big and I feel all clumsy and fumble-fingered even if I have to wind a ball of yarn. What I realized sitting on the porch that night listening to Momma and Mr Van Fleet go on and on was that those quilts would go places I'd never been and see sights I'd never seen, and probably never would. There I was, not able to admit to a soul that a bunch of patchwork quilts made by my grannie and great-aunts and women so long since dead I couldn't recall their names, that a bunch of old quilts had made me but one thing and that was jealous.

Get rid of them all, that's what I wanted to do. Then maybe I'd forget about them and not be made such a fool of. Let them go with Mr Van Fleet to Delray Beach, Florida, especially if his money is so hot it's burning a hole in his boiler-suit pocket.

'Sell,' I suddenly said out loud.

Mr Van Fleet slapped the arm of his rocker and said, 'That's what I've been telling her myself.'

Momma just kept on rocking like she hadn't heard a thing.

Mr Van Fleet finally left when it was good and dark, and we had to loan him a flashlight so's he could see his way to get to his car.

When he was gone, I asked Momma, 'You gonna sell him Widow's Mite?'

'I wish I had a nickel for every time you've asked me that. What makes you think I've changed my mind?'

'Because he leaves on Monday,' I said. 'And this is Saturday.'

'That ain't answering my question. What makes you think I have changed my mind?'

She didn't wait for me to say something, because I reckon she knew I didn't have nothing to say. Momma always was the best at calling somebody's bluff. We stood there for awhile in the darkness at the top of the stairs, watching the evening stars come up over Hogback Mountain, not saying a thing.

Finally Momma says Night, Esther, and I say Night, Momma, and that is that.

The next day Moon and his family came for Sunday dinner like they always do. It was Moon and his wife Betty and my two grandbabies, Mandy and Melissa. They had just started school the week before – kindergarten and second grade – and before their Momma and Daddy could even get out of the car they came rushing in with presents they had made for me during craft time. Mandy, the oldest one, brought a turtle she had made out of modeling clay and poked thumbtacks into its back to look like a shell.

'His name is Bill,' Mandy said.

'Where should I put him?'

'Up there.' She pointed to the shelf on the window above the kitchen sink.

I had to shift pots of African violets and a bunch of old orange juice cans I had wandering jew and coleus rooting in to make room for Bill. I even turned him so he could have a view down towards the valley and the althea hedge.

'Melissa brung something too.' Mandy reached for something in Melissa's hand but she jerked away.

'No!'

'Well show it, Melissa.'

Melissa lifted those little hands of hers up toward me, and laying there was this funny looking dark, round thing that I thought at first might be a cookie cutter. I picked it up and held it to where the light shone on it. It was a little, hard clay paper weight with Melissa's hand print right in the middle of it. The tips of my fingers would barely fit into the little scoops in the clay her own fingers had made.

I stood there awhile looking at it.

'It doesn't do nothing,' Melissa said.

'Yes it does. It sets up here on this window sill next to Bill and looks pretty.'

From the kitchen window I could see Moon in the backyard talking to Billy Walkingstick, the old Cherokee who's rented the cabin up above us for as long as I can remember. Moon and Billy had their hands in their back pockets, and every now and then they jabbed at the ground with their shoes. Betty leaned over a bed of petunias and marigolds and pinched off the dead blossoms.

It was times like these I found myself thinking about Cleeve. I should have seen it coming, should have known there was nothing to hold him here. He's not like Moon and Moon's not like Cleeve and I am not the first mother to birth out children who grow up so different you wonder if they can be brothers. Cleeve went and got mixed in with a bad bunch, and one night they went off and beat up an old man. Now Cleeve's down in Raleigh serving out a sentence for assault and battery. I lost something, with Cleeve. And I didn't know how to keep from losing it. It seems like I turned around one day and he was no longer there, like he'd slipped from me, right out of my hands. And right then I felt like I didn't know Cleeve anymore, anymore than I could know that funny looking clay turtle setting in my window sill. But the hurt was still there, I can tell you that.

I kept standing there looking out the kitchen window, leaning up against the cool enamel of the kitchen sink, and for a moment, I forgot where I was.

Then I heard Mandy and Melissa running through the house chasing Momma's six-toed tabby cat and Momma fussing at them. And then Moon and Betty came in the back door loaded down with pound cake and cobbler and okra. This was not time for standing at the sink moping about the way things chose not to turn out.

I gave up my place at the end of the table for Moon like I always did, and Momma sat at the other end. Melissa was still too little to sit in a regular chair, so we put her in the old high chair that her daddy and Cleeve and Mandy had all used. But she was almost too big for it and complained the whole time that it pinched her bottom.

If some stranger had walked in on our Sunday dinner he would have thought we just got through burying somebody. Moon should have felt like the cock o' the walk, what with being the only man there and setting at the head of the table, but I could tell his mind was on losing the sixteen acres and wondering what he could do to add to what he made at International. Betty was her usual quiet self, just chewing her food and looking at whoever happened to say anything.

And me of course. I was thinking about Cleeve, seeing him in some tiny gray room with no window in it.

But Momma was the one I couldn't figure out. What was her cause for setting there like she'd been smote dumb, barely looking at anybody and poking at her food like it might have been last week's oatmeal?

'Momma,' I finally said to her when we were by ourselves in the kitchen, 'something not suiting you? Why you setting there like death warmed over?'

'I got things on my mind.'

'What things?'

'Esther, you act like folks get old and they stop thinking on things. Sometimes I believe I've waited till I got old before I *begun* to do my thinking.'

'What's on your mind, Momma?'

'When I finish thinking on it I'll tell you.'

And with that she walked back in the dining room carrying a dish of blackberry cobbler and I knew it was no use trying to get it out of her until she was good and ready.

After dinner Moon and Betty took the girls for a walk along the river while Momma and me sat on the front porch in the cane bottom rockers and watched the cars that went down the old highway there in front of the house. Momma was fanning herself with the magazine from the Sunday newspaper, swishing the air around just enough to lift the hair up from the side of her face.

'What you looking at, Momma?' But I knew what she would say, and she did.

'Same thing I look at every time I set on this porch,' she said

169

and pointed with the magazine out towards the valley and the mountains. 'I reckon I've set here for nearly sixty years. We were setting here that spring evening when the man from Fort Jackson come to tell us about Hollis.' My brother Hollis got killed in Korea and the Army sent a man up here to tell us about it. Momma gave the man a piece of pie and a cup of coffee, then went in her bedroom and didn't come out again for two days. About the only time she talks of Hollis is when we set on the porch.

What she said next flummoxed me good.

'I have decided to let Mr Van Fleet have Widow's Mite.'

I stopped rocking.

'I've decided that,' she said, like I might not have heard her. She kept looking straight out at the valley and the mountains.

Times like this are strange, I tell you. You expect to leap up and whoop and holler, shouting 'Bout time, 'bout time! But that's never how it turns out with me. I just set there slack jawed and pop-eyed, holding my breath in case it won't last. I could hear my own heart beating, going Widow's Mite, Widow's Mite, Widow's Mite.

I took a few deep breaths and finally said, 'What made you change your mind, Momma?'

She kept fanning away. 'All of you did,' she said. 'Moon and the girls, and Cleeve. And you.'

'They said something to you?'

'Not a word.'

'What you mean they made you change your mind then?'

She finally stopped fanning and looked at me. 'You don't learn everything through your ears, Esther. I just set there looking at everybody today, setting where they always do for Sunday dinner. I was missing Cleeve, and thinking about those who've gone. And I decided I was a foolish old woman to try to hold on to one faded old quilt if what money it could bring in could help people setting around the table. Moon's losing land, you've lost Cleeve, why shouldn't I part with Widow's Mite?'

Way out across the highway on the narrow path that runs between the field of corn and an unused pasture, I could see Moon and Betty walking with the two girls. Melissa was up on Moon's shoulders, cupping her hands under his chin like the straps of a helmet. She towered above everybody, even the tassels of the corn, and moved back and forth in a right stately sway. She made me think of a movie I seen once on the television with an elephant carrying an Indian princess who sat in a high-backed golden throne under a canopy of satin and silk the very color of the sunset.

'To be honest, Momma, the money won't matter all that much.'

Momma rocked forward fast and brought her heels down on the floor with a clump.

'Just listen to you,' she said.

She was right put out with me.

I couldn't sleep that night so I got up and went into the kitchen to make a cup of Sanka and a bread and butter sandwich. Standing at the kitchen window I could see the light on in Billy Walkingstick's cabin and I knew he'd be asleep in his rocking chair with a copy of *National Geographic* spread out over his chest. Billy hardly reads anything else and the ladies in the bookmobile keep him stocked up. It's always struck me as funny to hear an Indian talking about places like Egypt and China and Timbuctoo. But I reckon Billy knows more about strange places in the world than anybody else around. And I know for a fact that he's never been to Delray Beach, Florida, either.

So there I was standing in my and Momma's dark kitchen looking at the light from Billy Walkingstick's cabin and the light from the moon that shone on the backyard and the flower beds and seemed to creep its way up towards me standing at the kitchen window. And up onto the presents from my grand-babies setting there on the window sill.

I picked them both up, in one hand even, they were so small, and brought them up close where I could see them good. They felt cool and I rubbed them against my forehead like folks like to do with a cold drink bottle. They still smelled like children do, sweet and sour at the same time. And they made my heart take a funny leap like I could have knocked down dead anyone who came in and tried to take them away from me.

Momma was right: You do have to get old before you do some thinking about some things.

Momma and I didn't say nothing to each other but we both knew he would show up at his usual time, just after supper but before the sun went down. For a man from Florida he seemed to like to do all his visiting in the dark. But I reckon he needed most of his daytime to look at golf balls and tennis balls and to shop in antique stores.

Something else Momma and I did without saying nothing to each other was dress up. Momma had on her lavender and beige polyester she's worn for the last couple Easters, and Grannie's mourning brooch. I could even see the corner of one of her special Irish linen handkerchiefs sticking out from under her sleeve. I put on my one good summer suit and the beads Mandy and Melissa had given me the Christmas before. It was like we both knew something important was going to happen.

We sat down on the porch to wait, not saying anything about each other's dress-up clothes, not even looking at each other hardly. It kind of made me feel the way you do when you see a man with his zipper down.

About fifteen minutes before sundown we see the lights from the car turn into our driveway, and pick and creep its way up to our house.

'Top of the evening to you.' Mr Van Fleet stood at the bottom of the porch steps, waiting for someone to invite him up. He had on khaki pants and a matching khaki jacket like hunters wear with big pockets and a belt and little flaps on the shoulders. If he'd had on one of those funny helmets he would a looked like somebody straight out of Africa.

'Evening,' me and Momma said. We went on rocking.

'The last night in the mountains is always a sad time. This time tomorrow I'll be in the panhandle of Florida, sweltering in the heat and fighting off the bugs.' He put one foot up on the first step. 'You folks are lucky, do you know that?'

'We know that,' Momma said.

'And I couldn't go without telling my favorite friends up here good-bye.' He moved his foot up to another step. 'That, and to come make one more offer to you for Widow's Mite, Molly. I'm even going to up it.' And he reached into one of those big pockets in his jacket and brought out a long envelope. 'Here's four hundred dollars. In cash – I thought you'd prefer cash. What do you say?'

Momma wasn't looking *at* him, but above him, towards the valley and the river. I was about to say something when she finally said, 'I say all right.'

Well, Mr Van Fleet's face cracked into the biggest smile I'd ever seen on anybody and he let out a funny little sound like Hah, and came bounding up the stairs like he was going to grab Momma and the chair she was setting in.

I stood up real fast.

'My momma has given you the wrong impression,' I said, putting myself between him and Momma. 'We have decided not to sell Widow's Mite. In fact, we have decided not to sell anymore quilts at all.'

He craned around me trying to see Momma and saying 'Molly, will you – Molly, wha – Molly?'

'You are welcome to come and visit us anytime you're in

these parts, but don't be asking for more quilts.'

Mr Van Fleet kept on sputtering away, saying things about having come to a decision, about being reasonable, and such like. And Momma the whole time wasn't saying nothing. Finally I heard her stand up. She put her hand on my shoulder and sort of turned me around. She stood there staring at me in the twilight, her face poked up right next to mine.

'Molly, let's try to keep this between you and me,' Mr Van Fleet said. One thing's for sure, he wasn't too happy by this time. He even tugged at her sleeve a little, like a whiny little boy might do.

But Momma paid him no heed, just kept looking at me until at last she smiled like I hadn't seen her smile in a long time.

Mr Van Fleet saw it too, and backed down the stairs a little bit. He stopped talking too.

'Mr Van Fleet,' Momma said, drawing herself up, 'my daughter is right. I am sorry I misled you. Old women sometimes do foolish things.' She set back down in her chair and stared out above his head again. 'You drive safely tomorrow. You've got a long trip ahead of you.'

He kept going but, but, but, but, sounding like a little motor boat, and flapping his hands around in the air. I felt sorry for him, I did. It seemed like he was more than just a long way from home.

He finally walked on down the stairs and out to his car. He slammed the door so hard it left a little echo in the air. I have to admire him for waiting to get good and angry.

Momma and me went on rocking. The evening star was up in the west, and the katydids were setting up their racket all around us. If Momma'd said anything she'd had to a shouted almost to have herself heard. So she set there not saying a word, because there's times, it seems to me, when it's best to just set. Billy Walkingstick would agree. He hisself says sometimes he sets and thinks, and sometimes he just sets.

And so we just set. A couple of old women looking out at the darkness and listening to the summer sounds, and grateful for a big old house with a good view.

MARION MOLTENO

The Uses of Literacy

It was only after Mr H. S. Ramgarhia died that I realised there was a Mrs Ramgarhia - Mrs G. K. Ramgarhia, to be precise – here with him, in England. Until then he had presented himself alone at the classes; he arrived alone, unconnected to any of the others, a tall, immensely dignified, heavy shouldered old man, his turbaned head carried processionally among the groups of women in saris.

He was there from the first time the Norwood Centre opened. Joyce and I had spent the previous weeks putting up posters in ante-natal clinics, health centres, Asian grocery shops – anywhere that women might be. We visited all the women we knew in the area – those who were being taught at home, those who had asked for help and not yet been allocated a teacher. We explained about the class, that there would be only women there, definitely only women, so please not to be nervous about coming. And on the first morning, in walked Mr H. S. Ramgarhia, unsolicited.

He had seen one of our posters. The poster has a picture of two women on it, but it does not explicitly repeat this message in words. It says, simply, in five Asian languages, 'Do you want to improve your English?' Mr Ramgarhia wanted to improve his English, and here he was.

That first morning, I taught him alone, sitting at a desk in a corner, while Joyce handled all other comers. I planned to give him a solid two hours' teaching, so he would not feel badly done by, and then at the end of the morning I would explain the situation to him gently, and direct him to the mixed class two miles down the road.

But at the end of the morning it was Mr H. S. Ramgarhia who made the speech, not me. He stood up, and put his hands behind his back in a way that made it clear what was going to happen. I stood up too, to receive it: 'I have to thank you for this most illuminating lesson,' he said, his craggy head inclined towards me with great simplicity. 'I have wished all my life to be an educated man, but until now the need to provide for my family has made it impossible. I left school very young. God has blessed my work, and enabled me to provide for my sons the education I could not have. Now my sons can support me, and I have the leisure to learn. All the English I know I have learnt without tuition. I listened to Englishmen speak in the days when the British were still in India. Now I am in the UK, I listen to the radio and television. But reading and writing have remained a difficulty for me. I spend time every day in the library, trying to read the newspapers, but many words escape my understanding. Now I have a teacher, I am sure I can begin to attain my life's ambition. I wish to thank you for providing me with this opportunity.'

'What could I say?' I asked Joyce, afterwards. 'Let me teach him again next week, and then I'll go with him on the bus to the other class, to show him there are good teachers there too.'

The following week, Mr Ramgarhia had done all the homework I had set him, and more. His speech was no formal wordspinning – he meant every word of it, and showed it in the total concentration he gave to each minute of the lesson. My heart sank slightly as the two hours came to an end, but I told myself not to be ridiculous. It was not as if we were throwing him out – the other class was just as good.

Mr Ramgarhia again stood up. He informed me that not only was the teaching excellent, but the class was most conveniently near to his son's house. This was a great advantage, since he suffered with aches in his legs, a thing that had not happened in the Panjab, and which he attributed to the damp climate rather than old age. He was grateful for the foresight which had led us to start a class in this area, because if it had been further away he would not have been able to attend.

The following week, Joyce made the speech, instead of me. To the women in her group. Explaining about Mr Ramgarhia's legs, she asked if they minded if he continued to attend, and perhaps join their group, since I would not be able to come every week, to teach him separately. It is all right, they said. He is old. He is respectable. Let him come. But not others.

He came, every week. For two years he did not miss a lesson. I visited the centre once a month or so, and each time I did he would approach me during tea break, to have one or two words with me about his progress, to ask politely about the other centres. When I say 'approach me' I should explain that he stood quietly behind all the women, not pushing to make any space for himself, waiting until I'd had a chance to greet the women I knew, or talk to Joyce and the other teachers who had since joined her. He stood still, waiting until I had time. He had instinctive tact; the women appeared to feel no restraint in his presence, because he made no move to exercise any male prerogative. For a while it was impossible for me to visit, and when I returned I found that it was Mr Ramgarhia who was now making the tea. He absented himself from the group ten minutes before eleven to put the kettle on, pushing his chair back very quietly so as not to disturb the class, and giving the teacher a slight bow of his turban by way of apology for walking out. Then at eleven he would come slowly up to each group, and announce that tea was ready. He served it, not as some men cook, to display their easy competence in an area normally beneath them – he served it as he studied English, as in fact he lived each moment of his life – with a concentration that transformed the act from a mundane one, to one of devotion.

Each time I visited, I made some excuse to spend ten minutes with him after tea break – a little individual lesson that was more for my benefit than his. He gradually gave me small bits of information about his family, his life in the Panjab. Not much, for his dignified reserve did not really allow the kind of easy warmth that sprang up so quickly with most of the women. And all that time I did not realise his wife was still alive, and here with him in England.

When he missed a lesson, Joyce knew there was something wrong. We phoned his home. It was the first contact we had made with him; before that he had come to us as if from a vacuum. We felt we were invading his privacy, but we were anxious, because of his legs, and because he had never missed a lesson in two years. The voice at the other end told us, abruptly, that he had died. A sudden heart attack.

It was difficult to cope with the idea. He had become a fixture, filling a space quite unlike that of any other person. Of course this is true of any individual, and my contact with him was after all limited to once a month, for a small controlled interaction, in an impersonal community hall. Nevertheless, there seemed to be sudden gaps in the pavement wherever I walked that day; I felt disoriented. I remembered his hands, an old man's hands like my father's in his last years, the skin mottled with old age, the hairs growing longer and more noticeable. He used to lay his hands on his knees as he inclined his head to listen to an explanation, or ask a question. Somehow I found them immensely comforting. There was a concentrated tranquillity about the way they rested on his knees. It is a quality I do not have myself, and therefore gravitate to in others, especially older people. I was thousands of miles away from my father when he died, so the event was difficult to mark emotionally. He was not there any more, but then he had not been there for years, since I had moved away. Now my father's hands had died again, and this time I was here.

Joyce and I went to see the family. She because she had been his teacher, and I because I needed to mark his death for myself. We did not know anyone else in the family, and it was unlikely that our visit would mean much. But we went.

His son and daughter-in-law were surprised, but welcoming. He had enjoyed the classes very much, they said. He had talked with great admiration of his teachers. We told them how much we had valued him. We had a cup of tea, and stood up to leave.

'Would you like to speak to my mother-in-law?' the young woman asked. 'She doesn't speak any English, but I think she'll be pleased to know you came.'

We followed her into a bedroom, where a tiny figure crouched in the foetal position on the bed, enveloped in a vast woollen shawl. The young woman shook her by the shoulder gently, and spoke to her in Panjabi. A head emerged, shrivelled with grieving. Dark eyes stared out at us, moving slowly from Joyce to me. Although she was perched on the high bed, she had to crane her neck to look up to us, so tiny was she. I thought of Mr Ramgarhia's height, and could not connect them. Why had he never mentioned her? Perhaps because the English class belonged to such a separate area of his life; although the others in the class were women, education had remained for Mr Ramgarhia part of the serious business of living, like going out to work. You did not discuss your wife among the other clerks in the office. Not if you respected her – which I had not the slightest doubt that he had.

Her eyes continued to stare, as if from a great distance. Joyce and I stood watching, wordless. It's difficult to know what we could have said even if we'd had a language in common with her, but without one I felt paralysed. I crouched down next to the bed, so that at least she would not have to stare up at us. Slowly, from out of the shawl, a thin, bird-like arm stretched – to touch my hand as it rested on the bed; and hold it. It was she who made the contact beyond words, dissolving the blockage.

We were silent for a minute. Eventually I turned my head to the young woman, and said, 'When her mourning period is over, perhaps she would like to come to the class sometimes. Just for company, if you are both out at work.'

The daughter-in-law translated for her. But her eyes had become vacant again, her hand had fallen away from mine. She had returned to nurse her pain. The daughter-in-law shrugged at me, as if to say, 'I'm sorry – she's too old. It's not relevant for her.'

I knew that; I had only said it because I had nothing else to give.

Two months later, Joyce said to me after a meeting, 'Do you know, she came?'

'Who?' I asked.

'Mrs Ramgarhia. Last week; her daugher-in-law brought her, to show her the way. She came back again on her own this week.'

I stared at her, unbelieving. It is just ten minutes' walk from the Ramgarhias' house to the centre, but it involves turning at least three corners and crossing several roads. I tried to imagine that tiny, shrunken figure in a shawl navigating the journey alone, and failed. As I walked towards the centre the next time, she was in my head; I saw the cars speeding, seemingly uncaring, as frail elderly women tried to cross the road on their fragile stick-like legs. But there, inside the building, there she was. More upright than I could have thought possible from that one image of her on the bed, but still no higher than my chest. She caught sight of me before I could go over and speak to her – someone else held me in conversation just inside the door. And from the corner of my eye I watched her behave just as her husband had always done, waiting quietly at the back, not making a move, until I should be free to spend time with her.

When I reached her, and sat down so as not to tower over her, she instantly stretched out and took my hand, in the gesture she had used before. It became, thereafter, her unfailing greeting.

Now that she was in the class, it became less difficult to talk to her. I could say simple things in English, and even if she didn't understand I knew it was part of my function to say them, so that gradually the phrases would become familiar. Hello, how are you? How's your family? It's cold today, isn't it? . . . To each she replied identically, by opening her face with a smile of pleasure at being spoken to, and saying, 'Mrs G. K. Ramgarhia.' Someone – presumably Mr Ramgarhia – had taught her that this was the correct answer to something; and she clung to that first and only lesson as to a magic charm, that would somehow make other learning follow if adhered to faithfully enough. The other women in the class called themselves 'Kulwinder' or 'Noorjahan'; initials and family names they saved for filling in forms. Once Kulwinder tried to convey this to Mrs G. K. Ramgarhia gently in Panjabi; she actually found out what the initials stood for – Gurmit Kaur – but none of us could bring ourselves to use them. The other women called her 'ma', because of her age. I called her what she called herself – Mrs G. K. Ramgarhia – which seemed to please her, fixing the magic charm more firmly, and giving it greater power.

So that was how we met from then on. I would come into the community hall, with its miserably inefficient overhead gas heaters, where the women huddled in their coats at their group tables. I would hover in the doorway, getting rid of my dripping anorak and boots, while people called out greetings.

Her group used the furthest corner; by the time I had made my way there, her eyes were waiting for me. To the others I said, 'Hello, how are you?' and they answered, 'I'm fine, thank you,' or 'I'm pine,' depending on how much in control they were of English pronunciation that day. And then I reached her and sat down next to her, and her face creased with pleasure. She took my hand, and I said, 'Mrs G. K. Ramgarhia, how are you?', and she held even tighter with her stiff, bony fingers, and said, 'Mrs G. K. Ramgarhia'; and I would feel as if nothing could go wrong with the day.

She was in Mumtaz's group – that is, the group for those who knew almost no English. In one way this was a good arrangement because Mumtaz, too, speaks Panjabi. But at first we were not sure how it would work out; Mumtaz is a Muslim, Mrs G. K. Ramgarhia a Sikh, and old enough to have been scarred by the fear and hatred between the two groups at the time of the Partition of India. Perhaps it would be difficult for her to relax with Mumtaz as her teacher? But it seemed that, on the contrary, she was comforted by Mumtaz's presence. It wasn't primarily a matter of language. Mrs G. K. Ramgarhia's Punjabi seemed very different from the city language Mumtaz used. Mrs G. K. Ramgarhia listened with great politeness, but it was clear that much of what was said was unintelligible to her. Yet the sounds must have made a familiar song for her, even when the words escaped her.

Beyond words, beyond religious divisions, she and Mumtaz understood perfectly how to behave with each other. Without having to think about it Mumtaz gave her the deference due to an elderly person, and she gave Mumtaz the respect due to a teacher, and would wait for Mumtaz to tell her what to do. Sometimes she would find it difficult to concentrate, and her eyes would close for a few minutes as she withdrew into herself. If this went on too long Mumtaz would give her shoulder a gentle shake, and tease her as a grandmother might tease a young child, laughing about her falling asleep and saying it was time to return to work. I cannot imagine myself or Joyce doing this without it seeming an intolerable intrusion; but Mumtaz never overstepped the limits of what was appropriate. Mrs G. K. Ramgarhia would beam when she felt this special attention being bestowed on her, and then would bend her head shyly to return to her work.

There were other elderly women at the centre, but none for whom age had assumed that quality of permanent clothing, as it did with her. The other women in the classes treated her accordingly – as if she was something precious, who might not be with them long. Perhaps this was because her husband had gone suddenly; her presence gave them a chance to pay their respects to him. At tea break the Panjabi speakers from the other groups made a point of going over to talk with her for a few minutes, and her face would move with pleasure. I think it mattered a lot to her that they had all known her husband, and respected him, that somehow she was here on his territory, and yet in a place appropriate for a woman. Even when she stood silent, with conversations swimming past her, she looked happy, as if the very bodies of the other women gave her a sense of being connected, part of society.

But it was when the class spent time practising reading that she enjoyed herself most. For the last twenty minutes of each lesson the women in her group worked their way slowly through very simple reading books. There was no way Mrs G. K. Ramgarhia could join this activity, so Mumtaz would give her letters to copy – round ones this week – a, o, c – stick ones another week – l, k, h – on large ruled lines in a special copy book. She would sit until after the class was over, unable to tear herself away from the work, slowly, very slowly, making more and more letters. If someone bent over her to see how she was getting on, she would lift her head back from the page and make a little graceful dancing movement with her hand, opening out away from the letters, inviting you to share them.

She was pleased to have praise, but it was not that she worked for; she loved the work itself.

It is now two and a half years since she joined the class. She has been there longer than her husband was before her. The last time I visited, I spent fifteen minutes working with her, helping her with her writing. She can copy, now, any simple text you put in front of her. Mostly she copies from the first reading book – an insipid little home-produced booklet in large print about a woman called Razia, who cleans her house, cooks her dinner, washes the dishes, all in the present tense, all within a vocabulary of twenty words. Mrs G. K. Ramgarhia tries to read what she has written: sometimes she gets a word, sometimes not. Mostly not. But she knows the names of the letters, and there is one whole sentence which she can write without copying, and read back: it is 'My name is Mrs G. K. Ramgarhia.' The first time she proudly showed me this sentence I remembered Mr Ramgarhia's speech, about how he had wished all his life to acquire education – and I longed so for her to have, just for a few moments, that power to make fluent speeches in words I would understand, so that she could tell me how exhilarated she felt at what she had achieved.

But she did it, anyway – with her face, and with that lovely sweeping little dance of her hand, as she lifted it off the page.

STEVIE SMITH

Autumn

He told his life story to Mrs Courtly
Who was a widow. 'Let us get married shortly',
He said. 'I am no longer passionate,
But we can have some conversation before it's too late.'

EDNA O'BRIEN

The Creature

She was always referred to as The Creature by the towns-
people, the dressmaker for whom she did buttonholing, the
sacristan, who used to search for her in the pews on the dark
winter evenings before locking up, and even the little girl Sally,
for whom she wrote out the words of a famine song. Life had
treated her rottenly, yet she never complained but always had
a ready smile, so that her face with its round rosy cheeks, was
more like something you could eat or lick; she reminded me
of nothing so much as an apple fritter.

I used to encounter her on her way from devotions or from
Mass, or having a stroll, and when we passed she smiled, but
she never spoke, probably for fear of intruding. I was doing a
temporary teaching job in a little town in the west of Ireland
and soon came to know that she lived in a tiny house facing a
garage that was also the town's undertaker. The first time I
visited her, we sat in the parlour and looked out on the
crooked lettering on the door. There seemed to be no one in
attendance at the station. A man helped himself to petrol. Nor
was there any little muslin curtain to obscure the world,
because, as she kept repeating, she had washed it that very day
and what a shame. She gave me a glass of rhubarb wine, and
we shared the same chair, which was really a wooden seat with
a latticed wooden back, that she had got from a rubbish heap
and had varnished herself. After varnishing, she had dragged
a nail over the wood to give a sort of mottled effect, and you

could see where her hand had shaken, because the lines were wavery.

I had come from another part of the country; in fact, I had come to get over a love affair, and since I must have emanated some sort of sadness she was very much at home with me and called me 'dearest' when we met and when we were taking leave of one another. After correcting the exercises from school, filling in my diary, and going for a walk, I would knock on her door and then sit with her in the little room almost devoid of furniture – devoid even of a plant or a picture – and oftener than not I would be given a glass of rhubarb wine and sometimes a slice of porter cake. She lived alone and had done so for seventeen years. She was a widow and had two children. Her daughter was in Canada; the son lived about four miles away. She had not set eyes on him for the seventeen years – not since his wife had slung her out – and the children that she had seen as babies were big now, and, as she heard, marvellously handsome. She had a pension and once a year made a journey to the southern end of the country where her relatives lived in a cottage looking out over the Atlantic.

Her husband had been killed two years after their marriage, shot in the back of a lorry, in an incident that was later described by the British Forces as regrettable. She had had to conceal the fact of his death and the manner of his death from her own mother, since her mother had lost a son about the same time, also in combat, and on the very day of her husband's funeral, when the chapel bells were ringing and re-ringing, she had to pretend it was for a travelling man, a tinker, who had died suddenly. She got to the funeral at the very last minute on the pretext that she was going to see the priest.

She and her husband had lived with her mother. She reared her children in the old farmhouse, eventually told her mother that she, too, was a widow and as women together they worked and toiled and looked after the stock and milked and churned and kept a sow to whom she gave the name of Bessie. Each year the bonhams would become pets of hers and follow her along the road to Mass or whenever and to them, too, she gave pretty names. A migrant workman helped in the summer months, and in the autumn he would kill the pig for their winter meat. The killing of the pig always made her sad, and she reckoned she could hear those roars – each successive roar – over the years, and she would dwell on that, and then tell how a particular naughty pig stole into the house one time and lapped up the bowls of cream and then lay down on the floor, snoring and belching like a drunken man. The workman slept downstairs on the settle bed, got drunk on Saturdays, and was the cause of an accident; when he was teaching her son to shoot at targets, the boy shot off three of his own fingers. Otherwise, her life had passed without incident.

When her children came home from school, she cleared half the table for them to do their exercises – she was an untidy woman – then every night she made blancmange for them, before sending them to bed. She used to colour it red or brown or green as the case may be, and she marvelled at these colouring essences almost as much as the children themselves did. She knitted two sweaters each year for them – two identical sweaters of bowneen wool – and she was indeed the proud mother when her son was allowed to serve at Mass.

Her finances suffered a dreadful setback when her entire stock contracted foot-and-mouth disease, and to add to her grief she had to see the animals that she so loved die and be buried around the farm, wherever they happened to stagger down. Her lands were disinfected and empty for over a year, and yet she scraped enough to send her son to boarding school and felt lucky in that she got a reduction of the fees because of her reduced circumstances. The parish priest had intervened on her behalf. He admired her and used to joke her on account of the novelettes she so cravenly read. Her children left, her mother died, and she went through a phase of not wanting to see anyone – not even a neighbour – and she reckoned that was her Garden of Gethsemane. She contracted shingles, and one night, dipping into the well for a bucket of water, she looked first at the stars then down at the water and thought how much simpler it would be if she were to drown. Then she remembered being put into the well for sport one time by her brother, and another time having a bucket of water douched over her by a jealous sister, and the memory of the shock of these two experiences and a plea to God made her draw back from the well and hurry up through the nettle garden to the kitchen, where the dog and the fire, at least, awaited her. She went down on her knees and prayed for the strength to press on.

Imagine her joy when, after years of wandering, her son returned from the city, announced that he would become a farmer, and that he was getting engaged to a local girl who worked in the city as a chiropodist. Her gift to them was a patchwork quilt and a special border of cornflowers she planted outside the window, because the bride-to-be was more than proud of her violet-blue eyes and referred to them in one way or another whenever she got the chance. The Creature thought how nice it would be to have a border of complementary flowers outside the window, and how fitting, even though *she* preferred wallflowers, both for their smell and their softness. When the young couple came home from the honeymoon, she was down on her knees weeding the bed of flowers, and, looking up at the young bride in her veiled hat, she thought, an oil painting was no lovelier or no more sumptuous. In secret, she hoped that her daughter-in-law might pare her corns after they had become intimate friends.

Soon, she took to going out to the cowshed to let the young couple be alone, because even by going upstairs she could overhear. It was a small house, and the bedrooms were directly above the kitchen. They quarrelled constantly. The first time she heard angry words she prayed that it be just a lovers' quarrel, but such spiteful things were said that she shuddered and remembered her own dead partner and how they had never exchanged a cross word between them. That night she dreamed she was looking for him, and though others knew of his whereabouts they would not guide her. It was not long before she realised that her daughter-in-law was cursed with a sour and grudging nature. A woman who automatically bickered over everything – the price of eggs, the best potato plants to put down, even the fields that should be pasture and those that should be reserved for tillage. The women got on well enough during the day, but rows were inevitable at night when the son came in and, as always, The Creature went out to the cowshed or down the road while things transpired. Up in her bedroom, she put little swabs of cotton wool in her ears to hide whatever sounds might be forthcoming. The birth of their first child did everything to exacerbate the young woman's nerves, and after three days the milk went dry in her breasts. The son called his mother out to the shed, lit a cigarette for himself, and told her that unless she signed the farm and the house over to him he would have no peace from his young barging wife.

This The Creature did soon after, and within three months she was packing her few belongings and walking away from the house where she had lived for fifty-eight of her sixty years. All she took was her clothing, her aladdin lamp, and a tapestry denoting ships on a hemp-coloured sea. It was an heirloom. She found lodgings in the town and was the subject of much curiosity, then ridicule, because of having given her farm over to her son and daughter-in-law. Her son defected on the weekly payments he was supposed to make, but though she took the matter to her solicitor, on the appointed day she did not appear in court and as it happened spent the entire night in the chapel, hiding in the confessional.

Hearing the tale over the months, and how The Creature had settled down and made a soup most days, was saving for an electric blanket, and much preferred winter to summer, I decided to make the acquaintance of her son, unbeknownst to his wife. One evening I followed him to the field where he was driving a tractor. I found a sullen, middle-aged man, who did not condescend to look at me but proceeded to roll his own cigarette. I recognised him chiefly by the three missing fingers and wondered pointlessly what they had done with them on that dreadful day. He was in the long field where she used to go twice daily with buckets of separated milk, to feed the suckling calves. The house was to be seen behind some trees, and either because of secrecy or nervousness he got off the tractor, crossed over and stood beneath a tree, his back balanced against the knobbled trunk. It was a little hawthorn and, somewhat superstitious, I hesitated to stand under it. Its flowers gave a certain dreaminess to that otherwise forlorn place. There is something gruesome about ploughed earth, maybe because it suggests the grave.

He seemed to know me and he looked, I thought distastefully, at my patent boots and my tweed cape. He said there was nothing he could do, that the past was the past, and that his mother had made her own life in the town. You would think she had prospered or remarried, his tone was so caustic when he spoke of 'her own life'. Perhaps he had relied on her to die. I said how dearly she still held him in her thoughts, and he said that she always had a soft heart and if there was one thing in life he hated it was the sodden handkerchief.

With much hedging, he agreed to visit her, and we arranged an afternoon at the end of that week. He called after me to keep it to myself, and I realised that he did not want his wife to know. All I knew about his wife was that she had grown withdrawn, that she had had improvements made on the place – larger windows and a bathroom installed – and that they were never seen together, not even on Christmas morning at chapel.

By the time I called on The Creature that eventful day, it

was long after school, and, as usual, she had left the key in the front door for me. I found her dozing in the armchair, very near the stove, her book still in one hand and the fingers of the other hand fidgeting as if she were engaged in some work. Her beautiful embroidered shawl was in a heap on the floor, and the first thing she did when she wakened was to retrieve it and dust it down. I could see that she had come out in some sort of heat rash, and her face resembled nothing so much as a frog's, with her little raisin eyes submerged between pink swollen lids.

At first she was speechless; she just kept shaking her head. But eventually she said that life was a crucible, life was a crucible. I tried consoling her, not knowing what exactly I had to console her about. She pointed to the back door and said things were kiboshed from the very moment he stepped over that threshold. It seems he came up the back garden and found her putting the finishing touches to her hair. Taken by surprise, she reverted to her long-lost state of excitement and could say nothing that made sense. 'I thought it was a thief,' she said to me, still staring at the back door, with her cane hanging from a nail there.

When she realised who he was, without giving him time to catch breath, she plied both food and the drink on him, and I could see that he had eaten nothing, because the ox tongue in its mould of jelly was still on the table, untouched. A little whiskey bottle lay on its side, empty. She told me how he'd aged and that when she put her hand up to his grey hairs he backed away from her as if she'd given him an electric shock. He who hated the soft heart and the sodden handkerchief must have hated that touch. She asked for photos of his family, but he had brought none. All he told her was that his daughter was learning to be a mannequin, and she put her foot in it further by saying there was no need to gild the lily. He had newspapers in the soles of his shoes to keep out the damp, and she took off those damp shoes and tried polishing them.

I could see how it all had been, with her jumping up and down trying to please him but in fact just making him edgy. 'They were drying on the range,' she said, 'when he picked them up and put them on.' He was gone before she could put a shine on them, and the worst thing was that he had made no promise concerning the future. When she asked 'Will I see you?,' he had said 'Perhaps,' and she told me that if there was one word in the English vocabulary that scalded her, it was the word 'perhaps'.

'I did the wrong thing,' I said, and, though she didn't nod, I knew that she also was thinking it – that secretly she would consider me from then on a meddler. All at once I remembered the little hawthorn tree, the bare ploughed field, his heart as black and unawakened as the man I had come away to forget, and there was released in me, too, a gigantic and useless sorrow. Whereas for twenty years she had lived on that last high tightrope of hope, it had been taken away from her, leaving her without anyone, without anything, and I wished that I had never punished myself by applying to be a sub in that stagnant, godforsaken little place.

ELIZABETH CAIRNS

Echoes

Each week the ritual was the same.

Tap of baton against stand. The swell of music stops, ragged voices trail away like ends of a frayed rope.

'Tenors, tenors! *Please!*'

Out of tune again. It's that G in the first chorus. *Exaudi orati-O-nem meam*, *listen to my words* – even if I can't quite reach the notes.

Why, when there are only five tenors, are they louder than the twelve altos and fourteen sopranos, not to mention the eight basses? Their voices stick out like gargoyles. Because, Melinda knows, the altos and sops are kind to their weaklings, they hide their mistakes. Jane Reeves sings sharp and Shirley Brown never comes in on the beat but that competent front row carries them through. And the choirmaster daren't take on two dozen middle aged women who know the work inside out.

You hear them humming it after rehearsals, drunk on the nectar of Mozart as they climb into their hatchbacks and unpadlock their bikes.

Et lux perpetua, eternal light . . . The middle part can have a kind of monotony but as you croon the notes to yourself you hear the rest of the voices, the silent harmonies, colouring the sound. First the sopranos' E flat, then their radiant G, *lu-ce-at, may it shine*. The sopranos soar, throats trembling as the music climbs. Old Mrs Bendix for instance; seventy five with the voice of a vibrato archangel. She goes downstairs backwards ('it's my balance, dear'). Melinda cups one fat elbow during their slow descent to the coffee break, words from another work, *O magnum mysterium*, forming in her mind. Big mysterious Mrs B, full of scorn at the tenors' hopelessness.

'I can still reach G; A flat on good days. Nonsense,' as Melinda suggests that high notes get difficult with age, 'these young men just don't bother to practise.'

She claws the bannisters like a cat climbing down a tree. A look of contempt darts out from under the thatch of permafrost curls.

'I'll tell you what age is: it's hitting the high notes because you've taken the time to practise them.' She stops in mid-descent and fixes Melinda with a marbly stare, 'I call it singing in tune with time, and that means getting your pace right, like going steady on the stairs. If you do that everything's easier, not just the music.' As the unrepentant tenors clatter past she gives a dismissive nod. 'They think they don't have to bother yet.'

In this choir the parts go in descending order of age. Sopranos pushing eighty, altos sixty, basses in their fifties (reversed order here), tenors forty-ish. Average age, near enough sixty.

That's me, Melinda thinks, bang in the middle; of choir, if not of life.

After the break the choirmaster, Luke, gives them a talking-to. The baton is laid down, hands raked through a coxcomb of taut hair. His face gleams like a polished shield.

'Imagine you are Mozart, listening; listening to your work, the work you have died in the middle of, sung *flat*.' He is five years younger than the youngest of them. This is not an easy task. He picks up the baton, lips chewing or are they moving in a silent prayer: God Mozart, descend to us we pray. 'Come on, have another try.'

The tenors shuffle and straighten up.

'Bottom of page 3; *exaudi –*'

The pronunciation no longer stumps them. But few of them really understand the words, or only the most obvious ones. *Dies irae, day of wrath*, that they all know, and ones like *lacrymosa* which are near the English. As for the rest, they don't worry. The music wrapping itself around these strange incantations is enough.

Before the fugue Luke baton-stops them again.

'If any of you know any men,' he ignores the titters, 'who know the work and could come along, tenors or basses . . .' He means tenors but hasn't the bottle to say it. The basses grin covertly. The sopranos and altos sit smugly waiting to go on.

Melinda looks along the rows. So many grey heads, so many pairs of specs. The uniform of the old. No wonder people see us as a race apart. My hair's not grey yet, only inside my head . . . She presses her copy of the music open, bracing herself for the fugue, but Luke for whatever reason decides to skip it.

'Page thirteen, top line. *Quantus tremor,*' *so much trembling* . . .

Which is what the tenors must be feeling as they come up to another G.

Luke's merciless tonight.

'Mozart. The Requiem.'

'I say, how fantastic! Lucky you.'

An arm circles her like an elephant's trunk and takes two sandwiches. 'Mm, these are nice. It's the emotion, you know – funerals give one a terrific appetite.' Then voice and trunk remove themselves.

What emotion, Melinda wonders. How much emotion can you feel for someone you haven't seen for forty years? So why has she driven two hours to get here if she doesn't care?

I didn't say not care, she corrects herself. The question is – how much? ('*If it be love indeed, tell me how much* . . .' The words float across her thoughts; from a long ago lawn where lights hung in trees and blossom breathed out of creepered walls. Who had she been with?)

They were a gang, a student gang; glued together by chance for three years, split in eight different directions for the next thirty-six. And life had happened in between. But you go to mark the ending of it – the ending of it for one of you, one of the once-inseparable gang – because with three down and five to go the scythe is getting nearer and each time you meet to mourn its sweep you think, next time it may be me.

Melinda knows that when you have a scythe in your hands (she uses one at home) the blade hisses on almost of its own volition. Slash, slash. *Sorry – I didn't mean to get you* . . . but the decapitated flower lies with the nettles and docks. Error.

'You're looking very serious.'

A new voice, just behind her. New – ?

'I'm thinking of scythes.' She isn't; she's thinking, as she turns, I know this voice.

'The Old Man, or meadows?'

'Both.'

It's a stranger, with a beard and grey hair. Inside them there's a face she knows. Take off that beard, darken the hair -

'David!'

She gulps. David, of all people. Of course he would be there, so why hasn't she expected it? And of course *he* would understand about the scythe. She says, plunging back into a conversation forty years old because excitement and a kind of nervousness suddenly make her mind jump grooves, 'Remember the Beethoven?'

He steps closer, as someone holding a cup of tea shoves past. 'We talked about scythes (and death) after the Bach, my dear, not the Beethoven. The day it snowed and I got you the daffodils.'

He's right of course. He always was; punctilious about detail in a way which had bothered her even in those scatty student days.

She looks at him, taking in the changed person, letting the memories spread over her; hers or his, it doesn't matter which when the details don't match. They never did, and that was the whole point, wasn't it?

He's got crows-feet that hold shadows of smiles in this older face he's grown. Crow's-feet around eyes you want to make light up.

She says, you haven't changed; and hears him say the same, feels his pleasure at their meeting like reflected warmth, their own little private electric fire.

He's shaking his head as if he can't quite believe she's there. There's something theatrical in the gesture: the older man's delighted disbelief. She's seen it on This is Your Life, then remembers how he always liked amateur dramatics. And –wonders, what is she doing which he's thinking 'ah!' about.

When did you hear about Clive, he asks. (This is, after all, a funeral. She notes his change of tone, the funeral timbre; as you get older you get good at it.) 'Did you see him at the end?'

No, not in touch with Clive, not in touch with any of the gang; just an occasional reader of obituaries – in case.

She'd let them all drop, let it drop: her past, her youth. The raw years when she'd piled up mistakes like a hampster storing grain. Get away from it as fast as possible, the future can't be worse. And it wasn't. At some point in the future she had moved into herself.

The crush around the sandwiches is dense. It pushes them to its edge.

'You don't even want a cheese straw?' he asks.

'Not even a cheese straw!' She senses him registering her quick watch-glance. 'I've got to go soon.'

'It's pelting outside.'

For a minute they both look out through the window at roofs running with shiny slate.

(Rain on summer leaves, like the patter of bare feet; an attic room where two people – can it be them? – lie like effigies, frozen in locked desire.)

She says, 'I'm parked round the corner.'

'Then you can drive me to my car.'

His umbrella is a huge segmented dome large enough for them not to have to link arms as they dodge the puddles.

The windscreen wipers brush tears across her mind. She asks herself, alone now and on the homeward route, would life have been different, what had gone wrong, had they just been too young?

Too young at nineteen! It was absurd. But inside adult bodies they'd had the instincts of terrified two-year-olds. Inside all that passion, fear. So the passion had flowed into letters, packets of them which she still kept in a dark cupboard like last year's bulbs, waiting to be planted again.

Age had made him better looking, taken away the soft look. All that grizzled grey firms a face, it concentrates the essence, pulls off the protective film.

How strange life is, she thinks (and wonders how many other people are leaving the funeral saying that, meaning, how strange death is. But she means life.) It's an accident who you end up with. Ripeness is all. No it isn't: wrong quote. The readiness is all. They hadn't been ready, simply that.

Her car is warm and music filled. Outside the motorway swishes past. Lorries spray like whales, lights reflect in dazzling spears. Inside, the *Benedictus* climbs and twines around its B flat scale. One minute it's a flower, an exotic brilliant plant, the next a cataract of coloured light. *Benedictus qui venit, blessed is he who comes* . . . They had not made love, she knows now, because they were not ready for it; and this realisation gives her an enormous sense of relief, as if things she had shut doors on forty years ago were still waiting, still alive. Like seeds taken from Tutenkhamen's tomb or Roman fortresses. Life, stored, waiting for the moment to be right to grow again.

When she reaches her road she parks the car and waits for the phrase to finish then sets the tape to rewind.

The tap on the window makes her jump. But before she has time to think it may be the police or a mugger or any of the people one doesn't want to tap on one's car window at midnight she knows it can only be David, although he's headed off in a totally different direction to drive to the other side of the country.

David it is. And as she unwinds her window he tells her he's left his umbrella in her car. Hasn't she noticed it, hasn't she seen him flashing for fifty miles of motorway?

No no . . . And though there's wonder in a corner of her mind at the fifty-mile detour to retrieve a brolly, her instant gladness smothers it.

'You drive very fast.' The reproach behind his words is affectionate but she thinks, yes, at our age people ought to drive more carefully. Something – the music? – has made her not watch her mirror or her speed.

'You're lucky I'm not a policeman!'

She smiles. 'I am. Lucky.'

She hears the click of the tape and has a sudden idea. 'David, do you still sing? Do you know the Mozart Requiem? Then come and help our tenors. On Saturday week, in St Martin's, just down the road. Rehearsal at two, concert at eight. I'll ring you about it.'

His address is sitting in her bag. He's given it to her, saying, we won't look so good after another forty years so let's keep in touch. Before letting herself into the house, under the light in the porch where he's left her, umbrella clamped under one arm with a quick brush of cheek against cheek (the ceremony has left a lot of those like layers of feathers, blown off as quickly as laid on), she checks that it's still there; which she knows it is.

She is met by her daughter.

'Mum you're back. How was it – was the funeral terrible? Joey's made you a cake to help you feel better!'

The proffered three-year-old's idea of victoria sponge looks like a drunken sand castle. Its warm vanilla smell releases a gush of appetite in her. She cuts herself a hunk.

Through the mouthful she answers, 'The funeral was . . . all right.'

Perhaps the dead are living still, looking over our shoulders, turning our heads at the right moment. Perhaps Mozart stalks the aisles whenever his Requiem is performed?

The final rehearsal took off. Luke shone like a beacon which helped laggards like Shirley Brown watch his beat, the tenors listened to each other for the first time and the soloists (loaned from a local madrigal group) sang like seraphs.

David arrived late. Melinda had smoothed the way with a surprisingly grudging Luke ('Yes, but does he know the work?' No, of course not, she wanted to say, but compassion at the speckled moistness of his face stopped her; he looks like an overwrought gingerbread man, she thought, overwrought and underbaked. He needs a thicker crust).

It was not till after the first chorus that the door of the church opened and David came in. Melinda saw his smile, apologetic for being late, as he took his place next to Mr Smythe (the tenor who most audibly could not reach G); she saw the crinkle of his eyes as he half turned his head to look for her. And she thought of Bach; of Bach and snow and daffodils and an evening which had ended, like the music, in tears of grief. They had sung in the same choir, been joined body and soul by music but then transported away from music's protective shell, the link that night had snapped.

('I want you, my darling . . . and I want to marry you.')

Marriage was what people talked about when they dared not take risks. Her answer, like the girl in the folksong, had been no.

Nil inultum remanebit. The alto, throaty as a blackbird, sang: *Nothing will remain unpunished.* Even a hasty decision of forty years ago, would she still be left with nothing but memories of a shredded relationship?

David turned his head. He was looking for her again. Now he had seen her. As she caught his eye the future – her future, their future – jumped into her throat like a beating pulse. It pounded in her ears. She could hardly hear for the hammering.

Quid sum miser tunc dicturus, what shall I, miserable one, say? The sound arched up to the church roof and the stained-glass filtered light. What am I going to say, she thought: how will we get from here . . . to there? But perhaps there won't be any *there*, perhaps we did shut the door on it forty years ago.

The tightness in her throat was tears now; church and music a blur. *Salva me fons pietatis, save me, fount of pity.* She tried to sing, three of the most beautiful bars in the whole work, but nothing came out. She stood silent, listening.

After the next chorus someone behind her said: 'Hark at those tenors! They got their Gs. Must be the new man. I wonder who he is.'

I wonder who he is. After forty years, was she the same person? So why should he be?

'We're going to sing ourselves out,' the voice went on. Melinda didn't bother to turn. Janet Stokes, who liked to talk and would use even a few bars' rest to have a chat. 'It's lucky we've got this gap. Last year Luke only gave us an hour.'

And this year we have four.

The gap between rehearsal and performance had worried her. I won't be back, she'd said at home, some deep reflex stirring in her, like the puff of a near-extinct volcano, telling her that she should free herself. And she had added, because her motives seemed so transparently base, 'Come to the concert – if you can get a sitter.' Just another concert, she'd implied, not going to be one of our best.

Families grow up with empathy their second language.

'Mum doesn't want us to go to the concert.'

'Probably because it's going to be a flop. Okay, evening at home then.'

They met on the stairs and created a small traffic jam while they decided what to do.

Lunch in a pub – and then a walk?

It was like being twenty again. Twenty, with sixty years of life to buttress you.

'Oh I say, Mellie, you are in a hurry. Is this your scarf?'

Yes, Janet, thanks –'

'I wouldn't leave it here, you know. Even in a church things get nicked. Why, last year –'

He was waiting outside the pub. She thought, I'm loading too much onto this.

He said, 'I was afraid you wouldn't turn up.'

She stood there while he laid his arms loosely around her as if shielding her from the people going in and out of the narrow swinging door. Breaths of pub gushed out each time it swung.

In there? He made a face. She knew what his next words would be because she had imagined them, she had hoped for them, she had willed them to be said from the moment she saw him come into the church till now. And, in a sense, she had known they were going to be said when he had told her on the phone that he was going to stay in Johnny's flat – remember old Johnny? as it's just across the river and he's away. Known, but not been sure.

'We'll go to Johnny's place. I've got some food . . . Why are you laughing?'

'A little thought from the requiem. *Mihi quoque spem dedisti,* *you too have given me hope.* 'I'll explain later.'

'You think you're going to have *spam* for lunch?' He tucked her arm into his. 'Not on your life!'

Johnny was a shell enthusiast. His flat was full of them. Bowls of whelks (she picked one up and heard, far away, the sea), razor shells in the bathroom, scallops fanning along kitchen shelves, a paper nautilus hanging from the ceiling on an invisible thread.

'He's a shell freak, this man.' She touched the nautilus and it spun round like a fragile flower. 'Aren't you afraid of breaking something?'

David stood in the kitchen door, dangling the drying up cloth. 'Only my luck.'

She had worried about how to get from here to there. As she looked at him standing there, twelve feet of carpet and two chairs away with the paper nautilus floating in between, she realised they were already there. She could see in his eyes that he was telling her what he'd said that night when marriage had been thrown in as a kind of safety net. *I want you, my darling.* Or was it her own voice she could hear? As always with David she had lost track of which were her feelings, which were his.

As her shoulder brushed it the nautilus did a little dance.

Melinda crossed back over forty years into his arms, into the completion of unfinished things which had been waiting to be resolved.

He said, I want to have a shower with you, and took her to the bathroom where the predictably shell-decorated glass box had room for them both; room to wash and to explore.

Bodies don't change, she thought, then remembered she hadn't known his. But our skins are smooth, our lusts still there. Does getting old diminish them? Not yet. It sharpens them, we're practised, we're honest, we go for what we want. There's no film between us now. It's like shedding old skins; underneath we're shiny and supple and ravenous.

The water made green and yellow smears across her eyes. With it streaming onto her head and down her face she could not see, only feel – the wet sleak of hair as she held his head and his lips moved across her breasts.

They dried themselves and wrapped themselves in more and drier towels and went over to the bed. He had grey hair on his chest and she became suddenly aware of all the years she hadn't known him, of all the things that had happened in those years. He seemed a stranger. Eyes so close to her, seeking hands. They were on separate islands, tremblingly linked.

But when their bodies joined the forty years ago was now. They were the same people, lovers; completing their love this time. They had left their age, like coats, hanging on the door. Bodies were the feelings that surged and spiralled in your core, not their outer case.

Benedictus qui venit, she thought; the refrain of their coming together after forty years.

'All those wasted years!' His fingers, charting the line of her body like a compass, lay curled across her hip.

She thought, it didn't happen then because it couldn't. And if it had, we wouldn't have it now.

'Not wasted,' she answered. 'Waiting.'

On her way out she picked up a whelk. Johnny could spare one. She cradled it in her palm, feeling its rough spiral bulge and pointed tip.

'Look,' she said, showing David.

He shook his head in mock disapproval. Then lifted up the shell to cup her hand against his lips.

Eight o'clock came and Luke was like one transfigured. The shine had gone (did he use powder?), the coxcomb tamed. He was a bow-tied magician ready to conjure music out of their souls.

Melinda knows the only thing she can or wants to do at that moment is sing. *Hostias et preces tibi domine, prayers and praise we offer you.* She leans into the music offering her gift of song. At moments of supreme happiness, those once, twice, thrice-in-a-lifetime moments you need someone to thank. Like the day Joey was born when she felt she was part of a tide of life that filled the universe. Like now, fused to earth and heaven on a pulse of music and desire.

The applause is prolonged and genuine. Everybody else's family and friends cluster round, the church is a hubbub of congratulations. Then benches start being shifted, chairs stacked and reminders about locking doors shouted across the aisles.

Melinda and David meet. He's got his bag and his car keys are in his hand. She knows he's going back to Johnny's and tomorrow morning will be off at six a.m. And she, back into her life. What with music and food and loving, she realises, they've hardly talked about their lives.

Mrs Bendix is waiting for her lift. 'So good of you, dear, are you sure you can manage it?' NO, Melinda wants to scream, NO. 'Of course I can.' She grasps fingers that are like a bunch of dried broad beans.

David's hand has touched hers, just touched. One quick squeeze before Janet and Shirley and all the rest bear down to lionise the older handsome tenor who has turned up like Shane to save the day. Before he is engulfed he smiles at her as he has done once before that day, with a half turned angle of his head and a deprecating, sorry, it can't be helped look.

The man who three hours ago was lying in her arms.

When she sits on her bed in her silent room, Melinda wonders who she is. She wonders how much life she has left and what it will do to her.

Her seven o'clock alarm call pads along the corridor on fat little feet, dapper in its nappies and purposefulness.

'Granny! granny!'

Melinda opens her bed; the magic cavern. Swiggle inside, stubby toes thrust against her thighs.

'Granny, what's that?'

For a minute, as a baby starfish hand reaches for the whelk, the bedside table turns into an aquarium.

'What is it, Granny?'

'It's a shell. Listen to it and you'll hear the sea.'

The solemn listening eyes of a three year old. The whelk telephone sticks up like a horn.

'It's not the sea.' He frowns. Does he know what the sea sounds like, she wonders? 'I can hear people talking.'

'What are they saying?'

'I'm not sure. I think, I *think* they're saying, "See you soon."'

He puts it down and looks at it questioningly, rolling it gently in his hand.

'Can I keep it, Granny?'

PAULE MARSHALL

To Da-duh, in Memoriam

'. . . Oh Nana! all of you is not involved in this evil business Death,
Nor all of us in life.'
– From 'At My Grandmother's Grave,' by Lebert Bethune

I did not see her at first I remember. For not only was it dark inside the crowded disembarkation shed in spite of the daylight flooding in from outside, but standing there waiting for her with my mother and sister I was still somewhat blinded from the sheen of tropical sunlight on the water of the bay which we had just crossed in the landing boat, leaving behind us the ship that had brought us from New York lying in the offing. Besides, being only nine years of age at the time and knowing nothing of islands I was busy attending to the alien sights and sounds of Barbados, the unfamiliar smells.

I did not see her, but I was alerted to her approach by my mother's hand which suddenly tightened around mine, and looking up I traced her gaze through the gloom in the shed until I finally made out the small, purposeful, painfully erect figure of the old woman headed our way.

Her face was drowned in the shadow of an ugly rolled-brim brown felt hat, but the details of her slight body and of the struggle taking place within it were clear enough – an intense, unrelenting struggle between her back which was beginning to bend ever so slightly under the weight of her eighty-odd years and the rest of her which sought to deny those years and hold that back straight, keep it in line. Moving swiftly toward us (so swiftly it seemed she did not intend stopping when she reached us but would sweep past us out the doorway which opened onto the sea and like Christ walk upon the water!), she was caught between the sunlight at her end of the building and the darkness inside – and for a moment she appeared to contain them both: the light in the long severe old-fashioned white dress she wore which brought the sense of a past that was still alive into our bustling present and in the snatch of white at her eye; the darkness in her black high-top shoes and in her face which was visible now that she was closer.

It was as stark and fleshless as a death mask, that face. The maggots might have already done their work, leaving only the framework of bone beneath the ruined skin and deep wells at the temple and jaw. But her eyes were alive, unnervingly so for one so old, with a sharp light that flicked out of the dim clouded depths like a lizard's tongue to snap up all in her view. Those eyes betrayed a child's curiosity about the world, and I wondered vaguely seeing them, and seeing the way the bodice of her ancient dress had collapsed in on her flat chest (what had happened to her breasts?), whether she might not be some kind of child at the same time that she was a woman, with fourteen children, my mother included, to prove it. Perhaps she was both, both child and woman, darkness and light, past and present, life and death – all the opposites contained and reconciled in her.

'My Da-duh,' my mother said formally and stepped forward. The name sounded like thunder fading softly in the distance.

'Child,' Da-duh said, and her tone, her quick scrutiny of my mother, the brief embrace in which they appeared to shy from each other rather than touch, wiped out the fifteen years my mother had been away and restored the old relationship. My mother, who was such a formidable figure in my eyes, had suddenly with a word been reduced to my status.

'Yes, God is good,' Da-duh said with a nod that was like a tic. 'He has spared me to see my child again.'

We were led forward then, apologetically because not only did Da-duh prefer boys but she also liked her grandchildren to be 'white,' that is, fair-skinned; and we had, I was to discover, a number of cousins, the outside children of white estate managers and the like, who qualified. We, though, were as black as she.

My sister being the oldest was presented first. 'This one takes after the father,' my mother said and waited to be reproved.

Frowning, Da-duh tilted my sister's face toward the light. But her frown soon gave way to a grudging smile, for my sister with her large mild eyes and little broad winged nose, with our father's high-cheeked Barbadian cast to her face, was pretty.

'She's goin' be lucky,' Da-duh said and patted her once on the cheek. 'Any girl child that takes after the father does be lucky.'

She turned then to me. But oddly enough she did not touch me. Instead leaning close, she peered hard at me, and then quickly drew back. I thought I saw her hand start up as though to shield her eyes. It was almost as if she saw not only me, a thin truculent child who it was said took after no one but myself, but something in me which for some reason she found disturbing, even threatening. We looked silently at each other for a long time there in the noisy shed, our gaze locked. She was the first to look away.

'But Adry,' she said to my mother and her laugh was cracked, thin, apprehensive. 'Where did you get this one here with this fierce look?'

'We don't know where she came out of, my Da-duh,' my mother said, laughing also. Even I smiled to myself. After all I had won the encounter. Da-duh had recognized my small strength – and this was all I ever asked of the adults in my life then.

'Come, soul,' Da-duh said and took my hand. 'You must be one of those New York terrors you hear so much about.'

She led us, me at her side and my sister and mother behind, out of the shed into the sunlight that was like a bright driving summer rain and over to a group of people clustered beside a decrepit lorry. They were our relatives, most of them from St Andrews although Da-duh herself lived in St Thomas, the women wearing bright print dresses, the colors vivid against their darkness, the men rusty black suits that encased them like straitjackets. Da-duh, holding fast to my hand, became my anchor as they circled round us like a nervous sea, exclaiming, touching us with their calloused hands, embracing us shyly. They laughed in awed bursts: 'But look Adry got big-big children!'/ 'And see the nice things they wearing, wrist watch and all!'/ 'I tell you, Adry has done all right for sheself in New York. . . .'

Da-duh, ashamed at their wonder, embarrassed for them, admonished them the while. 'But oh Christ,' she said, 'why you all got to get on like you never saw people from 'Away' before? You would think New York is the only place in the world to hear wunna. That's why I don't like to go anyplace with you St Andrews people, you know. You all ain't been colonized.'

We were in the back of the lorry finally, packed in among the barrels of ham, flour, cornmeal and rice and the trunks of clothes that my mother had brought as gifts. We made our way slowly through Bridgetown's clogged streets, part of a funereal procession of cars and open-sided buses, bicycles and donkey carts. The dim little limestone shops and offices along the way marched with us, at the same mournful pace, toward the same grave ceremony – as did the people, the women balancing huge baskets on top their heads as if they were no more than hats they wore to shade them from the sun. Looking over the edge of the lorry I watched as their feet slurred the dust. I listened, and their voices, raw and loud and dissonant in the heat, seemed to be grappling with each other high overhead.

Da-duh sat on a trunk in our midst, a monarch amid her court. She still held my hand, but it was different now. I had suddenly become her anchor, for I felt her fear of the lorry with its asthmatic motor (a fear and distrust, I later learned, she held of all machines) beating like a pulse in her rough palm.

As soon as we left Bridgetown behind though, she relaxed, and while the others around us talked she gazed at the canes standing tall on either side of the winding marl road. 'C'dear,' she said softly to herself after a time. 'The canes this side are pretty enough.'

They were too much for me. I thought of them as giant weeds that had overrun the island, leaving scarcely any room for the small tottering houses of sunbleached pine we passed or the people, dark streaks as our lorry hurtled by. I suddenly feared that we were journeying, unaware that we were, toward some dangerous place where the canes, grown as high and thick as a forest, would close in on us and run us through with their stiletto blades. I longed then for the familiar: for the street in Brooklyn where I lived, for my father who had refused to accompany us ('Blowing out good money on foolishness,' he had said of the trip), for a game of tag with my friends under the chestnut tree outside our ageing brownstone house.

'Yes, but wait till you see St Thomas canes,' Da-duh was saying to me. 'They's canes father, bo,' she gave a proud arrogant nod. 'Tomorrow, God willing, I goin' take you out in the ground and show them to you.'

True to her word Da-duh took me with her the following day out into the ground. It was a fairly large plot adjoining her weathered board and shingle house and consisting of a small orchard, a good-sized canepiece and behind the canes, where the land sloped abruptly down, a gully. She had purchased it with Panama money sent her by her eldest son, my uncle

Joseph, who had died working on the canal. We entered the ground along a trail no wider than her body and as devious and complex as her reasons for showing me her land. Da-duh strode briskly ahead, her slight form filled out this morning by the layers of sacking petticoats she wore under her working dress to protect her against the damp. A fresh white cloth, elaborately arranged around her head, added to her height, and lent her a vain, almost roguish air.

Her pace slowed once we reached the orchard, and glancing back at me occasionally over her shoulder, she pointed out the various trees.

'This here is a breadfruit,' she said. 'That one yonder is a papaw. Here's a guava. This is a mango. I know you don't have anything like these in New York. Here's a sugar apple.' (The fruit looked more like artichokes than apples to me.) 'This one bears limes. . . .' She went on for some time, intoning the names of the trees as though they were those of her gods. Finally, turning to me, she said, 'I know you don't have anything this nice where you come from.' Then, as I hesitated: 'I said I know you don't have anything this nice where you come from. . . .'

'No,' I said and my world did seem suddenly lacking.

Da-duh nodded and passed on. The orchard ended and we were on the narrow cart road that led through the canepiece, the canes clashing like swords above my cowering head. Again she turned and her thin muscular arms spread wide, her dim gaze embracing the small field of canes, she said – and her voice almost broke under the weight of her pride, 'Tell me, have you got anything like these in that place where you were born?'

'No.'

'I din' think so. I bet you don't even know that these canes here and the sugar you eat is one and the same thing. That they does throw the canes into some damn machine at the factory and squeeze out all the little life in them to make sugar for you all so in New York to eat. I bet you don't know that.'

'I've got two cavities and I'm not allowed to eat a lot of sugar.'

But Da-duh didn't hear me. She had turned with an inexplicably angry motion and was making her way rapidly out of the canes and down the slope at the edge of the field which led to the gully below. Following her apprehensively down the incline amid a stand of banana plants whose leaves flapped like elephants' ears in the wind, I found myself in the middle of a small tropical wood – a place dense and damp and gloomy and tremulous with the fitful play of light and shadow as the leaves high above moved against the sun that was almost hidden from view. It was a violent place, the tangled foliage fighting each other for a chance at the sunlight, the branches of the trees locked in what seemed an immemorial struggle, one both necessary and inevitable. But despite the violence, it was pleasant, almost peaceful in the gully, and beneath the thick undergrowth the earth smelled like spring.

This time Da-duh didn't even bother to ask her usual question, but simply turned and waited for me to speak.

'No,' I said, my head bowed. 'We don't have anything like this in New York.'

'Ah,' she cried, her triumph complete. 'I din' think so. Why, I've heard that's a place where you can walk till you near drop and never see a tree.'

'We've got a chestnut tree in front of our house,' I said.

'Does it bear?' She waited. 'I ask you, does it bear?'

'Not anymore,' I muttered. 'It used to, but not anymore.'

She gave the nod that was like a nervous twitch. 'You see,' she said. 'Nothing can bear there.' Then, secure behind her scorn, she added, 'But tell me, what's this snow like that you hear so much about?'

Looking up, I studied her closely, sensing my chance, and then I told her, describing at length and with as much drama as I could summon not only what snow in the city was like,

but what it would be like here, in her perennial summer
kingdom.

'. . . And you see all these trees you got here,' I said. 'Well,
they'd be bare. No leaves, no fruit, nothing. They'd be
covered in snow. You see your canes. They'd be buried under
tons of snow. The snow would be higher than your head,
higher than your house, and you wouldn't be able to come
down into this here gully because it would be snowed
under . . .'

She searched my face for the lie, still scornful but intrigued.
'What a thing, huh?' she said finally, whispering it softly to
herself.

'And when it snows you couldn't dress like you are now,' I
said. 'Oh no, you'd freeze to death. You'd have to wear a hat
and gloves and galoshes and ear muffs so your ears wouldn't
freeze and drop off, and a heavy coat. I've got a Shirley
Temple coat with fur on the collar. I can dance. You wanna
see?'

Before she could answer I began, with a dance called the
Truck which was popular back then in the 1930s. My right
forefinger waving, I trucked around the nearby trees and
around Da-duh's awed and rigid form. After the Truck I did
the Suzy Q, my lean hips swishing, my sneakers sidling zigzag
over the ground. 'I can sing,' I said and did so, starting with
'I'm Gonna Sit Right Down and Write Myself a Letter,' then
without pausing, 'Tea For Two,' and ending with 'I Found a
Million Dollar Baby in a Five and Ten Cent Store.'

For long moments afterwards Da-duh stared at me as if I
were a creature from Mars, an emissary from some world she
did not know but which intrigued her and whose power she
both felt and feared. Yet something about my performance
must have pleased her, because bending down she slowly
lifted her long skirt and then, one by one, the layers of petti-
coats until she came to a drawstring purse dangling at the end
of a long strip of cloth tied round her waist. Opening the purse

she handed me a penny. 'Here,' she said half-smiling against her will. 'Take this to buy yourself a sweet at the shop up the road. There's nothing to be done with you, soul.'

From then on, whenever I wasn't taken to visit relatives, I accompanied Da-duh out into the ground, and alone with her amid the canes or down in the gully I told her about New York. It always began with some slighting remark on her part: 'I know they don't have anything this nice where you come from,' or 'Tell me, I hear those foolish people in New York does do such and such. . . .' But as I answered, recreating my towering world of steel and concrete and machines for her, building the city out of words, I would feel her give way. I came to know the signs of her surrender: the total stillness that would come over her little hard dry form, the probing gaze that like a surgeon's knife sought to cut through my skull to get at the images there, to see if I were lying; above all, her fear, a fear nameless and profound, the same one I had felt beating in the palm of her hand that day in the lorry.

Over the weeks I told her about refrigerators, radios, gas stoves, elevators, trolley cars, wringer washing machines, movies, airplanes, the cyclone at Coney Island, subways, toasters, electric lights: 'At night, see, all you have to do is flip this little switch on the wall and all the lights in the house go on. Just like that. Like magic. It's like turning on the sun at night.'

'But tell me,' she said to me once with a faint mocking smile, 'do the white people have all these things too or it's only the people looking like us?'

I laughed. 'What d'ya mean,' I said. 'The white people have even better.' Then: 'I beat up a white girl in my class last term.'

'Beating up white people!' Her tone was incredulous.

'How you mean!' I said, using an expression of hers. 'She called me a name.'

For some reason Da-duh could not quite get over this and

repeated in the same hushed, shocked voice, 'Beating up white people now! Oh, the lord, the world's changing up so I can scarce recognize it anymore.'

One morning toward the end of our stay, Da-duh led me into a part of the gully that we had never visited before, an area darker and more thickly overgrown than the rest, almost impenetrable. There in a small clearing amid the dense bush, she stopped before an incredibly tall royal palm which rose cleanly out of the ground, and drawing the eye up with it, soared high above the trees around it into the sky. It appeared to be touching the blue dome of sky, to be flaunting its dark crown of fronds right in the blinding white face of the late morning sun.

Da-duh watched me a long time before she spoke, and then she said, very quietly, 'All right, now, tell me if you've got anything this tall in that place you're from.'

I almost wished, seeing her face, that I could have said no.

'Yes,' I said. 'We've got buildings hundreds of times this tall in New York. There's one called the Empire State building that's the tallest in the world. My class visited it last year and I went all the way to the top. It's got over a hundred floors. I can't describe how tall it is. Wait a minute. What's the name of that hill I went to visit the other day, where they have the police station?

'You mean Bissex?'

'Yes, Bissex. Well, the Empire State Building is way taller than that.'

'You're lying now!' she shouted, trembling with rage. Her hand lifted to strike me.

'No, I'm not,' I said. 'It really is, if you don't believe me I'll send you a picture postcard of it soon as I get back home so you can see for yourself. But it's way taller than Bissex.'

All the fight went out of her at that. The hand poised to strike me fell limp to her side, and as she stared at me, seeing not me but the building that was taller than the highest hill she knew, the small stubborn light in her eyes (it was the same amber as the flame in the kerosene lamp she lit at dusk) began to fail. Finally, with a vague gesture that even in the midst of her defeat still tried to dismiss me and my world, she turned and started back through the gully, walking slowly, her steps groping and uncertain, as if she were suddenly no longer sure of the way, while I followed triumphant yet strangely saddened behind.

The next morning I found her dressed for our morning walk but stretched out on the Berbice chair in the tiny drawing room where she sometimes napped during the afternoon heat, her face turned to the window beside her. She appeared thinner and suddenly indescribably old.

'My Da-duh,' I said.

'Yes, nuh,' she said. Her voice was listless and the face she slowly turned my way was, now that I think back on it, like a Benin mask, the features drawn and almost distorted by an ancient abstract sorrow.

'Don't you feel well?' I asked.

'Girl, I don't know.'

'My Da-duh, I goin' boil you some bush tea,' my aunt, Da-duh's youngest child, who lived with her, called from the shed roof kitchen.

'Who tell you I need bush tea?' she cried, her voice assuming for a moment its old authority. 'You can't even rest nowadays without some malicious person looking for you to be dead. Come girl,' she motioned me to a place beside her on the old-fashioned lounge chair, 'give us a tune.'

I sang for her until breakfast at eleven, all my brash irreverent Tin Pan Alley songs, and then just before noon we went out into the ground. But it was a short, dispirited walk. Da-duh didn't even notice that the mangoes were beginning to ripen and would have to be picked before the village boys got to them. And when she paused occasionally and looked out across the canes or up at her trees it wasn't as if she were seeing them but something else. Some huge, monolithic shape had imposed itself, it seemed, between her and the land, obstructing her vision. Returning to the house she slept the entire afternoon on the Berbice chair.

She remained like this until we left, languishing away the mornings on the chair at the window gazing out at the land as if it were already doomed; then, at noon, taking the brief stroll with me through the ground during which she seldom spoke, and afterwards returning home to sleep till almost dusk sometimes.

On the day of our departure she put on the austere, ankle length white dress, the black shoes and brown felt hat (her town clothes she called them), but she did not go with us to town. She saw us off on the road outside her house and in the midst of my mother's tearful protracted farewell, she leaned down and whispered in my ear, 'Girl, you're not to forget now to send me the picture of that building, you hear.'

By the time I mailed her the large colored picture postcard of the Empire State building she was dead. She died during the famous '37 strike which began shortly after we left. On the day of her death England sent planes flying low over the island in a show of force – so low, according to my aunt's letter, that the downdraft from them shook the ripened mangoes from the trees in Da-duh's orchard. Frightened, everyone in the village fled into the canes. Except Da-duh. She remained in the house at the window so my aunt said, watching as the planes came swooping and screaming like monstrous birds down over the village, over her house, rattling her trees and flattening the young canes in her field. It must have seemed to her lying there that they did not intend pulling out of their dive, but like the hard-back beetles which hurled themselves with suicidal force against the walls of the house at night, those menacing silver shapes would hurl themselves in an ecstasy of self-immolation onto the land, destroying it utterly.

When the planes finally left and the villagers returned they found her dead on the Berbice chair at the window.

She died and I lived, but always, to this day even, within the shadow of her death. For a brief period after I was grown I went to live alone, like one doing penance, in a loft above a noisy factory in downtown New York and there painted seas of sugar-cane and huge swirling Van Gogh suns and palm trees striding like brightly-plumed Tutsi warriors across a tropical landscape, while the thunderous tread of the machines downstairs jarred the floor beneath my easel, mocking my efforts.

ADRIENNE RICH

Aunt Jennifer's Tigers

Aunt Jennifer's tigers prance across a screen,
Bright topaz denizens of a world of green.
They do not fear the men beneath the tree;
They pace in sleek chivalric certainty.

Aunt Jennifer's fingers fluttering through her wool
Find even the ivory needle hard to pull.
The massive weight of Uncle's wedding band
Sits heavily upon Aunt Jennifer's hand.

When Aunt is dead, her terrified hands will lie
Still ringed with ordeals she was mastered by.
The tigers in the panel that she made
Will go on prancing, proud and unafraid.

PENELOPE GILLIATT

Foreigners

'Oh god, I wish the shops were open,' said the great atheist economist, near tears, to his terror. It was an ice-cold June Sunday. He had eaten roast mutton and apple charlotte. Three people in his Wiltshire drawing room slept, and so did his dogs. He looked at the fire hard enough to dry out his eye-balls, or perhaps to singe them.

'Sundays are impossible. I can't stand Sundays,' his voice said, again frightening him. The voice was shouting. His hands were shaking. Sunday lunch, sleep; radio, muffins, sleep; gin-and-lime, the cold roast, radio, sleep. His English life, his English wife. On the opposite side of their English fire-place, Sara was answering letters on her engraved English note cards: 'Mrs Thomas Flitch, the Dower House.' And so on and so on. His Indian mother was in a wheelchair by the bay window, reading. The sight of her brought back some Sunday in India. Himself a child on a bicycle. Dusk, nearly dark. Groups of young men sitting on the ground near a closed library, reading and talking by the light of flares in petrol cans.

His stepson, Simon, a tall stockbroker, guffawed for no obvious reason and kicked the chin of a sleeping dog off a pile of Thomas's books, although he didn't go on to pick up any of the spilled books.

'It'll be Monday all too soon,' Sara said, with the brotherly grimness that Thomas had learned to read in her as a style of intimacy. Now she was doing household accounts and checking the milk bill. She looked fatigued and drawn. He loved her, and wished to save her the frightful inroads of Anglo-Saxon activity, and hated her hat. She was still wearing the ugly straw that she had put on for morning church. She had cooked the lunch in it. Thomas liked her hair and loathed all her hats. In fifty-odd years of high regard for Englishwomen and awe of the fortitude and grace he saw in them, he had never accepted their defiling hats.

Simon's daughter, Pippa, a beauty of six who had one blue and one green eye, swarmed watchfully into the room on her stomach with Thomas's encouragement and bounced up with a war whoop behind the chairs of two sleeping visitors. So she was as oppressed by Sunday as he was. He admired her for dealing with it so capably. There was an interlude of chaos. A pot of coffee was spilled, and Sara had to get a damp cloth for the trousers of one of the visitors, who was involved in an unwise pretence that he hadn't actually been asleep. Thomas seemed to be seeing things through the wrong end of a telescope. People appeared to be very small, and their voices were too loud for their size. Pippa was much scolded.

'I've brought something for Great-Granny,' she said several times, while the storm went on around her pigtailed head and finally spent itself. She heard her father and Sara out, and meanwhile held the present in her closed hand.

After five minutes, Simon attended to what she was saying and assumed a look of astuteness. 'Have you got something in your hand?' he asked. Pause. 'Something for Great-Granny?' he carried on shrewdly. 'Let's have a look at it, in case it's one of the things Great-Granny doesn't eat.' He tried to force open her fingers. 'Let Daddy tell you. You're old enough to know by now that in the country where Great-Granny comes from they don't eat some of the things we eat. It's not that they're fussy, it's because they think it's wrong. You know that now, don't you, Pippa?'

'You told me before,' said Pippa.

'Ah, yes, you see; it's chocolate. So we're all right. I thought so. Why didn't you show it to me in the first place? Run and give it to Great-Granny,' he said, sometime after Pippa was already there. 'Granny, Pippa's brought you a special chocolate,' he went on, some time after the old lady had thanked the child.

Thomas's mother was named Arathra Chib. Although his father had acknowledged the son in due time – when the boy grew up to be phenominally educable – he had never married Miss Chib. She had stayed in a Delhi shack made of biscuit tins and a tarpaulin. Mr Flitch, not a bad man, had worked most of his life in India in the tea business. When his bastard turned out to be studious, the boy was accepted into the English bachelor's house for a short time before he was shipped off to prep school and public school in his father's country. He spent the holidays in England with any parents who would have him. If nothing worked out, he lived in the empty school. Some master, equally lonely, would be set to giving him extra essays and physical training to keep him occupied. Thomas bore England no grudge for the youth it dealt him; on the contrary. After getting a double first at Oxford he married Sara, scarcely able to believe his luck. She was a pretty young widow with a small son, and Thomas went to law to give the little boy his own surname.

'Well done, Pippa. Chocolates are perfectly safe,' Simon said laboriously in the direction of the wheelchair.

Thomas was already in the grip of a disorder not at all native to him, and now he suddenly confounded everything he believed he felt for Simon by remembering with hatred one of his adopted son's practical jokes. Some like Sunday long ago, the child Simon had crept up to his Indian step-grandmother when she was asleep in the same wheelchair and thrown a blanket over her, shouting that she was a canary in a cage. Thomas had kept the memory at arm's length until now, when it occurred to him that Simon's sensibility had not much changed. The insight cracked Thomas's heart slightly before he got rid of it again.

His mother's vegetarianism had been carefully respected at lunch, with the usual faint suggestion that it was aberrant and therefore embarrassing, although Sara did try to conceal her opinion. Before the apple charlotte, Miss Chib was given a bowl of pea soup with a spoonful of whipped cream on it. Thomas had noticed the cream, which represented effort. It also represented license, an unusual small expense on a treat beyond the necessities of Sara's food budget. Though Thomas was greatly revered he had never been well off, and now that he had retired from government advisory jobs he earned nothing much except by writing. Simon, who was well on his way to becoming a millionaire through his dealings on the stock exchange, had leaned over his pleasant young wife to peer at his step-grandmother's plate. 'I say,' he said jovially, 'I see my mama's been lashing out a bit.'

Thomas's house, which he could barely keep up, was run mostly on the income from a small chain of modern toy shops that he had built up for his wife over the years. He had given her the capital for the first one on their twentieth wedding anniversary, when he had already bought a Georgian pendant that he dearly wished her to have, but before he chanced giving it to her he had asked her what she would like, and she told him. She had ideas about how a toy shop should be run in these times. Strong plastics, instructive building toys, things that would save women trouble. After a long while of keeping the pendant hidden and unlooked at in his sock drawer, Thomas had to bring himself to hunt for someone to buy it back, for he couldn't afford both presents. He got nothing like the price of it. But Sara's idea had obviously been the better one, he told himself, though without believing a word of it, for where would they all be now without 'Mama's business venture,' as his stepson warmly pointed out to him on a walk round the garden this afternoon.

'Why don't you let me take over the accounts?' Simon said.

'What accounts?' Thomas asked, sheltering in slowwittedness. He seemed to be fending something off. Nothing he was doing was like himself, and Simon looked at him oddly before poking a black pig in the belly.

'You should keep more pigs and run the place as a farm,' Simon said. 'And all this could be plowed up, too.' He gestured across the lawn that ran down to a stream and then up again to his own cottage, which Thomas had given him as a wedding present. 'The expenses of this place are ridiculous. Mama's a Trojan, but she's looking pretty whacked.'

'She needs more help. I must see about more help.'

'As I say, I could do the papers of the business. You wear yourself out with them.'

'They seem to be taking longer at the moment. You wouldn't have time.'

'Oh, I could do them on the train to the City some morning every week.'

That fast? He probably could.

Simon looked around at the bigger house with an alert eye. 'This place is potentially a gold mine. It's madness to run it as a private house. If you turned it into a business, you could keep six maids and gardeners if you wanted and write them off against the pigs. Or whatever else you went in for. Mama's been talking of sugar beet.'

Sugar beet? Sugar beet hadn't come up. Thomas steadied his eyes on the Tudor stable yard and his library window. 'I won't have it,' he said, shaking.

'Buck up, Father. Nobody thinks it's your fault You're one of the world's thinkers. Been doing much writing?'

Thomas lied, against his temperament. 'Quite a bit.' Pause. 'Preliminaries.' Oh, come off it. But the ground seemed to be moving away. He felt as if Simon were lifting him by the collar and dangling him so that his feet were off the earth and his toes straining to reach something. Simon's big head and loose mouth loomed above him against the ridiculous English summer sky, which was the color of iron.

'Your last book was very impressive,' Simon said. 'Prunella and I both thought so. Reflected glow, you know.' He blew his nose on a red spotted handkerchief that he wore in yeoman moods. 'A bit above my level, I'm afraid, some of it.'

'Oh dear. Was it hard to follow?' Thomas asked, taking him to mean what he said. 'Which passages?' But Simon had never got beyond page 27, and after that he had merely left the book out in case his mother and stepfather came unexpectedly for drinks. So now he was at a disadvantage, which angered him, and he lost sight of the gratitude he usually summoned up for the stepfather who had spent much of his life obliging his adopted son's ambition for parents with a big house and a dashing car. At many moments of weakness, or love, Thomas had spent far more money than he could afford or even wished for the sake of Simon's joy in the holidays. The days when he could do it, or would, were now over. Their town house had been sold, lingeringly, with rearguard modernizing actions to keep up its price. The eventual loss kept Thomas awake at night. For the present, in the daytime, he was abruptly fed up with the lot: himself, his insufficiency, the toll that his financial state seemed to be taking of his wife, and the colossally polite head of his stepson, hanging over him now as if it had a miniature keg of brandy around its neck.

'Men are not made better by calamity,' he said. At the same time, he was engaged in disliking his own state of intellect at the moment, which appeared to own no responsibility for the production of that sentence and buzzed around small problems without much resource or repose.

'What's that from? Is it an Indian saying?'

'What? No. Where was she thinking of putting the sugar beet?'

'Hey, I say, chin up. No calamity in this house, eh? Mama's full of beans.'

'She's very tired.'

'Take her to the sun. Take her to Greece. A friend of mine's got a yacht. You could charter it.'

'It would be rather ludicrous.' When we can't afford someone to clean the house, Thomas added silently.

'I could put it against the farm and it wouldn't cost anything. A conference yacht.' Simon laughed loudly. 'Mama could be entertaining foreign buyers. I do think you should let me go into the pigs.'

Thomas told Simon to leave. He said he had work to do. Simon walked down to the stream and across the bridge to his own cottage, waving with his usual cordiality, which was unfailing because it depended on no cordial impulse. Thomas came back past the drawing room. He could see his mother, playing with Pippa, and his wife talking to a woman friend by the window. Thomas looked at them all, and then at Simon, who was now a small figure and in another sense no longer monstrous, because he was walking exactly as he had done when he was a very young child and most moving to Thomas, with his hands in his pockets and his back arched. The familiarity of everyone eased the strangeness in Thomas's head. I wish I had them all here, he thought. I wish we were together. I wish we were having a picnic and that it was hot, and I do indeed wish that we were all together; though even if I were to hold the whole world against my chest, it would probably save us from very little. The longing was unaccustomed. He came to the drawing-room window, which was open. His mind had at last found its way back to its usual cast when he heard Sara's friend talking to her.

'. . . start bestirring himself, for heaven's sake. Leaving you to do everything. What's a brilliant mind –'

'He is brilliant, that's so,' Sara said over her. 'But he's never made the career he could have done. He won't use his elbows.'

But I am not that man, Thomas thought, shivering in a heap on the flower bed where he had dropped onto all fours so as not to be seen. I am not that man, he thought again, straightening up now, for in the next instant it seemed entirely necessary that he should not hide, should visibly walk to the front door and into his library. I will not be that man. He sat behind his desk for a long time, skipping Sunday's cold-mutton supper, rousing himself to say goodbye to the visitors, trying to deal with the paperwork of Sara's business. Wholesale and retail prices, markups, running expenses, employment insurance. Nausea. Sara, beautiful Sara, appeared in the accounts as the manageress. Deductible, to be candid. *No. Once not.* She had left samples of toys and plastic playthings among his books and manuscripts. Garbage. Her piercing household face swam across his eyeline, even more changed from its former self than now, and hermetic in its enthusiasm for nursery objects properly researched by child psychiatrists to be fit for the middle class children who would lose them without a pang. There was a pale-pink celluloid rattle on his desk. It was decorated with an overdressed pale-blue rabbit in non-toxic paint. Long ago, he had found Simon a Hindu rattle made of chased silver with an ivory handle shaped for a child to hold. *What shall we leave behind us*, he thought. He stared at a Rajput scene on the wall among his books. 'Won't use his elbows.' I know as little of love as I do of painting, he thought. The days of smoking a pipe suddenly came back to him, and he realized that he was biting down on his own teeth. His mind seemed to be acting like mercury. He saw it slipping around in a pool and then dividing into drops that ran apart. He leaned back often for a rest and once he got up to type an envelope on an old typewriter in the window. The typewriter had been made in Delhi many years ago, copied from an English Underwood and reproduced in every detail except for the vital spring to drive the keys back. In the machine's hey-day, the deficiency had not been regarded as crippling. Labor was cheap, time ran slow, and a girl sat beside the man typist to return each key by hand as he pressed it. Thomas had grown up in the neighborhood of the machine and one day he had bought it, bringing it to England by boat and vaguely intending to explore the possibility of supplying a spring, though he also liked it well as it still was.

He delayed going upstairs for as long as possible, partly in a hopeless pretence of getting the papers finished with, and partly to avoid Sara. But she was lying awake. He guessed her to be worrying about money. Temper defeated pity and he attacked her rabidly for, of all things, going to her Anglican church. It appeared to him suddenly that there was a link between her flouted ambition for him and the ethic of a religion more alien to his own thought than he had ever dreamed. He sounded to himself like some tendentious student with balloon words coming out of his mouth.

'Jesus was the first Catholic and therefore the first Mr Success of the profit motive,' he said, putting on his dressing gown and feeling foolish. 'Christianity and capitalism are inseparable. Why do you go? Why do you spoil Sundays?'

Sara said, 'You're not well. You're losing your grip.' She watched him quite carefully. She got up.

'I daresay. We can't stay in this house. We simply can't keep it up.'

She was quiet.

So he snarled. 'Does it mean that much to you?'

'What do you think?' Now the rage poured out: All these years, our things, deserve, owe, our time of life, all we've been through.

Help, he thought. I can't go on. I can't manage any of it.

Earn, she threw at him.

Relearn, he thought, adding the first three letters to her word in his head as if they were playing a game. 'Church!' he shouted.

'You never shout,' she said, staring at him.

'You spoil Sundays!'

'Socrates was the first man who thought about thinking,' she said, sitting on the window seat and surprising him in every way.

'Uh?' he said over her.

'Jesus may have been the first man who understood the power of some actions. The power of forgiving an enemy, for instance.'

'You mean me, don't you?' He held his head.

On Monday, when Sara had left the house early to see to things in two of the toy shops on the other side of the county, he could find nothing at home that he felt up to doing. He drove to a café in the nearby market town and simply listened to pacify himself. It was a tea shop, with one half that sold honey and homemade scones and the other with tables where the walls were decorated with a mixture of horse brasses and psychedelic posters. One of the middle-aged women who kept the shop had ordered a set of posters about the Paris rising of May 1968, because she had gone to the Sorbonne to study when she was a girl. The tea shop was next door to one of Sara's branches. Remorse had drawn Thomas there and it kept him pinned, though he was also wild for flight. An arthritic woman came into the café, alone, with a paper bag carrying the name of Sara's shop.

'You feel safer at home than what you do further away,' she said after a long silence, addressing no one. 'Further away you might be a nuisance.'

Unplaced impatience felt like burrs on Thomas's skin. He leaned over to her and said, 'No, you should get out and about more,' which affronted her. He had broken the fourth wall.

In the late afternoon, slow to go home, he dropped in on an elderly doctor friend and played tennis. His hands shook and his friend prescribed a sedative.

'Work a strain at the minute?' said the doctor, watching.

'That sort of thing.'

'Take two a day,' said the doctor. 'Sleeping all right?' The whole circumstance startled him. He expected limitless serenity of a man half Indian, and indeed Thomas had sustained the expectation for twenty years or more.

'Mostly,' Thomas said.

'Let me know. Keep in touch.'

'I can't concentrate. I don't understand myself. Sara's being a brick.'

'Your English is more English than mine,' the doctor said, not really to make conversation but to find more time to see. Thomas's mind seemed to be elsewhere, and there was no perfunctory laugh in return.

The doctor was concerned enough about him to trail him on a journey that Thomas then made to London Airport. He merely sat at the coffee counter there, hour after hour, alone. The talk of strangers alleviated something. At one point, he inquired at the Air-India desk and made a booking. Then he went back to the coffee counter, where two girls were talking about pop singers.

'I wouldn't mind marrying Paul,' said the blonde girl of the pair. She had a beautifully high forehead and an upper lip that twitched softly, like a cow's in a fly-ridden summer.

'Paul?' said her freckled friend. 'Ringo any day.'

'I think Paul's sweet.'

'Ringo's more of a husband. More masterful.'

'Well, if you're talking about *masterful*,' the blonde said vaguely.

'Don't you want to be mastered?'

'Not much.'

'I don't think a marriage with Ringo would work if he wasn't the master.'

'There's always divorce.'

They paused and then the freckled girl said, 'What about the cooking? I can't see me cooking.'

'I wouldn't mind doing Paul a steak,' said the blonde. 'Or

spaghetti. As long as it wasn't fish with the eyes left in, or a chicken. Not a whole chicken. Nothing with innards.'

'Would you look after him if he was ill? That's what I'd have to do for Ringo, you know. I wouldn't mind. I should think he'd be very demanding. Anyone in the public eye.'

'Paul's kept his sincerity. He's not spoilt.'

Thomas quietly bought them another cup of coffee each, and they giggled when they realized it and clinked the thick coffee mugs with him before carrying on with their conversation as if he weren't there.

'What sort of ill, anyway?' said the blonde.

'Sick, say,' said freckles.

Thomas saw Sara in his mind's eye. She was never ill, but now she looked beaten and angered by something he must be doing to her. For richer, for poorer.

'What sort of sick? English sick or American sick?' said the blonde.

'What's the difference, then?'

'Cor, don't you know that?' American sick is just ill. When they mean English sick, they say throw-up sick or sick to your stomach.'

'English sick.'

'Come to think of it, I'd look after him anyway. So long as he didn't carry on about it. You wouldn't catch Paul carrying on.'

They ran for their plane, thanking Thomas for the coffee. He missed them and paced around and made another booking at the Air-India counter, stalling grandly about actually buying the ticket without even noticing that the people on duty were the ones who had humored him before. After a time, his doctor friend had seen enough of his extremity and took him for a drink in the airport bar.

'Funny, meeting you,' Thomas said, refusing any ordinary guess that it could be no accident.

'Off somewhere?' said the doctor.

Thomas suddenly started to shake so badly that the ice in his glass chattered. He fished the cubes out and put them into an ashtray and found it all he could do not to weep at the mess they made with the ash.

'You need help,' his friend said.

'What for?' Thomas said. 'The pills will do the trick. It's mostly that I can't sleep.'

'There are things that pills don't do so well as a rest and treatment. You need a rest.'

A county hospital treated Thomas that week for acute depression. He was greatly humiliated. He was also in fear. To the family, who were breezy, referring to 'Daddy's trouble,' he revealed nothing. Sara drove him scornfully to the hospital three times a week, for he wasn't supposed to drive. This on top of everything else, she seemed to be thinking, although she did what she might to eliminate exhaustion and scorn from her voice. On the car journey, which took an hour and a half each way, he would talk to her with all the will he could muster about the toy shops. It was barely manageable. He found it impossible to believe that he had ever been able to write a book, or give a lecture, or advise a government. Other scholars heard that he was unwell and sent him notes made remote by their instinct that his straits must mortify him. Sara felt many things, including affection, balked control, trouble over his loss of weight, and enmity toward one of the weak. Sometimes she tried talking to him about India, with a genuine impulse to do what she could. She did not feel shame, or any sense of partaking in the very view of life that was nearly extinguishing him.

At the end of the hospital treatment they went away to the Caribbean on holiday, by an airplane that belonged to a director of Simon's firm. An old friend of Thomas's lived on the island, but he was a Negro politician with a mind in the world that Thomas had lost for the moment. Sara had letters to people who owned polo ponies and valuable land for development. So Thomas played bridge with them, and swam, and learned to use an aqualung. He began to feel like a king, more or less. Or fit, at the least. One day he slipped off alone, out of interest, to look up a local doctor, who took him on a tour of hospitals. Maternity wards with two women to a bed. Children with rickets. He didn't tell Sara much of it.

When they got back to England Simon had a surprise waiting. He had exchanged houses with them. Sara and Thomas were to be in the cottage, and Simon's household of three in Thomas's place. The point was the running expenses. Most of the move had been accomplished already. Sara knew of it. 'We didn't tell you, because you were too ill,' she said. 'We decided to wait, so that there was a secret for you when you came back. When you were your old self.'

'It's a fine idea,' Thomas said to her, expounding it to himself and meantime walking around Simon's cottage with resentment for every stone of the place. 'They're an expanding family. There's less work for you to do here. It's very good of him. Where will I work?'

'I thought you'd be relieved. The financial burden. Young shoulders. Besides, he can write a lot of it off against tax, you know. So it's better in every way.'

(*Where will I work?*)

'It's very good of him,' he said, going across to the window to look at their house and then turning away in pain. He went on to bump his head on a beam. His state of mind was so much lighter than before that he laughed. 'If *I* hit my head, at five foot nine, no wonder Simon wanted to switch,' he said.

'It has nothing to do with his height,' Sara said stiffly.

The only things left to be moved were Thomas's books. The Sunday after they came back from the West Indies, he and Sara and his mother – who was living with them now in a room not much larger than a cupboard, although the view, as Simon constantly said, was staggering – went formally to lunch in their old house. Sara started off in her hat, left on from church.

'For heaven's sake, take your hat off,' Thomas said.

'Do you need one of your pills, dear?'

'No, I just hate your hat. We're going to our own house, aren't we? We're not going out.'

'We are going out. You've got to adjust. The doctor said that about the income.' This was the way she spoke of it: 'The income.' She meant his earnings, not the yield of the toy-shop business, but she had never been in the habit of referring to them so distinctly, let alone to the fact that they were thin on the ground at the moment. 'We *are* going out. We're lunching with Simon and Prunella in their new home.'

He threw a bottleful of his pills into the kitchen sink and tried to get them to go down the drain with the handle of a dishmop. 'I hate the word "home,"' he said. 'It's like "doggy." The place is a house.'

'It is my language,' Sara said. She saw then that saying this had been unpardonable, but the odd thing was that he did pardon her, and laughed, and quietly fished some of the soggy pills out of the sink in case he fancied one later after all.

Simon was sitting in Thomas's armchair, which was too big to be moved to the cottage. Prunella had nicely been trying to prise him out of it before they came, but she was timid of him. 'Better not to make an issue of it by my shifting,' Simon said. 'No need to treat him like an invalid.'

At lunch, where there were maids to serve, Sara kept watching Thomas's plate. 'Eat up,' she said when he left something.

'No, thanks.'

'The stomach shrinks. He's doing very well. He's put on six pounds,' she told the table. She looked splendid herself, said the table. She did. But it seemed to Thomas that she was too doughty for him, somehow, and the hat finished it. For years and years, her frailer beauty had made him feel physically famished for her, but he had generally subdued the longing because she seemed worn out with housework. And now she was as strong as a cart horse, and he didn't give a damn. He suddenly felt farcically drawn to Simon's Prunella, which seemed a sign of health if nothing else.

'What's the joke?' Prunella said gently.

'There's a Russian story about a peasant who dreams night after night of having a bowl of cherry jam and no spoon to eat it with. And then at last he goes to bed with a spoon, and he doesn't dream.'

Simon poured some port into the Stilton and talked of a hot tip about buying shares in a firm called North-East Gas Enterprises Limited. Thomas got up at last from his new place in the middle of the table, which he had quite liked because it had leg access to a rung where he could wriggle his feet when he was bored. He went to his old library, and Pippa followed him, equally enlivened to leave.

'Would you like to see my filthy sculptures?' she said.

'Very much,' he said.

'They're in your library.' They were made in Plasticine, and obviously based on photographs of Hindu sculpture in the art books on his bottom shelves. The six-year-old instinct had made them curiously abstract, and Thomas was much moved. The two were poring over them when Simon came into the room. He absorbed the little gray figures in a few seconds and his face bulged. He left the library and came back with a riding crop. Thomas found it hard to believe. He tried to block things but they went fast. The little girl was held by the back of her bent neck, and the lash of the crop swished down onto her cotton dress. When Thomas tried to grab the child away, the lash caught him in the eye.

'Stop!' he shouted, reaching again for the child and closing his red-hot eye.

'You speak of stopping,' said Simon. 'You led her on. Five, six, seven.' It went on to nine before Thomas put an end to it. Simon by then had heavily said, 'This hurts me more than it hurts you' to Pippa, and when the chaos was over Thomas began to laugh, for he had seen that the lash of the crop literally had curled round onto Simon's back between each stroke, probably quite stingingly, though the man had been too excited to notice it. Picking up the child, who was breathing in gulps like an oarsman at the end of a race, Thomas bent down to save her sculptures and carried her through to her mother. 'I want these kept always,' he said, thrusting the figures at her face.

'What are they?'

'They're sculptures of Pippa's. They're to be kept in my library. My books are to stay, too. I have a lot of work to do and there isn't enough room in the other place.'

Sara said, 'What was all that noise?' She looked more closely at the figures and turned away from him.

'What is it?' he said, watching her and flooded by a feeling that he had not expected. 'You're not weeping?'

'You don't seem to be any better than before.' She bent a little to lean her fists on the window seat, with her back to him. 'You're not trying. You give in to these willful tempers. You're not yourself. I've got more than enough to do. You were never like this.'

'Well I am now. Simon beat Pippa for these.'

'No wonder.'

'He'd better have beaten me.' Sara swung round, and Thomas was half touched by the horror in her. 'She must have liked a book of mine,' he said.

'They're in that wretched old-fashioned Plasticine,' she went on, switching ground and speaking as if that compounded things. 'Who could have given it to her? Prunella and I are so careful. She has plenty of the proper sort.'

'This kind smells nice,' he said.

'One of the *points* about the new kind is that it's odorless.'

'"Smell"!' he shouted. 'Not "odor." You even take away smells. Actually, I think I probably gave her the clay.'

'But we don't stock it.'

'No, I got it from an art shop.' In Sara's canon this was perfidy. She looked betrayed, and tight around the chin. 'You'll have to put up with it, darling,' he said gaily, refusing to fall in with her mood.

There was a pause while Sara collected herself, and then she said they must go back and do the accounts.

'I've got some work to do,' he said.

'Yes, we have.'

'No, my own work.'

'In that case there are all the books to move.'

'I'll go on with it here. There's more space.'

'Have you asked Simon?'

'Why the hell should I ask Simon?'

A dam burst again: All he's done for you. (Prunella left the room.) Picking up the pieces of your life for you. A foreigner accepted as if you were his own father. No real son could have done more. Difficult times for everyone. Your trouble. Everyone under great strain. You didn't mean. The subject of Pippa better not discussed (and then discussed at length). It occurred to Thomas as he listened to her that Sara had not changed a whit in the whole time they had been married. No hint or taint of him had touched her. She had remained her strong English self, and in truth she did put up with a good deal, for in her terms a scholar's life must always have stood for a life of privation, which would explain the furious resolve that clenched the lines in her face. All the same, he had work to do.

'Before you leave, you'd better apologize to Simon,' she said.

He left the room, picking up the little erotic figures and locking them into his desk drawer.

Sara followed him. 'What are you doing?' she said.

'Nothing,' he said.

'What are you thinking about?' She pursued him.

'Nothing,' he said again, smiling at her, for she was Sara. ('Remember the nine tenets of resistance in a country occupied by foreign forces,' he said to himself. '"We know nothing, we recognize nothing, we give nothing, we are capable of nothing, we understand nothing, we sell nothing, we help nothing, we reveal nothing, we forget nothing."')

'Doesn't it hurt your pride? It must,' she said, not unkindly but in a rare and urgent search for a response of any sort at all.

After contemplation, he replied quite seriously, 'A little. Very little. At first. Not now. I think it's harder on you.'

'You've never been properly recognized.'

'You mean well paid.' He waited. 'To choose to do the work one wants, I suppose one will quite often have to renounce the idea of making a fortune. Yes? I'm sorry, my dear.' A few minutes before, he had tried to add 'We apologize for nothing' to the rules in his head, but he knew that Sara would always move him to compunction.

Alone then in his library, feeling fine, his spirits began to mount. He thought about some work, and also about the world, as he had not since he was in India. The sense of being part of a general flux had been lost for years. There grew in him a wish to touch with his fingers a future that he knew was that of many others. The disorder that had seemed to him for decades to determine the course of events regrouped itself like a pile of iron filings suddenly organized by a magnet, and he had a flash of optimism when it appeared quite possible that men in the days to come might wish to find out more than concerned them at the moment. Probably this curiosity will be quite superficial, he thought to himself, as it is in me until I have more time to spend on it. But it will be better. He considered for several hours, making notes and getting up now and then for books. He felt he had his hand on a way to proceed, and one that might be of some consequence, with luck. Simon's heavy tread moved about upstairs and his voice shouted something at a maid. He was calling for a sherry and a tonic water with ice for Mr Flitch in the library. No gin. He doesn't drink. Remember that. Pru, he is still here, isn't he? He hasn't drifted back to his own place yet, eh? Do you think we have to offer him a meal?'

Thomas looked out of the window. I'll leap into my life, he thought, if it splits my face to bits.

AUTHOR NOTES

———— ••• ————

SARAH BARNHILL lives in the mountains of western North Carolina, USA. She has a BA and MA from Clemson University, a secondary education certificate from Jordanhill College in Glasgow, USA, and a PhD in 20th century American Literature from the University of South Carolina. Her fiction and non-fiction have appeared in numerous magazines in the USA, among them *Appalachian Heritage, Cold Mountain Review* and *Summit*. She is currently running an international trading and procurement business which specialises in American-made textiles, finding fabric for American and foreign buyers. (Her company, she says, does not deal in quilts.)

JULIA BIRLEY is the eldest daughter of the distinguished novelist and playwright Margaret Kennedy, and she cannot remember a time when she did not have the urge to write herself. She is the author of five novels, short stories (mainly for children), articles and radio sketches. Amongst her range of themes perhaps the strongest is that of her last novel, *Dr Spicer* (1988): the myths and realities of 19th century Britain which have left their mark on contemporary social life and imagination. At different times she has taught classics and worked in hospital administration, and confesses to belonging to the last generation of educated women who could get by without a proper job. With her husband, a psychiatrist now retired, she has recently settled in Herefordshire. Her interests include grandparenthood, gardening and work for the London committee of Age Concern, an organisation she greatly admires.

ROSALIND BRACKENBURY was born in 1942. She was educated at Sherborne School for Girls and at Girton College where she read History. After university she taught in a secondary modern school in London. She married in 1966 (later divorced) and had two children. Her first novel, *A Day to Remember to Forget*, was published in 1971. It was followed by a further seven novels, among them *Into Egypt* (1973), *A Superstitious Age* (1977), *The Woman in the Tower* (1982) and *Crossing the Water* (1986). She has published three poetry collections: *Telling Each Other It Is Possible* (1987), *Making For The Secret Places* (1989) and *Going Home The Long Way Round The Mountain* (1993). She lives in Edinburgh and has taught courses in creative writing at Edinburgh University. She has received three awards from the Scottish Arts Council.

ISMAT CHUGTAI (1915–1991) was born in India. She was one of the most famous of the school of Urdu short story writers who were associated with the All-India Progressive Writers' Association, founded in 1936, which stood for independence from foreign rule and against exploitation. 'Tiny's Granny' is symbolic of the oppressed women whose lives provided the material for many of her stories. According to her translator, Ralph Russell, her mother tongue was Urdu but she had to reacquire it after her predominantly English education. She developed a vivid and idiomatic style, using the unique language of Muslim women which has its own vocabulary and idioms. These were sometimes shocking to her readers; in 1944 she defended herself successfully against a charge of obscenity for her short story *Lihaaf* (The Quilt) in which she explored areas which were considered taboo. Her central concern was to tell the truth. An intense individualist and iconoclast long before it was fashionable to be so, her writing became an inspiration in the struggle against conservatism. Her output was prolific and her work widely proclaimed both in India and Pakistan. She also wrote plays, film scripts, essays and an autobiographical novel, *Terhi Lakir* (Crooked Line).

COLETTE (1873–1954) was born in a village in Burgundy. She went to the local school where her skills at composition made her an outstanding pupil. When she was twenty she was taken to Paris by her first husband, Henri Gauthier-Villars, under whose pseudonym 'Willy' her first novels, the *Claudine* series (1900–1903), were published. After their divorce in 1906 she spent six years on the stage. In 1910 she married Henri de Jouvenal by whom she had a daughter. In 1916 she dropped the name 'Willy' in favour of

'Colette'. Four years later her novel *Chéri* was published and its immediate success established her as a leading author. In *Chéri* the theme of the older woman and the younger man, one that recurs in many of her stories, has its fullest and most famous treatment. Colette was a prolific writer, every aspect of her life, whether Paris society or the provinces, the stage or marriage, was food for her talent. Her works include over fifty books – novels, short stories, reviews, essays and autobiographical pieces. In spite of increasingly crippling arthritis as she grew older her interest in the world around her never waned. She married her third husband, Maurice Goudeket, in 1935. Colette was the first woman President of the Goncourt Academy and the first French woman to be given a state funeral.

MARY COWAN was born in 1914 in Edinburgh, of mixed Scottish and English parentage. A grey childhood in her native city was brightened by holidays in Galloway and Northumberland and access to a dream world of treasured books. After a short spell at art college she worked in Bethnal Green as a health worker for the LCC. This experience and, later, the shock of the Spanish civil war, made a socialist out of her; she joined the Communist Party. At the age of twenty–three she made a romantic *mésalliance* and went to live on a Thames sailing barge till conjugal discords were interrupted by war. After the war she returned to Scotland where she brought up her four children and cultivated acres of garden, selling its produce. At the age of sixty–one she went to Vietnam for two and a half years to work in a government publishing house in Hanoi on a translation of the Anthology of Vietnamese Literature. She translated and published *Our Motherland*, a collection of Vietnamese poetry, after which she returned to the Scottish house, now shared by four generations of her family. She still struggles with the garden and makes occasional sorties 'to explore the world in search of truth'.

KATHLEEN DAYUS was born in 1903 in Birmingham. She was the youngest of six surviving children out of a family of thirteen. Her father worked as a brass cutter, her mother as a cleaner; their house was typical of the city's slum area, with three habitable rooms and a water standpipe in the yard. She left school at 14 to work in various jobs, ending up as an expert enameller. When she was 18 she married, but ten years later was left a widow with four children. Her industrial skills enabled her to see her family through their early years. Now, sixty years later, she has twelve grand-children and eight great-grandchildren. Her life provides the material for her writing. Her first book of autobiography, *Her People* (1982), covers the period of her childhood. In 1983 it was awarded the JR Ackerly Prize for autobiography. Its sequels, *Where There's Life* (1985), *All My Days* (1988) and *Best of Times* (1991) carry her story through the First World War, when she worked in a muni-tions factory, to the Depression when she was forced to put her children in Dr Barnado's homes until she could support them again herself. Her latest book, *The People of Lavender Court*, was inspired by the people in Birmingham she visits and whose memories, like her own, offer a unique and rich glimpse into the past.

PAM GIDNEY is a retired English teacher. She left school towards the end of the war at the age of sixteen and later married and had two sons. When she was 38 she went to college and emerged four years later with a degree in English and the Philosophy of Education. She belonged to Mensa for a number of years. For ten years she taught English in a large London comprehensive, then was home tutor to an autistic boy for five years. Now she spends her time writing novels, short stories and poetry. Her poems have been published in a number of anthologies and also in numerous small-press magazines, her short stories in *Woman's Own*, *Best*, *Weekend*, and the *London Evening News*.

PENELOPE GILLIATT (1932–1993) was born in London. She was brought up in Northumberland, educated there by private tutors and at Queen's College London and Bennington College, Vermont. She also studied music and played the piano and harpsichord. Her professional life as a writer was divided between London and New York. She was film critic of *The Observer*, wrote for *The Guardian* and numerous magazines, and was a contracted writer for the *New Yorker*. She published seven collections of short stories, among them *Nobody's Business* (1972), *Splendid Lives* (1978), *Quotations from Other Lives* (1982), *They Sleep Without Dreaming* (1985) and *Lingo* (1990). Her five novels include *A State of Change* (1967), *The Cutting Edge* (1979) and *A Woman of Singular Occupation* (1988). Her last work, *To Wit* (1990), is a critical study of comedy. A sense of comedy, sharply observed, runs through her fiction as counterpoint to the dramas of her characters' lives. Her original screenplay for John Schlesinger's film *Sunday, Bloody Sunday* won multiple awards including an Oscar nomination. She also wrote two one-act plays, a libretto for the English National Opera and films for television. She was a fellow of the Royal Society of Literature and received a grant from the American Academy of Arts and Letters in recognition of her work. At the end of her life she lived in London. She had one daughter.

DAPHNE GLAZER was born and brought up in working-class Sheffield and now lives in Hull. She spent five years in Nigeria teaching German to adults. On her return to Britain she worked in a toffee factory and taught in a maximum security prison and a borstal. At present she runs writing workshops in further education and teaches German. She is the Quaker chaplain at Hull prison. She has published one novel, *Three Women* (1984) and stories in magazines (*New Statesman & Society*, *Critical Quarterly* and *Panurge*) and has featured on Radio 4's *Morning Story*. She says the models for her stories are often the women she sees around her, like those who clean the college or serve in cafés: 'toughies, indomitable survivors'. She says she believes 'life is a journey and that every part of it unfolds something new and vital. It is up to each one of us to be conscious of its awesomeness and surprise.'

NADINE GORDIMER was born in 1923 in Springs, South Africa, a small gold-mining town east of Johannesburg where her father settled after emigrating from Lithuania. She left school at nine owing to a heart complaint and dates her starting to write to that period of lonely childhood in a community of mixed race and uprooted people. She has said: 'You put your hand deep down into the world that you know around you, into your own society. And whatever is there you come up with, this is what being a writer's about.' She is a world famous author now with eighteen books and an array of awards to her name. *Friday's Footprint* (1961) won the W. H. Smith Literary award, *A Guest of Honour* (1962) the James Tait Black Memorial Prize and *The Conservationist* (1974) was joint winner of the Booker Prize. In 1991 she was awarded the Nobel Prize for Literature. The political context of her life informs all her work: *Enemies* is one of the few stories where it is not overtly evident, yet it can be felt in the sense of hierarchy between the different characters, healthism and the mistress–servant relationship creating their own apartheid. She has been described as 'South

Africa's conscience'. She is a co-founder of the Congress of South African writers, aimed to assist anti-apartheid writers, and is now a member of the African National Congress. She lives in a suburb of Johannesburg with her husband, Reinhold Cassirer, and has two children and one step-child.

SUSAN HILL was born in Scarborough in 1942. She studied English at King's College, London, and published her first book, *The Enclosure* (1961), soon after leaving university. This was followed by nine further works, then after her marriage in 1975 to Stanley Wells, the Shakespeare scholar, and the birth of their first child she took a break from writing fiction. When she did publish again it was after two more children (the second of whom had died) and in a different genre: ghost stories and non-fiction titles. Her novel, *The Woman in Black* (1983), has been turned into a play which is currently enjoying a record West End run. She has received several awards. At the age of thirty she was made a Fellow of the Royal Society of Literature. *I'm the King of the Castle* (1971) won the Somerset Maugham Prize; *The Albatross and Other Stories*, the John Llewelyn Rhys Memorial Prize; *The Bird of Night* (1972) the Whitbread Award, and one of her children's books, *Can It be True?* won the Smarties Prize. She has written several radio plays and is a regular broadcaster and reviewer. She said of 'A Bit of Singing and Dancing' that the idea for the story came from seeing an old man dancing to a gramophone outside South Kensington station. She and her husband live in a village in Oxfordshire.

SUSAN KATZ lives in New York. Her poetry has been published in numerous magazines in the United States. She has published three poetry collections, *The Separate Sides of Need* (1984), *Two Halves of the Same Silence* ((1985), *An Eye for Resemblances* (1991) and her work has been included in a dozen anthologies. From 1985 to 1991 she was book review editor of the poetry magazine *Bitterroot*. She has run poetry courses and workshops and been an active member for fifteen years of the New York State Poets in Public Service programme. Her work has received numerous awards and she has been elected a Fellow of the International Academy of Poets, a member of the Academy of American Poets and of the Poetry Society of America. She is currently working on a poetic exploration of Greek mythology.

MARGARET LAURENCE (1926–1987) was born in Neepawa, a small town in Manitoba, Canada. She studied Arts at United College (now Winnipeg University). In the same year she graduated she married John Laurence, a civil engineer, with whom she had a daughter and a son. Her husband's job took them abroad – to Somaliland, Ghana and England. Margaret, who had written from an early age, used the experiences of their travel as background for her books. *A Tree for Poverty* (1954) was a collection of translated Somali poetry and folk tales, and her first two novels, *This Side of Jordan* (1960) and *The Tomorrow-Tamer* (1963) are set in West Africa. She also published four children's books and two volumes of essays. Her Canadian childhood was drawn on for her five major works, the Mannawaka sequence: *The Stone Angel* (1964), *A Jest of God* (1966, made into a film, *Rachel Rachel*, directed by Paul Newman), *The Fire-Dwellers* (1969), *A Bird in the House* (1970) and *The Diviners* (1974). The fictional Mannawaka is the symbol of the small prairie town and Margaret Laurence's terse powerful style a fitting voice for its characters. *A Jest of God* and *The Diviners* received Governor General Awards. Acclaimed as one of Canada's best modern writers, in 1972 she was made a Companion of the Order of Canada and in 1977 she became a Fellow of the Royal Society of Canada.

PENELOPE LIVELY was born in Cairo in 1933. She grew up in Egypt but came to England after the Second World War and did a history degree at Oxford. In 1957 she married Professor Jack Lively with whom she had a son and a daughter, and now has two granddaughters. From 1970 onwards she published a book a year, sometimes more. Her first eleven published works were children's books. In 1977 her first novel, *The Road to Lichfield*, was shortlisted for the Booker Prize. Ten years later (after six more novels and six more children's books), her novel *Moon Tiger* (1987) was awarded the Booker Prize. The theme of her fiction is often the past – both the shared and individual past – and the ways in which it can be interpreted and used. She says: 'In writing fiction I am trying to impose order upon chaos, to give structure and meaning to what is apparently random,' as the central character in her story *Party* does when she tries to impose order on social chaos. 'The short story,' Penelope Lively has said, 'can act as a concentrated beam of light.' Her writing has this searchlight quality of finding the cracks as well as the strengths beneath the surface, with humour and unswerving insight. Her first collection of short stories, *Nothing Missing but the Samovar* (1978), won the Southern Arts Literature award. Two of her children's books received awards: *The Ghost of Thomas Kempe* (1973) the Carnegie Medal and *A Stitch in Time* the Whitbread Award. She is a Fellow of the Royal Society of Literature and a member of the Society of Authors.

PAULE MARSHALL was born in the United States in 1929 where her parents had immigrated from Barbados during the First World War. She graduated from Brooklyn College in 1953. She worked as a magazine writer and researcher and published her first novel, *Brown Girl, Brownstones*, in 1959. She went on to publish three more novels: *The Chosen Place, The Timeless People, Praisesong for the Widow* and her latest work, *Daughters* (1993). Her two short story collections are *Soul Clap Hands and Sing* (1961) and *Merle and Other Stories* (1983). Considered one of America's leading contemporary writers she uses her heritage from two cultures to evoke powerful characters and situations in a language of rich imagery. She sees Da-duh, the eponymous grandmother in her story, as 'an ancestor figure, symbolic for me of the long line of black women and men – African and New World – who made my being possible'. In 1989 she received the Dos Passos Award for Literature, in 1984 the American Book Award. In 1992 she won a MacArthur Fellowship. She is now Professor of English and Creative Writing at Virginia Commonwealth University in Richmond, Virginia.

MARION MOLTENO grew up in South Africa but left with her husband because of their opposition to apartheid. She spent eight years in Zambia where her two daughters were born and where she taught, and worked on a community education project. In 1976 her husband, a lecturer at the university, was detained without trial along with other lecturers and students. Eventually with the support of Amnesty International they were released and she and her family settled in Britain. For the past sixteen years she has worked in adult education, writing and lecturing widely on intercultural issues. She is a founder member of the South London Refugee Project, a self-help organisation in which refugees and local people work together to meet the needs of recently arrived asylum seekers. Her published works include *A Language in Common* (1987), a collection of short stories about Asian women in

Britain, and *A Shield of Coolest Air* (1992), a novel about Somali refugees in Britain. Both books grew out of her close involvement with minority communities and her own parallel experiences. She has recently taken up the violin at what she feels, at forty–nine, is a late-starter age, but has happily found a niche in a 'late starters' orchestra'.

GRACE NICHOLS was born in 1950 in Georgetown, Guyana, and grew up there. She studied at the University of Guyana where she took a degree in Communications. She worked as a reporter and freelance journalist before coming to Britain in 1977. Since then she has published several children's books and two poetry collections, *i is a long memoried woman* which received the Commonwealth Poetry Prize in 1983 and *The Fat Black Woman's Poems* (1984). She has also published a novel, *Whole of A Morning Sky* (1986) which evokes the Guyanese world of her childhood. She lives in Lewes, Sussex, with the poet John Agard. She has one daughter.

EDNA O'BRIEN was born on a farm in County Clare, Ireland, and educated at Irish convents. She worked for a brief time as a pharmacist in Dublin. Her first novel, *The Country Girls* (1960) dealt with what has became the theme of all her books, the suffering and pain women experience through loving. She explored this with an honesty which led to some of her early works being banned in Ireland (the ban has since been lifted). Between 1960 and 1978 she published nine novels and three collections of short stories. Her books include *Girl with Green Eyes* (1962, originally titled *The Lonely Girl*) which was filmed starring Rita Tushingham and Lynne Redgrave, *August is a Wicked Month* (1965), *A Pagan Place* (1970) which was acclaimed as a minor masterpiece, and *Night* (1972). In 1979 she edited *Some Irish Loving*, an anthology of Irish poetry and prose about love. *The High Road* (1988) takes up the theme of love but this time between two women, with dramatic and tragic outcome. 'I've only got to put pen to paper and the melancholy comes,' she has said. But the sadness is shot through with the warm colours of a vivid, musical prose. She has two sons whom she brought up after the early break up of her marriage. She lives in London.

ADRIENNE RICH was born in Baltimore in 1929. Her first volume of poetry was published in 1951, the year she graduated from Radcliffe college. Since then she has published nine volumes of poetry, one of which, *Diving Into The Wreck* (1973), was co-winner of the 1974 National Book Award of America. She is also one of the great feminist writers and thinkers of her generation. 'I am a feminist,' she wrote in the 1970s, 'because I feel endangered, psychically and physically, by this society and because I believe . . . we have come to an edge in history when men have become dangerous to children and other living things, themselves included.' It has been said of her that she is 'the poet who has most roundly and significantly expressed women's feelings about their sexual identity and value in society'. She lives in Massachusetts and is Professor of English at Douglass College, Rutgers University.

ELIZABETH SMART (1913–1986) was born in Ottawa, Canada. She was educated at private school in Canada and at King's College, London. After the Second World War she worked as a journalist and in advertising in London, and in 1963 she became the literary and associate editor of *Queen* magazine. She achieved literary fame with the publication of her book, *By Grand Central Station I Sat Down and Wept* (1945). This poetic prose novel, hailed as a masterpiece, was based on her love affair with the poet George Barker (whom she never married but by whom she had four children). The calm confidence of the late poem, *Why Can't An Old Woman Learn To Fly*, in contrast to the passion and at times despair of *By Grand Central Station*, is evidence of the changes wrought by the thirty-odd years that separated them. Her *Collected Poems* were published in 1977 when she was sixty four. Towards the end of her life she retired to Suffolk.

MURIEL SPARK was born in Edinburgh in 1918 and went to private school there. At nineteen she married and travelled with her husband to Central Africa where her only child was born. The marriage did not last and after the outbreak of war she returned with her son to Britain. War work took her to the Political Intelligence Department of the Foreign Office producing 'black propaganda'. This taught her, she said, 'a lot about fiction which is what making propaganda is'. After publishing some poems and two successful biographies, of Mary Shelley and Emily Bronte, she decided to concentrate on novels, with the backing of Graham Greene, a fellow Catholic (she had converted to Catholicism in 1954) who offered her £20 a month while she wrote her book. The result was six novels in four years. *The Comforters* (1957) was her first. Two years and two books later came *Memento Mori*, an acclaimed masterpiece which explored human feelings about mortality with mordant humour. 'I don't like to express serious things too seriously,' she said, 'I write to make people smile.' *The Prime of Miss Jean Brodie* (1961), in which she drew on her own experiences of schooling in Edinburgh, brought her world wide fame. It was turned into a very successful play and then into a film (with Maggie Smith in the title role). She received literary awards – the Italia Prize and the James Tait Black Memorial Prize – and in 1967 was awarded the O.B.E. She now lives in Tuscany.

STEVIE SMITH (1902–1971) was born in Hull, but from early childhood until her death she lived in Palmers Green, first with her parents and after they died with a beloved aunt. Her real names were Florence Margaret; she acquired the nickname 'Stevie' when she was eighteen after some boys shouted 'Come on, Steve!' as she cantered past on horseback (a reference to the jockey Steve Donaghue). After going to Palmers Green High School and the North London Collegiate School for Girls she worked as a private secretary until retirement. Her first published work, *Novel on Yellow Paper* (1936) was written after being told by a publisher to whom she had shown her poems, 'Go away and write a novel and we will then think about poems.' A year later her first volume of verse, *A Good Time Was Had By All*, appeared and established her reputation as a poet of subtle directness. Seven more collections were published, many of them illustrated by her own drawings, and two more novels, *Over the Frontier* (1939) and *The Holiday* (1949). She won the Cholmondeley Award for Poetry and, in 1969, the Queen's Gold Medal for Poetry. Two posthumous collections of her works were published: *Collected Poems* (1975) and selections from her short stories, reviews, poems and letters in *Me Again: The Uncollected Writings of Stevie Smith* (1981).

ELIZABETH TAYLOR (1912–1975) was born in Reading, Berkshire. She went to the Abbey School in Reading and after leaving school worked as a governess and later in a library. When she was twenty–four she married John Taylor, a businessman with whom she had two children. Most of her married life was spent in the village of Penn in Buckinghamshire. Her first novel, *At Mrs Lippincote's* (1945), was written during the war while her husband was in the RAF. This was followed by a further fifteen adult books – novels, short stories – and a children's book. In 1984 her novel *Angel*, based loosely on the life of Marie Corelli, was selected as one of the Book Marketing Council's 'Best Novels of Our Time'. Her penultimate work, *Mrs Palfrey at the Claremont* (1971), a study of old age, is a masterpiece of humorous and compassionate observation. *Blaming* (1976), published posthumously, deals with the theme of bereavement and guilt.

MARI B. WAAGAARD was born in 1927 and brought up in Oslo. She took a Masters degree in Philology at Oslo University. She has taught in grammar school and at Oslo University and has written for newspapers and magazines. She produces programmes on literature and music for NRK (the Norwegian Radio). She has been writing short stories for the last twenty years and in 1991 *The Sweet Old Lady Who Cried Wolf* won a prize in a Scandinavian crime story contest. Part of the background to this story about the sweet (tough) old lady are memories of the Nazi occupation of Norway which the writer herself experienced as a teenager. She lives in Oslo and is married with three children and three grandchildren.